STERLING
Test Prep

AP
U.S. History

Complete
Content Review

4th edition

www.Sterling-Prep.com

Copyright © 2019 Sterling Test Prep

4 3 2 1

ISBN-13: 978-1-9475563-4-8

Sterling Test Prep products are available at special quantity discounts for sales, promotions, academic counseling offices, and other educational purposes.

For more information contact our Sales Department at:

Sterling Test Prep
6 Liberty Square #11
Boston, MA 02109

info@sterling-prep.com

© 2019 Sterling Test Prep

Published by Sterling Test Prep

 Printed in the U.S.A.

Congratulations on choosing this book as part of your AP U.S. History preparation!

Scoring well on AP exams is important for admission to college. To achieve a high score on the AP U.S. History exam, you need to develop historical thinking skills to properly analyze historical evidence and quickly respond to the exam's questions. You must learn to apply chronological reasoning, draw comparisons and contextualization and craft arguments from historical evidence.

This book provides a thorough and curriculum-oriented review of all periods and Key Concepts per the College Board's most recent AP U.S. History course outline. The content is organized into nine historical periods and is centered around all Key Concepts tested on the AP U.S. History exam.

The information is presented in a clear and easy to understand style. You can focus on one historical period or one Key Concept at a time to fully comprehend and internalize important historical relationships.

This book can be used both as accompanying text during your AP U.S. History course and as a review guide before the exam. By using it as your study tool you will develop the necessary skills and will be well prepared for the AP U.S. History course and exam.

The content is developed and edited by highly qualified history teachers, scholars and education specialists with an emphasis on the curriculum and skills outlined by the College Board for the AP U.S. History course. It was examined for quality and consistency by our team of editors who are experts on teaching and preparing students for standardized tests.

We wish you great success in your future academic achievements and look forward to being an important part of your successful preparation for the AP U.S. History!

Sterling Test Prep Team

190111gdx

We want to hear from you

Your feedback is important to us because we strive to provide the highest quality prep materials. Email us if you have any questions, comments or suggestions, so we can incorporate your feedback into future editions.

Customer Satisfaction Guarantee

If you have any concerns about this book, including printing issues, contact us and we will resolve any issues to your satisfaction.

info@sterling-prep.com

We reply to all emails – please check your spam folder

Thank you for choosing our products to achieve your educational goals!

Table of Contents

Our Commitment to the Environment

Sterling Test Prep is committed to protecting our planet's resources by supporting environmental organizations with proven track records of conservation, ecological research and education and preservation of vital natural resources. A portion of our profits is donated to help these organizations so they can continue their critical missions. These organizations include:

 For over 40 years, Ocean Conservancy has been advocating for a healthy ocean by supporting sustainable solutions based on science and cleanup efforts. Among many environmental achievements, Ocean Conservancy laid the groundwork for an international moratorium on commercial whaling, played an instrumental role in protecting fur seals from overhunting and banning the international trade of sea turtles. The organization created national marine sanctuaries and served as the lead non-governmental organization in the designation of 10 of the 13 marine sanctuaries.

 For 25 years, Rainforest Trust has been saving critical lands for conservation through land purchases and protected area designations. Rainforest Trust has played a central role in the creation of 73 new protected areas in 17 countries, including the Falkland Islands, Costa Rica and Peru. Nearly 8 million acres have been saved thanks to Rainforest Trust's support of in-country partners across Latin America, with over 500,000 acres of critical lands purchased outright for reserves.

 Since 1980, Pacific Whale Foundation has been saving whales from extinction and protecting our oceans through science and advocacy. As an international organization, with ongoing research projects in Hawaii, Australia, and Ecuador, PWF is an active participant in global efforts to address threats to whales and other marine life. A pioneer in non-invasive whale research, PWF was an early leader in educating the public, from a scientific perspective, about whales and the need for ocean conservation.

With your purchase, you support environmental causes around the world.

AP U.S. HISTORY EXAM

The AP U.S. History Exam is 3 hours and 15 minutes long and includes both a multiple-choice/short-answer section (105 minutes) and a free-response section (90 minutes). Each section is divided into two parts, as shown in the table below. Student performance metrics on these four parts are compiled and weighted to determine an overall AP Exam score.

Section	Question Type	Number of Questions	Timing	Percentage of Total Exam Score
I	Part A: Multiple-choice questions	55 questions	55 minutes	40%
	Part B: Short-answer questions	4 questions	50 minutes	20%
II	Part A: Document-based questions	1 question	55 minutes	25%
	Part B: Long essay question	1 question (chosen out of 2)	35 minutes	15%

The content of the new AP U.S. History curriculum and exam is divided into nine chronological periods. The table below shows the specific years included in each of the nine periods and their approximate presence on the exam.

Period	Date Range	Approximate Percentage of AP Exam
1	1491 – 1607*	5%
2	1607 – 1754	10%
3	1754 – 1800	12%
4	1800 – 1848	10%
5	1844 – 1877	13%
6	1865 – 1898	13%
7	1890 – 1945	17%
8	1945 – 1980	15%
9	1980 – present*	5%

* No document-based question or long essay question focuses exclusively on events prior to 1607 (Period 1) or after 1980 (Period 9)

The coverage of the periods in the exam as a whole reflects the approximate period weightings. Students write at least one essay—in either the document-based question or long essay—that examines long-term developments spanning historical time periods.

Assessment of Student's Learning on the Exam

The following are general parameters about the relationship between the components of the curriculum framework and the questions on the AP Exam. AP US History exam assesses:

- Students' understanding of all nine periods of U.S. history.

- Students' achievement of the thematic learning objectives.

- Students' use of historical thinking skills.

Multiple-Choice Questions

The multiple-choice section contains several sets of questions with 2-5 questions per set. These sets ask students to respond to stimulus materials (primary or secondary sources) including texts, images, charts, graphs, maps, etc. The stimulus material reflects the types of evidence that historians use in their research. The set of multiple-choice questions draws upon knowledge required by the curriculum framework, and each question addresses one of the learning objectives for the course. While a set may focus on one particular period of U.S. history, the individual questions within that set may ask students to make connections to thematically linked developments in other periods.

Multiple-choice questions assess students' ability to evaluate the stimulus material *in tandem with* their knowledge of the historical issue at hand. The possible answers for a multiple-choice question reflect the level of detail present in the required historical developments found in the concept outline for the course. Events and topics contained in the illustrative example boxes of the curriculum framework do *not* appear in multiple-choice questions (unless accompanied by text that fully explains the topic to the student).

Short-Answer Questions

Short-answer questions directly address one or more of the thematic learning objectives for the course. At least two of the four questions have elements of internal choice, providing opportunities for students to demonstrate what they know best. All of the short-answer questions require students to use historical thinking skills to respond to a primary source, a historian's argument, non-textual sources such as data or maps, or general propositions about U.S. history. Each question asks students to identify and analyze examples of historical evidence relevant to the source or question; these examples can be drawn from the concept outline or from other examples explored in depth during classroom instruction.

Document-Based Question

The document-based question measures students' ability to analyze and synthesize historical data and to assess verbal, quantitative, or visual materials as historical evidence. As with the long essay, responses to the document-based question are judged on students' ability to formulate a thesis and support it with relevant evidence. The documents included in the document-based question are not confined to a single format, vary in length, and illustrate interactions and complexities within the material.

Where suitable, the documents include charts, graphs, cartoons, pictures, and written materials. In addition to calling upon a broad spectrum of historical skills, the diversity of materials allows students to assess the value of different sorts of documents. The document-based question typically requires students to relate the documents to a historical period or theme and, thus, to focus on major periods and issues. For this reason, outside knowledge beyond the specific focus of the question is important and must be incorporated into the student's essay to earn the highest scores.

Long Essay Question

To provide opportunities for students to demonstrate what they know best, they are given a choice between two comparable long essay options. The long essay questions measure the use of historical thinking skills to explain and analyze significant issues in U.S. history as defined by the thematic learning objectives. Student essays must include the development of a thesis or argument supported by an analysis of specific, relevant historical evidence. Questions are limited to topics or examples specifically mentioned in the concept outline but are framed to allow student answers to include in-depth examples of large-scale phenomena, either drawn from the concept outline or from topics discussed in the classroom.

Tested Skills

There are nine historical thinking skills that students must demonstrate on the AP U.S. History exam. They are grouped into four skill types as shown in the table below.

Skill Type	Historical Thinking Skill
I. Chronological Reasoning	1. Historical causation 2. Patterns of continuity and change over time 3. Periodization
II. Comparison and Contextualization	4. Comparison 5. Contextualization
III. Crafting Historical Arguments from Historical Evidence	6. Historical argumentation 7. Appropriate use of relevant historical evidence
IV. Historical Interpretation and Synthesis	8. Interpretation 9. Synthesis

Skill Type I: Chronological Reasoning

Skill 1: Historical causation – the ability to identify, analyze and evaluate the relationships among multiple historical causes and effects, distinguishing between those that are long-term and proximate, and among coincidence, causation and correlation

Proficient students are able to:

- compare causes and/or effects and distinguish between short- and long-term effects.
- analyze and evaluate the interaction of multiple causes and/or effects.
- assess historical contingency by distinguishing among coincidence, causation, and correlation as well as critiquing existing interpretations of cause and effect.

Skill 2: Patterns of continuity and change over time – the ability to recognize, analyze and evaluate the dynamics of historical continuity and change over periods of time

Proficient students are able to:

- identify, analyze and evaluate historical patterns of continuity and change over time.
- connect patterns of continuity and change over time to larger historical processes or themes.

Skill 3: Periodization – the ability to describe, analyze, evaluate and construct models that historians use to organize history into discrete periods

Students should be familiar with different ways that historians divide time into historical periods and identify turning points in the past. Students may develop this skill by examining and evaluating the model of periodization provided in this framework. Students may then compare this periodization against competing models, such as the one used in their textbook.

Proficient students are able to:

- explain ways that historical events and processes can be organized within blocks of time.
- analyze and evaluate competing models of periodization of U.S. history.

Skill Type II: Comparison and Contextualization

Skill 4: Comparison – the ability to describe, compare and evaluate multiple historical developments

This skill asks students to compare related historical developments and processes in various chronological and geographical contexts within one society or between different societies. This skill also involves the ability to identify and compare multiple perspectives on a given historical experience.

Proficient students are able to:

- compare related historical developments and processes across place, time and/or different societies or within one society.
- explain and evaluate multiple and differing perspectives on a given historical phenomenon.

Skill 5: Contextualization – the ability to connect historical events and processes to specific circumstances of time and place and to broader regional, national, or global processes

The "context" for world history is the world as a whole; for European history, it is Europe as a whole and for U.S. history, it is primarily the United States itself. The skill of contextualization, therefore, takes on different forms depending on the scope of time and geography. One of the central questions of world history is: How does the history of this specific region or era fit into the larger story of world history as a whole? For U.S. history, that same contextualization question is: How does the history of a particular group, region, or era fit into the larger story of the development of the United States?

Proficient students are able to:

- explain and evaluate ways in which specific historical phenomena, events, or processes connect to broader regional, national, or global processes occurring at the same time.
- explain and evaluate ways in which a phenomenon, event, or process connects to similar historical phenomena from other times or places.

Skill Type III: Crafting Historical Arguments from Historical Evidence

Skill 6: Historical argumentation – the ability to define and frame a question about the past and to address that question through the construction of an argument

Over the span of the course, students should move from describing to evaluating the conflicting historical evidence used in making plausible historical arguments. In U.S. history, the skill of historical argumentation often operates in conjunction with other skills and with course themes that transcend several periods. A plausible and persuasive argument requires a clear, comprehensive and analytical thesis supported by relevant historical evidence—not simply evidence that supports a preferred or preconceived position. In addition, argumentation involves the capacity to describe, analyze and evaluate the arguments of others in light of available evidence.

Proficient students are able to:

- analyze commonly accepted historical arguments and explain how an argument has been constructed from historical evidence.
- construct convincing interpretations through analysis of disparate, relevant historical evidence.
- evaluate and synthesize conflicting historical evidence to construct persuasive historical arguments.

Skill 7: Appropriate use of relevant historical evidence – the ability to describe and evaluate evidence about the past from diverse sources

This skill asks students to analyze documents (including written documents, works of art, archaeological artifacts, oral traditions, and other primary sources). It involves the capacity to extract useful information, make supportable inferences and draw appropriate conclusions from historical evidence while also noting the context in which the evidence was produced and used, recognizing its limitations and assessing the points of view it reflects.

Proficient students are able to:

- analyze features of historical evidence such as audience, authorship, content, purpose, point of view, format, argument, limitations, and context related to the evidence considered.
- make supportable inferences and draw appropriate conclusions based on analysis and evaluation of historical evidence.

Skill Type IV: Historical Interpretation and Synthesis

Skill 8: Interpretation – the ability to describe, analyze, evaluate and construct diverse interpretations of the past

This skill asks students to both describe and evaluate varied historical interpretations while being aware of how particular circumstances and contexts in which individual historians work and write also shape their interpretation of past events. Historical interpretation requires analyzing evidence, reasoning, determining the context and evaluating points of view found in both primary and secondary sources. To help students create their own interpretation of U.S. history, students should examine changing historical interpretations over time, such as the different ways that historians have interpreted the institution of American slavery or evaluated Reconstruction.

Proficient students are able to:

- analyze diverse historical interpretations.
- evaluate how historians' perspectives influence their interpretations and how models of historical interpretation change over time.

Skill 9: Synthesis – the ability to develop meaningful and persuasive new understandings of the past by applying all of the other historical thinking skills

This skill asks students to demonstrate an understanding of the past by making an argument that draws appropriately on ideas from different fields of inquiry or disciplines and creatively fuses evidence from different works.

Synthesis takes distinctive forms depending on the subdiscipline because each history course grapples with diverse materials. Unlike other histories, in U.S. history there is a predisposition of developing a single narrative that consolidates and merges many different cultures. Yet, the development of such a narrative raises the historiographical question about which groups are included or excluded from the story. Students should attempt to challenge the narratives to which they are exposed in order to have a better understanding of their place in an increasingly globalized and diverse world.

Proficient students are able to:

- combine disparate, sometimes contradictory evidence from primary sources and secondary works in order to create a persuasive understanding of the past.
- apply insights about the past to other historical contexts or circumstances, including the present.

PERIOD 1

1491-1607

Contact among the people of Europe, the Americas and West Africa created a new world on a North American continent controlled by American Indians.

Major historical events of the period:

1492 – Columbus lands in the Bahamas

1520 – Spanish explorers bring smallpox to the Mexican mainland

1521 – Hernàn Cortés conquers the Aztec capital, Tenochtitlán

1598 – New Mexico is founded by Juan de Oñate

1600 – East India Company is founded

1602 – Dutch East India Company is founded

PERIOD 1: 1491-1607

> **KEY CONCEPT 1.1:** Before the arrival of Europeans, native populations in North America developed a wide variety of social, political and economic structures based in part on interactions with the environment and each other.

The spread of maize cultivation from present-day Mexico northward into the American Southwest and beyond supported economic development and social diversification among societies in these areas; a mix of foraging and hunting did the same for societies in the Northwest and areas of California.

Indians in the Southwest (present-day Arizona, New Mexico, and surrounding areas) made a living from agriculture for thousands of years before the Europeans arrived. They mainly grew maize (corn), introduced from Mesoamerica around 2,100 B.C. A variety of sedentary cultures developed in this arid region, relying on irrigation and other techniques to collect and conserve the water needed for agriculture.

Maize cultivation spread fairly quickly across the dry lands of the Southwest, possibly carried along by migrant agriculturalists heading north from Mexico. Despite the rapid rate of diffusion, maize did not become the primary source of nutrition right away for the hunter-gatherers who already lived there. Instead, they incorporated maize farming into their wide selection of food sources, trying, as foragers normally do, to limit the risk that the failure of one food source might have catastrophic consequences. At first, maize was only a minor component of their diet and way of life.

Pueblo girl winnowing beans

Before the dawn of agriculture, bands of hunters and gatherers tended to be small. Except for special circumstances, such as an important ritual or a task that required extensive collaboration, their groups typically consisted of only ten to fifty people. It was only over time that the role of maize expanded, allowing for larger and more sedentary settlements. Hunting and gathering remained important, but the productivity of agriculture allowed populations of 2,000 or more to congregate in one community. Others lived in smaller settlements of a few hundred people or continued to live in tiny groups dispersed across the region.

Among the Ancestral Puebloans (the best-known farming society of the prehistoric Southwest) the size of settlements eventually became so large that the actual fields could be some distance from the tillers' dwellings. Even though this could be a disadvantage, the ability to join together to pool food and other resources and to protect and defend the community was highly advantageous.

However, the forces of centralization and dispersal never reached a stable equilibrium. Instead, farming conditions and environmental changes caused communities to enter cycles of abandonment and regeneration. The intensive agriculture of the Pueblos ultimately proved to be unsustainable when sustained droughts began to occur in the 12th century. Droughts resulted in widespread famine, and many great settlements were left behind as the Pueblos sought new lands and new ways to survive. The traditional centers of population and civilization experienced an irreversible decline.

Pueblo cart

In the Pacific Northwest, an abundance of fish in the rivers and along the coastline allowed for an unusual phenomenon: the development of complex, settled communities among peoples who remained hunters and gatherers. Upon arrival, European explorers witnessed complex coastal societies unfamiliar with agriculture but still home to large villages and elaborate social hierarchies. The Northwestern Indians had large, durable houses and economies that were specialized enough to participate in wide-ranging networks of trade. In the interior, some of the diverse Indian tribes retained the mobility and egalitarianism typical of hunter-gatherer groups. However, other communities, especially along the Columbia and Fraser Rivers, lived sedentary lifestyles and exhibited wealth and social inequality.

Among the latter peoples were the Chinook, who lived by the Columbia River (in present-day Washington and Oregon). They excelled at hunting elk and fishing salmon, and especially depended on the abundance of fish in the river. Their society was very stratified, with a minority of shamans, warriors, and traders who limited their contact with less privileged commoners who made up the majority of the population. They even prevented their children from playing with peers from less prestigious backgrounds.

To mark their status, they would flatten the heads of infants to distinguish them and maintain their superiority over round-headed people. Since those without deliberately deformed heads could be used as slaves, having a round head implied not only inferiority but servility as well. The Chinook apparently picked up the practice of slavery from other tribes farther north.

In California, the Indians were not exactly farmers but engaged in horticultural practices to increase their access to food and medicinal plants. They employed these gardening practices in a variety of environments, including forests, grasslands, and wetlands. They also used fire to facilitate the growing of crops (fertilizing the soil by ashes) and to reduce the risk of larger, disastrous fires. Burning also prepared new areas for cultivation or allowed new, wild growth that would attract game. Even old, cultivated areas could be put to the torch to enable continued use, leading toward a more sedentary lifestyle.

Societies responded to the lack of natural resources in the Great Basin and the western Great Plains by developing largely mobile lifestyles.

The high desert region between the Rocky Mountains and the Sierra Nevada is known as the Great Basin. It is an arid region, most of it poor in flora and fauna, but in some small areas, water is plentiful, affording some plants and animals opportunities to thrive. Overall, the land is not suitable for farming, nor is there much game for hunting. Seemingly inhospitable, the land has nevertheless been a site of human habitation for thousands of years. In the Great Basin, Indians had to be extremely mobile and knowledgeable to successfully exploit the few ecological niches, often spread dozens of miles apart, which allowed them to eke out a living. Their familiarity with local microenvironments was crucial to survival, as was the ability to utilize a wide range of wild plants as food and fiber—the Southern Paiute gathered seeds from more than forty species of grass.

In this unyielding environment, bands remained small, with no more than thirty people in the desert and maybe up to one hundred in slightly more forgiving areas. They were almost always on the move but knew of places near water sources which could be used to set up camp. Leadership was not authoritarian, but a matter of leading by example, advising juniors in the band and working towards consensus decisions that everyone could accept. At any rate, those who did not agree were free to leave. Membership in these small bands was quite fluid, even though members were often closely related.

On the Great Plains east of the Rockies, some Indians farmed and lived a semi-sedentary lifestyle in small villages along the rivers. The main challenge to plains agriculture was that rainfall could be insufficient for raising maize. In the northern areas, the growing season was shorter as well. Consequently, the progress—or rather fluctuations—of agriculture on the plains followed trends in precipitation, conquering drier lands to the west in wetter periods and falling back toward the east when the threshold was not met. Some Indians lived in fortified villages of up to several hundred people along the Missouri River, raising corn, beans, and squash.

For most of those who lived on the plains, much depended on the bison. Even men engaged in farming would typically leave the village to follow the great buffalo between planting and harvest. The Indians used fire to engineer the grasslands where the bison thrived, and also tried to regulate the bison. Before the Europeans brought horses and guns to the Americas, bison had to be hunted on foot, herded or rather chased and trapped into corridors and corrals where they could be killed or stampeded across high cliffs called buffalo jumps. This elaborate system of hunting large numbers of bison often provided a considerable surplus that encouraged not only feasting but significant trade as well. This enabled some groups to maintain a nomadic hunter-gatherer lifestyle, exchanging meat and hides for corn from the farming villages.

In the Northeast and along the Atlantic Seaboard, some societies developed a mixed agricultural and hunter-gatherer economy that favored permanent villages.

The Eastern Woodland culture consisted of Indian tribes inhabiting the eastern United States and Canada. These woodlands stretched from the Atlantic Ocean to the Mississippi River and the Great Lakes and were favored with relatively moderate climates and ample precipitation. Across such a vast area there was, of course, some variation in terms of both climate and specific natural resource endowments, but in general, conditions were good for hunting in the great forests and farming along the numerous lakes and rivers.

Algonquin Indian

There were, of course, differences in ways of life, including diet, housing, clothing and modes of transportation. Nevertheless, the Indians of the woodlands lived in similar ways. Their societies were stratified and distinguished between chiefs, noblemen, and commoners. Intertribal disputes over land, the audacity of young men, and quests for revenge made brutal warfare a staple of everyday life. Fortified villages were a necessity.

But mostly, these Indians were farmers and deer hunters. They made bows and arrows, stone knives and war clubs for hunting and war, and they made pottery and vessels made from wood and bark for cooking. The Iroquois, a confederation of northeastern Indian tribes in the Great Lakes region and the Northeast, were mainly farmers but combined agriculture with gardening, hunting, fishing, and foraging.

The Iroquois cultivated a number of plants, including pumpkin and tobacco, but their main crops—the "three sisters," a special providence from the Creator—were corn, beans, and squash. They knew how to combine these organisms in single plots where bean plants climbed the corn stalks, with the big leaves of the squash underneath keeping the soil moist and shaded, thus preventing the growth of weeds. This technique could keep the soil fertile for decades. When it eventually lost that fertility, the whole community would have to uproot and move. The Iroquois also knew how to conserve meat, fish, vegetables, and berries for the winter.

Iriqouis dwellings

The success of the Iroquois adaptation to their rich environment enabled strong population growth. Large numbers of warriors provided the foundation for a culture of imperialist expansion, with frequent wars against the less sedentary Algonquian tribes in the surrounding areas. Over time, Iroquois expansion was only halted by the Algonquian move toward farming, which raised their populations sufficiently to withstand the Iroquois onslaught. In southern New England, Algonquian tribes relied predominantly on slash-and-burn agriculture. They cleared fields by burning, farmed for a year or two and then moved the village to a different location to repeat the process. Many Algonquians continued, however, to depend largely on hunting, fishing, and gathering, especially in the Far North.

The Algonquian economy continued to revolve around the seasonality of food resources. They lived in villages of a few hundred people belonging to the same clan, but these villages often dissolved into smaller groups of people roaming around to sites where food was plentiful at a particular time of year. Later, these groups could join together again in a new village or join with others in new ways. It was a flexible system adapted both to the availability of foodstuffs and the threat of war.

> **KEY CONCEPT 1.2: European overseas expansion resulted in the Columbian Exchange, a series of interactions and adaptations among societies across the Atlantic.**

Millions of years ago, the supercontinent Pangaea was torn apart by continental drift, and North and South America were separated from Eurasia and Africa. The long journey of separation and divergence caused evolution to take different directions in the Old and the New World, leading to the emergence of new species that had no counterparts across the ocean. After 1492, one species—human beings—began to reverse this process by establishing connections that transferred plants, animals, and microorganisms between Afro-Eurasia and the Americas. This transfer is called the Columbian Exchange and represented not only a spectacular ecological reversal but also a major turning point in world history.

The arrival of Europeans in the Western Hemisphere in the 15th and 16th centuries triggered extensive demographic and social changes on both sides of the Atlantic.

Spanish and Portuguese exploration and conquest of the Americas led to widespread deadly epidemics, the emergence of racially mixed populations and a caste system defined by an intermixture among Spanish settlers, Africans and Native Americans.

Spanish explorers: Cortés, Coligni, de Soto and Verazzani

Before the Columbian Exchange, the peoples of Eurasia and the Americas differed in ways that would have spectacular effects once regular communication between the two hemispheres was established. Eurasian civilizations had more centers of high population density, kept a much wider range of domesticated animals and suffered from a number of infectious diseases unknown in the New World. Trade, migration, and war allowed these diseases to spread widely across Europe and Asia. However, as these diseases became endemic over time, Europeans also developed some level of resistance or immunity to smallpox and other epidemics.

The Indians of the Americas, on the other hand, had not had the same opportunity to develop natural immunity to many of the diseases common in Europe. Deadly epidemics followed in the wake of European explorers, and once established, they were able to spread from one Indian population to the next without direct contact with whites. Microorganisms could of course travel in the other direction as well; it appears that the voyages of Columbus brought syphilis, a harrowing and deadly venereal disease, from the Americas to Europe. In general, however, the exchange of diseases was highly asymmetric and took a far greater toll in the New World.

The rapid spread of smallpox in the Americas was one of the most devastating events of world history. It cost far more lives than all the wars and conquests initiated by the conquistadors and other European colonists, and a much greater proportion of the population died than in the Black Death, the catastrophic epidemic which hit Europe in the 14th century. Only about 10 percent of indigenous populations survived the spread of smallpox and other epidemic diseases between the late 15th and the early 17th centuries. In some cases, entire cultures disappeared and lands were laid waste, forever altering the demographic composition of two continents and facilitating the rapid establishment of European dominance.

In 1520, a group of Spaniards from the smallpox-ravaged island of Hispaniola (today divided between Haiti and the Dominican Republic) landed on the Mexican mainland. They were defeated by another Spanish force under the leadership of Hernán Cortés, who had arrived in the previous year. One of his men, however, contracted smallpox, and when his party set off for the Aztec capital Tenochtitlán, they brought the deadly disease with them. The Spanish soldier eventually died, but smallpox had already spread to the Aztec population.

Meeting of Cortés and Montezuma

Having been forced to flee after an initial confrontation, Cortés returned in 1521 to find the large city completely devastated by disease and death. Large numbers had already perished, including most of the Aztec army. Unable to mount a proper defense of the capital, the Aztecs were easily defeated by Cortés and his Indian allies. The Spanish entered in triumph only to see streets covered in the dead and dying, as well as houses that had become tombs as all the inhabitants had passed away.

The Inca Empire was similarly overwhelmed and demoralized by the effects of smallpox. There, the disease had arrived and began to wipe out the population even before the Spanish conquerors appeared on the scene. The efficient road system that tied the empire together also had the unfortunate effect of aiding the rapid spread of disease. Within months, both the old emperor and his immediate successor had died, along with most other persons of authority.

Warring factions emerged in this power vacuum, and a young leader, Atahualpa, eventually came to power. After this brutal civil war had already further destabilized and weakened the Inca, a small group of highly motivated Spaniards led by Francisco Pizarro was able to capture Atahualpa, take Cuzco (the capital) and swiftly establish Spanish authority over what had once been an impressive indigenous empire. Much of the Inca population succumbed to smallpox, and other European diseases led to further devastation.

As the Europeans began to bring African slaves to the Americas, they also brought yellow fever along. This disease was endemic in Africa, so many Africans were immune. However, this was not the case with those of European descent, who suffered high mortality rates in American yellow fever epidemics all the way into the 19th century.

Heroic defense of Cuzco

Part of the reason why the Europeans were able to establish their hegemony in the Americas centuries before they achieved the same result in Africa was the great difference in the impact of disease: tropical diseases made Africa a "white man's grave," while in the Americas, conquest and control was made easy by the collapse of indigenous cultures in the face of shocking epidemics.

Early conquistadors and settlers were typically men. As they desired female companionship, intermarriage became common in Spanish America. This gave almost instantaneous rise to a mixed-race population, called *mestizos,* which quickly became the numerically superior part of the population in many of the Spanish colonies. Some indigenous women were forced to become wives or concubines. Over time, the amount of European, Indian and African "blood" a person possessed became one of the main organizing principles of Spanish American society, and a kind of hereditary caste system evolved.

The racial hierarchy created by the Spanish elite was based on the assumption that people could be meaningfully classified according to racial and ethnic origins because these determined the differences between people. The caste system was more than a way of ascribing social status; it had economic implications as well. Those who belonged to the lower end of the system met proportionally higher demands for taxes and tribute payments. Socioeconomic status largely corresponded with skin color, appearance and family background.

The Peninsulars (those born and raised in the Iberian Peninsula) occupied the most important government offices and held much of the wealth, while darker skin and non-European ancestry entailed poverty, inferiority, and servitude. Being white allowed a person to claim status and respect, while people of color faced obstacles and prejudice. Even whites born in the colonies faced discrimination by the Peninsulars, which eventually led the former group, known as *criollos*, to seek independence for the Latin American countries in the early 19th century.

The term *zambo* was used to identify individuals of mixed African and Indian descent. Marriages and liaisons between Africans and Indians took place throughout the Spanish colonies and their borderlands. At times, groups of runaway slaves would mix with local Indian populations. In one unconquered region of present-day Ecuador, a group of shipwrecked slaves actually took control of an indigenous community. Another group, who had revolted on a slave ship and wrecked it on the border between Honduras and Nicaragua, united with the local Miskito people. They eventually came to dominate that society and engage in extensive slave raids.

Spanish and Portuguese traders reached West Africa and partnered with some African groups to exploit local resources and recruit slave labor for the Americas.

The Atlantic slave trade took place across the Atlantic Ocean from the 16th to the 19th centuries. Most of those who came to the Americas by way of the brutal Middle Passage were from Central or West Africa, sold by other Africans to European traders who arrived at the many forts and trading posts established primarily for this purpose. The number of slaves was so great that more blacks than whites came to the Americas before the late 18th century.

Only about 5 percent of the slaves were taken to North America; the rest were brought mainly to South America (especially Brazil) and the islands of the Caribbean to work on plantations. They labored to produce coffee, tobacco, cocoa, and sugar for European consumers who held these new commodities in high esteem and were able to create new, pleasant lifestyles for themselves. The slaves also grew cotton and rice, toiled in gold and silver mines, built houses and cut timber. Some were skilled laborers, craftsmen, or domestic servants.

The first African slaves in the New World came from Europe rather than directly from Africa. In the early 16th century, they arrived on ships carrying a variety of goods for sale rather than on dedicated slave ships. This was an extension of the already existing Portuguese traffic in slaves, which had been carried on for decades before Columbus' first voyage. Portuguese mariners had grown accustomed to buying African slaves on the West African coast and taking them to the Atlantic islands or even to mainland Portugal, where black slaves had become common in Lisbon and on some of the great estates.

The arrival of the first slave ship directly from Africa may not have come until 1526. By 1550, many transatlantic slave ships were headed for the Spanish colonies in the Caribbean, and the first slave vessels had also begun to arrive on the Spanish Main. In this early period, many were sent to work in the mines, especially the gold mines on Hispaniola.

Colonial slave market in the 17th century

Since the Spanish did away with some of the more unsavory parts of the slave trade business, the Portuguese remained dominant. They also served their own needs for manpower, with the traffic to Brazil eventually accounting for almost half of the Atlantic slave trade. Starting around 1560, it was the demand for sugar in Europe and the corresponding demand for labor on Brazilian sugar plantations that drove this trade.

By 1630, Africans had basically replaced the original Indian labor force operating Brazilian sugar mills, and these mills were producing almost all the sugar consumed in Europe. Later, sugarcane planting spread to islands in the Eastern Caribbean, rendering the sugar complex the central fact of life in many colonial societies, including possessions of the Spanish, Dutch, English, and French. The success of sugar, in turn, encouraged the great westward expansion of slave systems across Latin America and the present-day United States.

While the demand for plantation commodities, the environment of the tropics and European ideas about race and identity were important determinants of how the slave trade developed, African agency was also a key factor. Both Europeans and Africans had long traditions of slavery, but unlike the Europeans, Africans did not use skin color to determine someone's eligibility for slavery. Instead, they often chose to make criminals, debtors, and prisoners of war into slaves. As the transatlantic slave trade expanded, some African wars were initiated with the specific purpose of taking slaves.

The merchants who sold slaves to the Europeans and the chiefs who supplied those merchants usually had strict criteria for who could be made a slave. As a consequence, the supply of slaves depended not only on whom plantation owners wanted to purchase, but also on whom powerful Africans wanted to sell. The victims of the slave trade were also able to exert agency at times. Slave rebellions occurred frequently, and the risk of such events probably increased costs to the point that it somewhat reduced the scope of the overall traffic.

The introduction of new crops and livestock by the Spanish had far-reaching effects on native settlement patterns as well as on economic, social and political development in the Western Hemisphere.

When the Europeans arrived in the New World, wheat, barley, and rice did not grow there, nor were corn, potatoes, and sweet potatoes found in Europe and Asia. The Americas had very few domesticated animals: llamas and alpacas, dogs, guinea pigs and some species of fowl. There were no horses, cattle, sheep or goats. The Columbian Exchange would change all this and transform the environment on each of the continents.

The exchange of crops affected both hemispheres. When corn made its way to China, or potatoes to Ireland, the supply of food increased and supported higher population levels. Similarly, wheat and cattle shaped the post-Columbian future of the Great Plains and the Texas grasslands, the Argentinian Pampas and the Brazilian interior.

The introduction of horses proved a great opportunity and advantage to many Indians. Especially in the case of the Plains Indians, horseback riding created an entirely new way of life. It changed how people lived, how they interacted with their environments and how they felt about themselves. Yet, with time, horses also aided the Europeans in their eventual quest to "pacify," or rather subdue, the Indians.

Typical Cayuse and his mount

The Spanish had a famous equestrian tradition, one of the most successful horse cultures Eurasia had ever seen. After 1492, they used their skill as mounted combatants to conquer vast swaths of lands in the Americas. From Mexico, conquistadors also struck north into the American Southwest, continuing onto the Great Plains.

Even with the presence of Spanish horsemen, it took a long time before the use of horses spread to the indigenous population in North America. The Spanish in New Mexico were well aware that their monopoly on horses was key to maintaining control in a vast and sparsely populated region. However, the Indians began to help themselves to horses, starting with the Pueblo uprising in 1680. After that, horse culture spread at breakneck speed. Trading and stealing horses from other tribes became a prominent activity among the Indians in the Southwest, the Great Plains, and the Great Basin. Fifty years after the Pueblo rebellion, horses had become integrated into Indian culture as far away as the northern Rocky Mountains, and another fifty years later horse culture had become predominant throughout the Trans-Mississippi West.

Having horses allowed for a new way of life, partially by promoting more efficient hunting expeditions. Assaulting the bison was a much less daunting task from horseback than on foot. The horse facilitated long-distance trade and travel in ways that opened the indigenous groups to new goods, impulses, and ideas. At the same time, horses once again proved to have tremendous military consequences. Adopting horses early gave some tribes the advantage they needed to punish their enemies and expand their hunting lands, which in turn forced the other tribes to exploit the reach and power of the horse in order to survive rapidly changing conditions. For some, the world simply seemed to have greater potential when seen from horseback—endless possibilities on the horizon filled mounted warriors and huntsmen with a spirit of freedom, pride, and confidence.

Christopher Columbus

The first cattle were brought by Christopher Columbus on his second voyage across the Atlantic to Hispaniola. The imported cattle reproduced rapidly, and soon imports were no longer needed. A generation later, Caribbean cattle were brought to Mexico and within a few decades had reached north into what is now Texas and south into Colombia and Venezuela. The cattle adapted to this new ecological setting and roamed the verdant grasslands in great herds. Wild cattle sometimes constituted a nuisance for Indian farmers, but the Indians also soon found the cow to be very beneficial for them. Cattle provided meat, milk, tallow, hides, transportation and a source of labor.

Even as the Indian population declined due to the smallpox scourge and other epidemics, there was a rapid increase in European livestock as cattle, sheep, and horses flourished on new farms or formerly unclaimed lands. In a way, the Indian population of Mexico, for example, was replaced by European livestock.

In the economies of the Spanish colonies, Indian labor, used in the *encomienda* system to support plantation-based agriculture and extract precious metals and other resources, was gradually replaced by African slavery.

Since the Spanish needed the Indians as workers and payers of tax or tribute, they strove to uphold some aspects of Indian life to the extent that it served their own goals and did not contradict Spanish domination or the tenets of Christianity. Even in Mexico and Peru, where indigenous religion and clergy essentially disappeared, the traditional aristocracy remained, with the backing of Spanish colonial authorities. These noblemen served as middlemen, imposing tax and labor demands on the population at large.

By the middle of the 16th century, taking Indians (other than prisoners of war) as slaves had become illegal in Spanish America. New forms of imposing labor and taxes had been introduced. So-called *encomiendas* were granted to conquistadors and other members of the Spanish elite. These grants meant that Indians were "commended" to an authority figure who was supposed to offer protection in return for service and taxes.

Although the Inca and Aztec Empires also had demanded labor and tribute from their subjects, the new demands of the *encomenderos* who held Spanish grants were often excessive, while the responsibility of protection was too frequently neglected. Thus the sense of reciprocity usually encountered in traditional Indian culture was often lost somewhere along the way. *Encomiendas* covered the region from New Mexico in the North to Chile in the South, usually proving destructive to indigenous communities. Even the holders of grants were often troubled and disappointed by the performance of the *encomiendas*, especially as the Indian populations continued to decline.

The government in Spain also had concerns about the system, as they feared the establishment of a powerful aristocracy so far from their own seat of authority. The institution was dismantled by limiting the ability of children to inherit *encomiendas*, and by prohibiting certain kinds of labor demands. *Encomiendas* remained in some areas of the empire, but mostly in marginal areas. Instead of grants of people, grants of land would form the new basis of wealth.

Meanwhile, the colonial government used royal officials to demand Indian labor and tax more directly. Indian communities were required to offer laborers to work on state projects, such as building churches and roads, or in labor gangs working in mines and on plantations. Thousands of Indians were recruited for this forced labor, and although they were paid a wage, they often encountered systemic abuse and work requirements that could have grave consequences both for individuals and the community at large.

Some Indians decided to leave their communities to avoid taxes and forced labor, going to work for Spanish landowners or city dwellers instead. Uprooted Indians thus became mobile wage laborers for mines, farms and urban enterprises.

Introduction of slavery

At the same time, the decline in Indian populations also encouraged a corresponding increase in the use of African slaves to meet labor requirements in the colonies. African slaves were with the Spanish from the very beginning, even among Cortés's army as he went to conquer the Aztecs and occupy Tenochtitlán. Later, slaves were put to work farming sugar and rice in Mexican fields. The numbers were quite a bit smaller than in Brazil and Haiti, but the black population nevertheless outnumbered the Spanish settlers in the colony.

The Spanish colonies which valued sugar plantations and gold and silver mines often made widespread use of slave labor. This was the case in Cuba, Venezuela, Colombia, Peru, and Ecuador. In parts of Spanish America where plantation agriculture and giant mines were not so dominant, Africans were rather few and far between, although some slaves were engaged as craftsmen or house servants.

Portuguese Brazil, rather than the Spanish colonies, was the world's leading sugar producer. Unlike most agricultural produce, sugarcane had to be processed with the use of expensive and sophisticated machinery on the spot. It was cut and pressed in a sugar mill, and the juice was then heated to make the sugar crystallize. In other words, sugar production actually was a combination of farming and manufacturing, requiring unusual amounts of both capital and labor. The labor was also unusual in that it was exceptionally strenuous and intense in the harvest season, and the mortality rates on the plantations were correspondingly high. Some free workers participated in this process as skilled laborers or artisans, but most of the work was done by slaves. In Brazil, African slaves soon constituted half of the total population.

Based on a single crop produced by slave labor, Brazil became the first great plantation colony and a model that would later be followed by other European nations in their own Caribbean colonies. Ever since, despite diversification of the economy, Brazilian society has continued to reflect its origins in plantation hierarchies and slavery. The white planter families emerged as a powerful and wealthy aristocracy taking control of local communities. They established connections to merchants and government officials to maintain their control of the flow of money and the use of force.

At the bottom of the social hierarchy were the slaves who were treated merely as property. This harsh, unmerciful version of slavery was quite different from African circumstances where slaves, despite their lowly social status, were treated as human beings with a certain dignity, and in many cases included as part of the extended family. American slaves, on the other hand, were subject to a new form of trade, where they were essentially interchangeable commodities. Most slaves only survived for a few years in the New World, but others replaced them from the ships plying the triangular trade between the Americas, Europe, and Africa.

European expansion into the Western Hemisphere caused intense social/religious, political and economic competition in Europe and the promotion of empire building.

European exploration and conquest were fueled by a desire for new sources of wealth, increased power and status and converts to Christianity.

From the 8th to the 15th centuries, the Christian kingdoms of the Iberian Peninsula sought to drive out the Moors, Muslims from North Africa who had conquered most of the peninsula in the early years of Islam. The gradual *Reconquista*, or Reconquest, was not complete until 1492. In 1479, two of the Spanish monarchs, King Ferdinand of Aragon and Queen Isabella of Castile, had married and united their kingdoms. Thirteen years later, their armies expelled the Muslims from their last stronghold.

The *Reconquista* was not a mere political conflict, but a crusade driven by devotion to the Christian religion and hatred of infidels. Whereas Iberian Muslim rulers offered Christians and Jews considerable religious freedom, the Christian rulers sought to use a somewhat intolerant Christianity to unite their subjects and vanquish a common enemy. *Reconquista* fighters saw themselves as obviously superior to enemies who rejected Christ and developed rules of war reflective of this view, rules that made it legal to enslave any conquered people. As soon as the *Reconquista* was complete, Muslims and Jews faced a choice of conversion or expulsion from Spanish lands.

The *Reconquista* nourished not only religious devotion but a markedly militaristic mindset and a romantic understanding of war. Spanish fighters, especially the Castilians who were to conquer the Americas, also had roots in an agricultural society where personal relationships, reputation, and honor were the key elements in determining a man's worth. At the same time, materialistic motives were apparent as well.

As the Spanish kings frequently lacked the funds to finance military actions, military leaders would risk their own money, securing in turn rights to conquered land and a share of the spoils. These pre-existing notions of simultaneously seeking monetary reward, divine favor and a glorious reputation in romantically inspired military adventures made the conquistadors a perfect fit for their demanding roles of conquerors of a New World across the enormous ocean and of people they saw as savages and heathens. They were prepared for an adventure, and Columbus gave them one.

Thanksgiving before the image of the Virgin

The Crusades had brought Europeans into contact with eastern cultures again after centuries of relative isolation. Temporarily recapturing the Holy Land allowed them to once again gain familiarity with the abundance of spices, silk, jewels, gold and other goods flowing from China, India and other parts of Asia beyond the Middle East. Unfortunately, South and East Asia were thousands of miles away, across deserts, mountain ranges, and lands where both the climate and the inhabitants were inhospitable. The long and treacherous journey from the East made spices and other goods terribly expensive by the time they reached the West.

Columbus, vastly underestimating the distance to the Indies (Asia), proposed to open up new sources of wealth and glory by sailing westward rather than following the route around Africa then being explored by the Portuguese. In 1492, his persistent lobbying finally resulted in funding for his expedition. Ferdinand and Isabella did not have complete faith in Columbus, but they realized that the potential benefits were great and the costs relatively low.

Upon arrival, Columbus was quite disappointed by the people he found. Although they were friendly and peaceful, they did not have any of the vast riches Marco Polo and other travelers had written about. Indeed, they did not know how to work metals and they had no weapons other than simple spears. Profitability was the main problem Columbus faced, and it derived from his poor understanding of geographical realities. To the very end, he thought of the islands as part of the Indies, thinking that Hispaniola was Japan and Cuba the Asian mainland.

Landing of Columbus

However, it was obvious that the rich ports and cities he had heard about were nowhere to be found, and that none of the people he met had any contact with the Great Khan of the Mongols. Columbus had hoped to form an alliance with the Khan against the Muslims, as part of a farfetched scheme to use profits from the new possessions to reconquer Jerusalem. It had been prophesized that the reconquest of Jerusalem would bring about the Second Coming of Christ.

The fortress and trading post system that the Portuguese had set up on the coast of Africa was not a realistic option for the Caribbean either. Trading posts would only be useful if there was a sizeable trade going on already, and there was no indication of that. Thus, Columbus soon realized that the only way of making the new lands profitable was colonization by European settlers and the exploitation of Indians as slaves.

While the colonies served primarily as sources of wealth and power, they continued to be imbued with religious purpose. In the Latin American colonies, the preaching orders of the Roman Catholic church—Franciscans, Dominicans, and Jesuits—played key roles. Friars took part in most expeditions, and conquest and conversion often went hand in hand (though with a questionable degree of success). Within ten years of Cortés landing in Mexico, one Franciscan friar claimed to have personally converted more than 200,000 Indians to Christianity.

Most prominent in these activities were the Jesuits, the order established as a kind of special operations force of the Counter-Reformation. In Brazil, the Jesuits pushed European settlement inland, as they pressed farther up the rivers in order to create new, tightly knit frontier settlements of Christian Indians isolated from the sinfulness of the conquistadors. In Paraguay, their settlements were so numerous and successful, that it almost appeared as a separate country. The territory had its own army and about 100,000 Indians under Jesuit tutelage.

New crops from the Americas stimulated European population growth, while new sources of mineral wealth facilitated the European shift from feudalism to capitalism.

Corn was not known in the Old World before the voyages of Columbus, but it quickly became a staple crop in the earliest stages of the Columbian Exchange. By 1630, Spain was heavily invested in the commercial production of corn, far surpassing the traditional subsistence farming in Mesoamerica.

Similarly, potatoes and sweet potatoes were unknown in Europe before the exploration of the Americas. The white potato came from the Andes Mountains in South America, where the indigenous people had developed a multitude of varieties adapted to varying microenvironments. It eventually became a staple crop in Europe and was brought to North America by Scotch-Irish immigrants in the 18th century. The potato is a good source of many nutrients, and in many European locations, a plot of potatoes was much more productive in terms of calories than an equivalent plot of other food crops. The sweet potato also became an important crop in Europe.

Peppers were grown in Central and South America. Spanish explorers took pepper seeds back to Spain as early as 1493, and the plants soon spread across Europe. Today, they are grown in tropical areas of Asia and Africa, as well as in the Americas. Tomatoes also originated in the New World, specifically in the highlands of South America. They were brought to Mesoamerica in an intercolonial exchange, but of course also to Spain, where their use in new sauces earned the label "Spanish" cuisine. The explorers also took peanuts back to Spain, where they are still grown. From Spain, traders and explorers took peanuts to Africa and Asia. Peanuts were brought to the southern part of North America along with the Africans who were shipped there as slaves.

Some Indians used cacao beans as currency, and Columbus took some to Europe as an example of American money. Cortés watched the Aztec court drinking chocolate, and eventually, this drink also became familiar and appreciated by European colonists. By the early 17th century, the drink was becoming popular in Europe itself, and later in that century, the first chocolate house was opened in England.

New crops from the Americas made the European diet more varied and sophisticated but also contributed greatly to population growth. This is especially true of corn, and even more importantly, potatoes. Incorporating potatoes into the European diet allowed higher food production and a form of insurance against catastrophic grain harvest failures that could result in misery and famine. The highly nutritious potatoes also strengthened the immune systems of Europeans suffering from debilitating diseases like dysentery, measles, and tuberculosis. The introduction of potatoes was accompanied by higher birth rates, lower mortality rates and a rapid rise of the population in both Europe and the United States.

Spaniards gambling

The abundance of gold and silver in the mountain ranges of the Americas revolutionized the European economy. In the 16th century alone, the supply of these precious metals multiplied by a factor of eight. This flood of new currency was so overwhelming that it tended to destabilize rather than strengthen the old order of things in Europe, although this had certainly not been the intention of the Spanish monarchs. The feudal system where land ownership was paramount was challenged as money, a new measure of wealth, came into play in a much more significant way.

The new money could be used to invest in new ventures in trading and manufacturing and was of course much more liquid and accessible than land. The feudal aristocracy in Spain, moored to the land by regulations that prevented them from participating in middle-class business activities, was left out as a new economic order emerged, where elites in other more dynamic and mercantilist countries came to the forefront. Since the Habsburg monarch Charles was both King of Spain and Emperor of the Holy Roman Empire (Germany and the surrounding areas), money spread easily across Austria, Germany, Italy, the Netherlands, and Switzerland.

The wastefulness and warmongering of the Spanish kings meant that most of the bullion from America had to be devoted to paying off debts, and on several occasions the Crown was even forced to default on those debts, meaning that despite the enormous riches obtained in the Americas, Spain was essentially bankrupt. Precious metals rather than land now became the foundation of power and status. A new class of merchants and capitalists emerged that would eventually dominate not only Europe but the whole world.

Even on the fringes of Europe, the Ottoman Empire which controlled Turkey, the Balkans and most of the Middle East and North Africa were far from immune to the impact of American silver. The impact was suddenly felt in 1584 when the Ottoman currency fell precipitously amidst shocking price inflation. The currency fell to half of its former value and never regained its significance in world trade again.

Arguably, the influx of silver from the Americas did more to undermine the worldly power of the Islamic countries in the centuries that followed than any other factor. In fact, throughout the world, the new European wealth eroded the value of holdings in every other country in the Old World, while allowing Europe to expand and form a Eurocentric system of world trade. The silver of America made possible a world economy for the first time, as much of it was traded not only to the Ottomans but to the Chinese and East Indians as well. All the great civilizations of Eurasia were thus brought under the influence of American silver and its destabilizing effects. Europe's prosperity boomed, and its people wanted all the teas, silks, cotton, coffees and spices which the rest of the world could offer in the new global economy.

Improvements in technology and more organized methods for conducting international trade helped drive changes to economies in Europe and the Americas.

The exploration of the Americas was made possible in part by prior technological developments in Europe. The Spanish and Portuguese had pioneered a vessel called the caravel, which made oceangoing exploration possible. These were relatively small, narrow, but sturdy ships, often with two lateen (triangular) sails. Their larger counterpart, the carrack, usually had a full rig, that is to say, two square sails and one lateen sail. They were slower, but they were harder to board and could carry more cargo. European navigators had acquired the magnetic compass from the Muslims.

Caravel with oars

Portuguese galleons and carracks

However, it was probably the Portuguese who first used mariner's quadrants to accurately measure the angle from the North Star (or the Southern Cross, in the Southern Hemisphere) and thus determine latitude, which was crucial in unknown waters. Determining longitude accurately, on the other hand, was impossible. Navigators would generally try to follow a certain latitude from east to west and then try to estimate the ship's speed by observing the hull's movement and the hourglass. Having guessed what the speed was, they could guess what their position was, although with limited accuracy.

The importance of oceangoing ships was such in the new world economy, that Europeans continued to pursue new navigational technologies. By the 18th century, they had developed octants that made the measurement of latitude even simpler and more accurate. Around the same time, astronomers developed a method for predicting the angular distance between the moon and other celestial bodies.

Using this technique, the navigator at sea could use a new device, a sextant, to measure the angle between the moon and a planet or star, calculate the time at which the moon and the celestial body would be at that angle, and then compare local time with the standardized time of the national observatory. Knowing the time difference between the two points allowed a precise determination of longitude. After millennia of navigation, seafarers were finally able to determine the exact position of their vessel at any given time.

Spanish Armada

The expansion of European economic interests into new areas around the world also led to innovations in the field of business organization. This was not so much the case with the Spanish and Portuguese, whose ambitions of honor, glory and aristocratic leisure were in a sense feudal and medieval. However, later Dutch and English colonial projects had much more of a mercantile and capitalist flavor. Among the innovations they pioneered in response to the quest for colonial riches were two of the most important financial innovations of all time, the joint-stock company and the stock exchange.

The earliest joint-stock company in England was the Company of Merchant Adventurers to New Lands, chartered in 1553. More significant and vastly more wealthy and influential was the East India Company, granted a royal charter by Queen Elizabeth I in 1600. This charter gave the Company, as it became known, enormous trade privileges in India, effectively a temporary monopoly on trade between England and Indian ports. The Company went far beyond mere trading ventures, however, supporting its mercantile clout with veritable armies and navies, and eventually expanding its political power until it was essentially the government of a colonized subcontinent.

Similarly, the Dutch East India Company was a tremendously powerful political, military and economic force. Starting in 1602, it issued shares that could be traded on the Amsterdam Stock Exchange, a brilliant financial innovation that made it easy for joint-stock companies to attract investor capital since it became much easier to both buy and sell shares.

Henry Hudson

The Dutch East India Company was arguably the world's first modern corporation and was allowed to operate with limited liability, meaning that investors could only lose what they had invested, and were not liable for any further debts incurred by the company.

Henry Hudson sailed on the river which now bears his name on behalf of the Dutch East India Company, and his explorations led to the establishment of New Netherland (present-day New York). Eventually, Dutch interests in the Americas would come to be pursued by a separate Dutch West India Company. But before that time, the joint-stock Virginia Company established in England in 1606 had already established a settlement at Jamestown.

KEY CONCEPT 1.3: Contacts among American Indians, Africans and Europeans challenged the worldviews of each group.

European overseas expansion and sustained contacts with Africans and American Indians dramatically altered European views of social, political and economic relationships among and between white and nonwhite peoples.

With little experience dealing with people who were different from themselves, Spanish and Portuguese explorers poorly understood the native peoples they encountered in the Americas, leading to debates over how American Indians should be treated and how "civilized" these groups were compared to European standards.

Establishing contact with the Indians was shocking to the minds of Christian Europeans: the indigenous people of the Americas did not appear in the Bible or in the other main source of authoritative knowledge, the writings of the ancient Greeks and Romans. At the outset, it was not even clear whether or not the Indians should be considered human. From the perspective of Christian Europe, this would require the Indians to have the ability to reason and a soul which could be saved from eternal suffering through conversion to the true faith. Once the pope had declared that Indians were human, the Spanish began to recognize their humanity as well. They saw them as a part of the united community of God and recognized that they had certain rights.

Spanish explorers raising memorial cross

Europeans generally and the colonists especially had few qualms about subjecting American Indians and Africans to harsh discipline and hard work or taking away other peoples' lands or humanity. The only major exception before the second half of the 18th century was the dissent of some highly articulate Spanish friars and theologians. Dominican friars on Hispaniola had come to convert the heathen but witnessed death and destruction on an unprecedented scale.

Mostly because of diseases the Europeans brought, with the added effect of violence and forced labor, the population of Hispaniola dropped from maybe several million in 1492 to less than 30,000 twenty years later. One day in 1511, Antonio de Montesinos gave the first sermon on the treatment of the native peoples: "Tell me, by what right of justice do you keep these Indians in cruel and horrible servitude? On what authority have you waged a detestable war against these people, who dwelt quietly and peacefully on their own lands? . . . Are these not men? Have they not rational souls? Are you not bound to love them as you love yourselves?"

The colonists were outraged by this attack, but the Dominicans continued to question the legality and morality of the colonial enterprise and forced a protracted debate among lawyers and theologians in Spain. The Dominican theologian Francisco de Vitoria used the medieval conception of natural law to demonstrate that Indians were rational beings with rights to life, liberty, safety and property which could not be abridged either by the pope or by the king of Spain. His writings went far in the direction of creating a foundation for international law, as well as suggesting the basic equality and dignity of all human beings.

But the most famous defender of Indian rights was Bartolomé de Las Casas, originally a priest who owned former Indian lands worked by forced Indian labor. He experienced a crisis of conscience in 1514, became a Dominican friar, and spent most of his life working for better treatment of the Indians. He argued that the European purpose in the New World should be peaceful conversion. In 1550–51, he argued the case of the Indians at a hearing in Valladolid, Spain, debating for several months about the legal and theological aspects of colonization and empire. His main opponent was the scholar Juan Ginés de Sepúlveda, who argued the Aristotelian point that the civilized had every right to rule over barbarians.

Las Casas and his supporters had some influence on the development of Spanish colonial law, but most of the time the protections guaranteed to Indians and Africans existed only on paper. Because of his tendency to exaggerate, Las Casas was also used to propagate the so-called "Black Legend", the idea that Spanish rule was more cruel and unjust than that of the other colonial powers. In reality, it would be difficult to argue that the other powers of the 16th and 17th centuries were significantly better.

Many Europeans developed a belief in white superiority to justify their subjugation of Africans and American Indians, using several different rationales.

Three early modern developments were responsible for the entry of racial stereotypes into the European view of the world: the emergence of the transatlantic slave trade, the formation of social structures in colonies settled by Europeans, and the *Limpieza de Sangre* (i.e., purity of blood) on the Iberian Peninsula. The latter had an indirect link to colonial development in the New World, while the first two were intimately connected with it.

Controversy exists regarding whether racial concepts already existed at the beginning of the slave trade. When Africans were sent to the New World as slaves, it may in part have been because they were already seen as inferior. However, the slave market system followed its own logic and led to the further development of concepts of race.

The establishment of the transatlantic slave trade was governed by the rules of the early markets. Besides, the Europeans usually did not take slaves themselves, but rather purchased the slaves from other Africans or from Arab middlemen. In other words, they needed to build business relationships with African merchants and chiefs on a basis of equality or at least some element of mutual recognition and respect. Nevertheless, the trade increasingly contributed to the perception that Africans in the New World were inferior.

Dutch selling slaves to the Virginia planters

The widespread use of African slaves necessarily contributed to the racialized social structures of the New World, although the structures usually preceded the explicit and eventually elaborate justifications for their creation and maintenance. The social system of the Spanish Colonial Empire appeared to be organized strictly according to racial origins with clear distinctions between whites, blacks, Indians and intermediate categories.

However, this system was much more rigid in theory than in practice, and some people were able to transcend racial boundaries and improve their position in society. As this shows, the racial elements of the system of social stratification did not necessarily indicate ubiquitous racism. Unlike later developments in the British colonies, the Spanish and Portuguese Colonial Empires allowed the intermingling of peoples and the crossing of racial lines, rather than seeing the mixing of races as an abomination and a threat to society.

Native peoples and Africans in the Americas strove to maintain their political and cultural autonomy in the face of European challenges to their independence and core beliefs.

European attempts to change American Indian beliefs and worldviews on basic social issues such as religion, gender roles within the family and the relationship of people with the natural environment led to American Indian resistance and conflict.

A basic justification for the Spanish conquest of the New World was the Christianization of the Indian population and its adoption of Spanish values and ways of life. A good example of the challenges involved in this program is New Mexico, founded in 1598 when Juan de Oñate, the scion of a wealthy mining family, established a colony in the upper Rio Grande Valley. At the time, the Pueblo Indians in the area lived in villages called pueblos, and Franciscan missionaries built mission churches on the outskirts of these existing villages. By 1680, they had established thirty missions and a similar number of religious stations in the region.

The relationship between the Pueblo and the Spanish was always strained. As many as twenty thousand Pueblos converted to Christianity; they adopted Christian marriage and burials and participated in feast day processions and other rituals. Yet, while the Pueblos were baptized, attended church, accepted communion and so on, they also continued to perform traditional religious ceremonies considered anathema by the Spanish.

The Franciscan missionaries were frequently outraged by such transgressions and would seek to punish indigenous beliefs and behaviors by desecrating shrines, destroying religious objects and imposing corporal punishment on traditional religious leaders. At the same time, the Pueblos were forced to build new churches and to pay tribute to the *encomenderos* who were supposed to offer military protection from warlike tribes in the region.

Spaniards destroying Mexican idols

By the 1630s, the Pueblos erupted in rebellion against the Spanish colonizers and their assault on the Indian way of life. In the following decades, tensions continued to mount as epidemics, drought, poor harvests, and raids by the Apache and the Navajo negated the anticipated march to progress. In the 1670s, a missionary accused Indian villagers of witchcraft, and a number of Pueblos were executed or flogged. By the 1680s, Pueblo discontent was unleashed in a rebellion of unprecedented scale and ferocity.

Led by a victim of religious persecution, the Indians sought to remove every trace of the European way of life. They killed their livestock and cut down their trees, and took river baths to wash away the effects of baptism. Many missionaries were killed, and the city of Santa Fe laid to waste. Almost 400 people were killed in the uprising, and it took twelve years before the Spanish returned.

By that time, some of the Pueblos actually welcomed the Spanish. They wanted the Spaniards to protect them against enemy raiders and to regain the benefits of trading with the Europeans, who had access to goods otherwise not available. The Spanish also decided to reach a new understanding with the Pueblos. The *encomienda* system was no more, and fewer labor demands were made. They granted land to the Pueblo villages, and appointed an advocate to protect their rights and argue their cases in court. Even the Franciscans became more tolerant, avoiding the subject of traditional Pueblo ceremonies as long as they were performed in secret. In general, the Spanish colonizers attempted to define norms and roles in the new colonial societies.

New notions of gender were constructed in the context of the Roman Catholic family and religious structure. Spanish women were seen as naturally more virtuous and valuable than others; their virginity was "protected" and a woman's adultery was punishable by death. The women of other races or of mixed blood were seen as having exotic bodies; although they could also be portrayed as innocent mothers and wives in the mold of the Virgin Mary, they were more typically regarded as highly sexual beings, seductive and available for Spanish men.

The Spanish sometimes married indigenous women, and even more frequently had sexual relationships with them, often resulting in mixed-race offspring. Thus many never became "proper" mothers and wives, but rather mistresses raising illegitimate children. Latin American life had a strong flavor of patriarchy, a system women could really only escape by joining a convent.

In spite of slavery, Africans' cultural and linguistic adaptations to the Western Hemisphere resulted in varying degrees of cultural preservation and autonomy.

The Middle Passage, or the slave voyage to the Americas, was a traumatic experience for the slaves. After being captured, they could be branded, shackled, forced to walk long distances and confined to dark dungeons for long periods even before they boarded ships where filth, disease, and abuse were the order of the day. Some chose to commit suicide either before or during the long journey to the Americas. Despite these traumas, Africans were also able to keep some of their culture, language, belief systems, traditions, and memories. Some even organized rebellions and took control of slave ships.

Differences between European cultures as well as the various origins of the slaves in Africa and the environmental settings of the Americas meant that slave societies differed considerably from each other, but there were many similarities as well. Every slave system differentiated between African-born slaves and American-born descendants. Status systems also evolved with hierarchies where free whites were at the top, slaves at the bottom and free people of color, often mixed race, held an intermediate position.

Color and "race" played a role in American slavery it had not played in Africa. Slaveholders gave American-born slaves more opportunities to acquire skills and perform domestic duties, especially if they were mixed race—often a consequence of abuse or sexual relationships between slave women and male members of the slaveholding family. They were less likely to do the excruciatingly mindnumbing and backbreaking work in the fields and mines, and more likely to be given their freedom by masters, a process of liberation called manumission.

This system, created by those who owned slaves, did not necessarily correspond with notions of status among the slaves themselves. Africans who had been nobles or fetish priests in their homelands sometimes continued to exercise authority, or at least influence, within the community of slaves. However, differences in origin, birth, and color did have a tendency to split slave communities along racial and ethnic lines, which slaveholders usually saw as an advantage. After all, they did not want the slaves to be capable of collective action on their own terms.

Sugar plantation

In the Americas, Africans kept at least some features of their traditional cultures alive, whether language, art, or traditional practices and beliefs. The exact level of continuity was very variable, depending on the extent to which members of the same tribe were transported together in sufficient numbers to obtain a critical mass. Ongoing connections between the Old World and the New also enabled slaves to maintain their culture over time.

Yoruba culture, for example, virtually flourished in northeastern Brazil due to the frequent trade contacts with the Bight of Benin. Members of the various Akan groups were predominant in Jamaica, while Ewes were plentiful in Haiti. Slaveholders could make efforts to obtain a mix of slaves from different ethnic groups, but the regular patterns of the slave trade often undermined such efforts.

Despite Africans' hopes of retaining their identities, the brutal facts of reality indicated that they had to adapt and change, and they also had to be open to developing new forms of culture based on the heterogeneity of cultures on diverse plantations. In addition, they had to bow down to the culture and manners of the slaveowners, so that the new Afro-American cultures reflected adaptions of African cultures to American realities. In this sense, the new cultures were dynamic and creative, but their development was of course by no means free or unfettered.

Religion was one important aspect of culture where both forced adaptation and creative syncretism occurred. The Spanish and Portuguese colonists and missionaries were eager to convert Africans to Catholicism, and some slaves also became very devout Christians. They even organized in new Catholic fraternities divided by African origins. Still, beliefs and practices carried from Africa remained important and raised the ire of the Inquisition which investigated paganism, heresy, and demonic deeds. Africans were frequently accused of witchcraft.

In the English islands, Africans continued to perform religious rituals rooted in African tradition. These practices were called obeah, and those who served as ceremonial leaders had high status in the slave communities. Similarly, religions derived primarily from African sources, such as candomblé and Vodun, remain significant to this day in Brazil and Haiti, respectively. They have survived centuries of attempted suppression.

It was easier to bring beliefs and customs across the Atlantic than religious institutions. Without a class of clergy or religious specialists, most aspects of religion were subject to change in a new and extremely challenging setting. Slaves often held both Christian and traditional beliefs simultaneously or attempted a syncretic fusion of the two. For Muslim Africans, this was far more difficult. As late as the 19th century, a major slave rebellion among Muslim slaves of Hausa and Yoruba origins targeted both whites and infidel blacks.

While the drudgery, brutality, and isolation of plantation slavery certainly discouraged it, resistance and rebellion were nevertheless an import feature of black history in the Americas. Wherever there were slaves, there were people evading work, running away, or even directly confronting owners and overseers. From the outset in the early 16th century, slaves in Spanish America disrupted communications, plotted rebellions, and sought other ways to subvert or escape authority. Communities of runaways formed throughout the Americas and such communities especially flourished in Colombia, Venezuela, Brazil and some of the islands in the Caribbean. Some of these communities became veritable towns or small kingdoms.

For example, 17th century Palmares (in Brazil) contained numerous villages and possibly as many as 10,000 inhabitants. This society of runaways was made up of both African and American-born slaves, organized and led by Angolans. They successfully fought back against Portuguese and Dutch aggression for a century. Similarly, the "Maroons" of Jamaica managed not only to break away from their chains but also to be recognized as a virtually independent community.

Slave rebellions organized by various African ethnic groups were a regular feature of life in the Caribbean and Brazil. In North America, where slave survival and reproduction rates were higher, and the American-born contingent correspondingly larger, such rebellions based on ethnic unity were much more difficult to orchestrate. Nevertheless, other, more subtle forms of resistance were an important part of slave existence in North America as well.

John Brown at Harper's Ferry Raid

In Suriname, large numbers of runaways fought a protracted war against the authorities in the 18th century. Despite the brutal prosecution of the war by slaveowners and the government, the war eventually came to a standstill, and the Maroons were able to create a kind of separate society based on West African cultural forms fused with the ways of Europeans and Indians, a new and truly Afro-American culture. Today, many descendants of these runaways live in Suriname and French Guiana, still maintaining some of their traditions, customs and beliefs.

PERIOD 2

1607-1754

Emergence of distinctive colonial and native societies as Europeans and American Indians maneuvered and fought for dominance, control and security in North America.

Major historical events of the period:

1739 – Stono Rebellion

1676-1677 – the rebellion of Nathaniel Bacon

1744-1748 – King George's War

1686 – Dominion of New England

1730s-1740s – the Great Awakening

1732 – Hat Act and Debt Recovery Act

PERIOD 2: 1607-1754

> **KEY CONCEPT 2.1: Differences in imperial goals, cultures and the North American environments that different empires confronted led Europeans to develop diverse patterns of colonization.**

Although the various European colonial powers, including England, Spain, France, and the Netherlands, had some shared goals for the colonizing process, the substantial differences in the home cultures of these countries, as well as the variety of environments encountered in the New World, led to a remarkable diversity in the patterns and outcomes of imperial ventures. The divergent considerations and purposes of governments played a large role in creating differences in how countries administered and ruled the distant lands they claimed.

For example, the Spanish government was far more actively involved in governing its colonies than England. The Spanish model of centralization and control led to different trajectories of development than the largely hands-off approach of the English. The land and its natural resources also greatly affected trajectories of development; areas suitable for growing export commodities, like sugar and tobacco, imported large numbers of slaves, while areas characterized by more mixed agriculture evolved in a different way.

In some of the latter areas, the economy became significantly more diversified, allowing the development of crafts, commerce, and small-scale manufacturing. Other factors, including warfare, laws, religion, disease, racial sentiments, gender roles and relations between colonists and Indians also made a difference and ensured that the American colonies—despite their commonalities—ended up as something of a mosaic of social, economic and cultural patterns.

Cultivation of tobacco at Jamestown

Seventeenth-century Spanish, French, Dutch and British colonizers embraced different social and economic goals, cultural assumptions and folkways, resulting in varied models of colonization.

One of the most significant differences between the colonial powers was the difference in cultural perceptions of economic development, or more simply, the meaning of making money. To the Spanish elite, made up of the monarchy, nobility and the church who dominated society and stamped their cultural values on the process of colonization, it was ultimately titles, honor, luxury and the glory of God that mattered. There was no glory in working hard or accumulating capital; money was supposed to be spent on luxuries and leisure, or even more prudently, on conquests, wars and the conversion of heathens. They sought wealth primarily through extracting mineral resources or demanding tribute and labor from native populations and placed little emphasis on economic development in the sense of modernization or progress.

In short, the Spanish outlook was aristocratic and pre-capitalist, and despite the many manifestations of their greed, they valued money as a means to an end rather than an end in itself. Even Columbus himself died an unhappy man despite the great wealth he had accumulated, feeling that he had not been recognized as an administrator and a religious pioneer.

The Dutch, who were essentially trying to gain their independence from Spain between 1568 and 1648, had a very different culture and a different order of priorities. In the 17th century, the Netherlands became the world leader in shipping, commerce, and finance. The government was a federal republic where merchants were heavily influential, and colonial ventures were directed by joint-stock companies rather than the Crown. These companies had their own armies and navies and utilized force whenever it was necessary to secure profits, but capitalist gains rather than glory or honor were usually the ultimate aim. Over time, however, their overwhelmingly commercial orientation and impressive financial savvy were not enough to protect their leading position in the world economy, as they were surpassed by other nations that were militarily stronger.

The British colonies were unusual in that the government exercised very little control in their development compared to other colonial powers. The colonies were created almost haphazardly and for a variety of economic, religious and political reasons. There was little or no uniform administration, and the colonists in America grew accustomed to having various rights and privileges relatively independent from the Crown.

The North American colonies were generally seen as unattractive because they did not bring immediate profits from high-value commodities like gold, silver or sugar. Those who were already rich and powerful saw little reason to waste their time or energy on these projects. Instead, they became opportunities for Europeans from middle- or lower-class backgrounds who wanted to improve their status, become rich or create religious utopias.

The cultural development of these colonies was in turn heavily influenced by the beliefs and customs of the immigrants who arrived there. Puritans in England, Germans in Pennsylvania and Scottish Highlanders in the North Carolina hinterland all brought a unique set of behaviors and lifestyles that remained influential despite the necessary adaptations to the New World environment and the colonial system.

Settlers in North Carolina

With the decline of Spanish power in the 17th century, France emerged as the greatest power on the European continent. However, this power relied on the ability of the government to extract soldiers and taxes from a large population in order to fight large-scale and expensive wars. This led the French government to discourage mass emigration to the colonies, and a reluctance to use scarce resources and manpower to defend American settlements. Canada and Louisiana seemed to have few natural resources that could be easily exploited, and efforts to develop these areas tended to be halfhearted. The French were more concerned with Haiti, which promised to be a major supplier of highly demanded sugar.

Spain sought to establish control over the process of colonization in the Western Hemisphere and to convert and/or exploit the native population.

The voyages of Columbus soon turned into a diplomatic issue. The lands Columbus had found were south of the Canary Islands (outside the northwesternmost part of Africa) and thus conceivably reserved for the Portuguese under the 1479 Treaty of Alcáçovas. Ferdinand and Isabella hurried to secure their claim by seeking support from the pope, who proposed a western boundary for Portuguese claims.

This eventually led to the Treaty of Tordesillas, signed in 1494, which divided Castilian and Portuguese claims along a north-south line 370 leagues west of the Cape Verde Islands. This would eventually justify the Portuguese claim to Brazil and the Spanish claims elsewhere in the Americas, as the treaty formally divided the non-European world between Spain and Portugal.

Queen Isabella of Castille (left) and King Ferdinand V of Aragon (right)

However, as early as the peace treaty signed by France and Spain in 1559, the two parties agreed that attacks west of the Azores or south of the Tropic of Cancer should not be a reason for war in Europe. In practice, this meant that all colonial areas were subject to continual warfare outside the customary rules of declaration of war, Christian ideas of "just war", etc. Spain reserved the right to attack anyone trying to trade in the Caribbean, and the other nations reserved the right to attack and capture the Spanish treasure fleets. Outside Europe, anything was fair game. This principle became known as "no peace beyond the line."

The English started their American involvement as privateers and smugglers in the 16th century. But after 1600, they set up several colonies on the mainland of North America and in the Caribbean, disregarding Spanish claims. In 1655, they even took Jamaica, a colony already set up by Spain. In 1670, the Spanish finally faced reality and recognized the English settlements as legitimate. This ended the anarchic era of "no peace beyond the line," and it became possible to some extent to distinguish between pirates and lawful traders. This was not the end of piracy; on the contrary, the first half century after 1670 is often considered the golden age of pirates and buccaneers.

An example of the sometimes chaotic colonial rivalry between the European powers before 1670 was the early white settlement in Florida. The first colonial outpost there was established by the French in 1564, with the specific purpose of attacking Spanish treasure galleons sailing past. The following year, a Spanish expeditionary force was sent out to destroy the settlement, and the Spanish commander ordered summary executions of the surrendering Frenchmen.

A few years later, in 1573–74, the Spanish government changed its policies toward the Americas, deciding that the church, rather than the military, should be the main representative of the Crown in the Americas. Part of the rationale behind this new policy was that the missionaries would be less ruthless and exploitative in their dealings with the indigenous people. However, the Franciscan missions in 17th-century Florida turned out to have very disruptive effects on the Indians. They now had to live in mission villages and become full-time farmers, incorporating European crops and animals into a new way of life. They were very vulnerable to the diseases brought by the colonists, resulting in many deaths and a steady decline in population. Military assaults by English and French forces further destroyed the population.

French and Dutch colonial efforts involved relatively few Europeans and used trade alliances and intermarriage with American Indians to acquire furs and other products for export to Europe.

The French sent numerous explorers to North America and made pioneering discoveries around the Great Lakes and in the Mississippi Valley, founding settlements from Quebec and Montreal in the North to New Orleans and Baton Rouge in the South. However, peopling these settlements proved a tremendous challenge. The Company of New France (Canada) failed to bring the promised number of colonists across the Atlantic. The imposition of direct royal rule in 1660 did make a difference, but these areas were never able to compete with the English colonies in terms of population.

Instead, they became largely dependent on friendly Indian tribes militarily, commercially and in terms of finding wives for French men. Indians who joined the settlements were legally accepted as French and in principle eligible to take up residence in France itself without any process of naturalization. Despite the French efforts to invite Indian partners and allies, however, the lack of actual colonists gave France a severe disadvantage in the colonial rivalry with England.

After 1660, competition between French and English colonists over the lucrative fur trade escalated. The English challenged the monopoly of the French by chartering the Hudson Bay Company, while at the same time French and mixed-race individual traders also sought to circumvent regulations. Eventually, a system emerged where wealthy merchants in Montreal were able to send out licensed traders far and wide to procure furs.

Indians at a Hudson Bay Company trading post

Most of the actual trapping continued to be done by the Indians, and the fur trade played a significant part in the many wars between the various Great Lakes tribes throughout this period. Thus, the European competition over the furs of beavers and other animals, due in great part to the popularity of beaver hats across the Atlantic, ended up severely destabilizing a large region in the Americas. The expansion of fur trading and exploration into the Mississippi Valley led to the foundation of the vast colony of Louisiana, stretching in parts the entire north-south length of the present-day United States and from the Rockies to the Appalachians.

However, the lack of easily accessible natural resources and the failure of the French government to provide the infrastructure, commercial facilities and physical safety necessary to make the colony attractive for settlement meant that few Europeans chose to migrate there.

The Dutch in New Netherland (encompassing present-day New York and parts of the surrounding states) were also primarily interested in the fur trade. Like the French, they relied to a great extent on building alliances and trading with the local Algonquian and Iroquois tribes. The port of New Amsterdam, today's New York City, became an important hub for exporting furs and other American commodities to Europe. The Dutch West India Company tried to support colonization and population growth by granting vast tracts of land to so-called *patroons* who would, in turn, invite immigrants to become tenant farmers on their land, but this policy was only moderately successful. After the Anglo-Dutch wars of the 1660s–70s, New Netherland was ceded to the English.

The Dutch trading with the Indians

Unlike their European competitors, the English eventually sought to establish colonies based on agriculture, sending relatively large numbers of men and women to acquire land and populate their settlements, while having a relatively hostile relationship with American Indians.

Unlike the Spanish quest for precious metals and the Dutch and French involvement in the fur trade, English colonization of the North American mainland sought to reproduce a European way of life by focusing on family farms. This was especially true of the northern colonies because the southern colonies featured slave-based plantation agriculture more closely resembling Caribbean models than anything seen in Europe. Access to land, combined with a measure of political and religious autonomy, made these colonies attractive to immigrants, including couples, families and single men and women. Heads of immigrant families could be rewarded with land grants. Others received grants directly from the Crown, bought or rented land or simply chose to squat on land that had not yet been distributed to other white settlers.

The new landowners were often mobile and opportunistic, utilizing farmlands in an unsustainable way and then moving on to greener pastures when the soil was exhausted. The access to ample, fertile land nevertheless made farming by far the most important activity in the English colonies, engaging the vast majority of the population until the 19th century. In addition, English settlers also engaged in shipping, shipbuilding, fishing, and trade.

The British hunger for farmland and other natural resources combined with the lack of racial intermixing in these colonies led to a pattern of frequent and often enduring hostilities between the colonists and the indigenous people. Although there were many examples of cooperation, peaceful trade and even military alliances between whites and Indians, tensions were often persistent and resulted in raids, plunder, and retribution as well as outright wars leading to conquests and massacres.

Part of the problem stemmed from different conceptions of rights to land; the Indians generally believed that such rights only extended to specific uses of the land and its resources at a given time or season, while the British equated landownership with absolute and unrestricted control of the land to the exclusion of others. The introduction of crops and domestic animals from Europe also disturbed existing ecological systems and posed a further challenge to the Indian way of life.

The British–American system of slavery developed out of the economic, demographic and geographic characteristics of the British-controlled regions of the New World.

The sale of slaves to the British colonies in North America accounted for a very small proportion of the transatlantic slave trade as a whole. At first, most slaves did not even arrive directly from Africa, but rather from other colonies in the Caribbean. Even though African captives arrived in Virginia as early as 1619, the British system of slavery in the Americas really developed on the islands during the first half of the 17th century.

Following the Brazilian model, these Caribbean colonies thrived by focusing on the production of sugar on large plantations where almost all the workers were black slaves. Slaves became the majority on these islands; their rights were extremely limited and their lives often short. The treatment of slaves differed significantly from the African tradition where slaves were more commonly treated as inferior members of the family with the ability to gain their freedom after some years of service.

Slavery on the North American mainland was initially of a more complex and humane nature, with Africans sometimes treated more like indentured servants or at least as people who eventually might gain freedom for themselves or their children. The term "slave" was not even used, and for some time there were no laws clearly specifying the conditions of these workers. However, as the availability of indentured servants from England declined and Africans became a larger proportion of the workforce, political leaders in the southern colonies took steps to ensure that the institution of slavery would ensure a lasting supply of laborers. They turned to the models of the Caribbean and sought to define slavery as a permanent situation where people would be treated as property for life.

Domestic slave trade

In the northern colonies, which were unsuitable for plantation agriculture, slavery was less common. Maintaining slaves over the long northern winters made less sense as there was little farm work to be done. Still, there were substantial numbers of slaves, especially in the cities, where they more typically performed household chores or worked in shops and workshops. Some historians argue that northern whites tended to own slaves as a status symbol rather than primarily to make a profit. However, the New England colonies were also heavily involved in slave trading, where there was a lot of money to be made.

Unlike Spanish, French and Dutch colonies, which accepted intermarriage and cross-racial sexual unions with native peoples (and in Spain's case, with enslaved Africans), English colonies attracted both males and females who rarely intermarried with either native peoples or Africans, leading to the development of a rigid racial hierarchy.

In the Spanish colonies, intermixing of races had been taking place since the very beginning and resulted in a complex but, to a certain extent, flexible status hierarchy based on skin color and birth. When the French and Dutch established colonies in the Americas, there were few Europeans involved, and especially few European women. As in the Spanish case, this led to widespread intermarriage, and mixed-race offspring could rise to important positions in colonial society. Louisiana law prohibited Catholics from marrying non-Catholics, but there were no restrictions based exclusively on race.

By contrast, some of the English colonies began to legislate against marriages between whites and slaves, and later between whites and any black or mulatto person. The Chesapeake planters were especially fearful of a coalition of white and black laborers and sought to ensure rigid separation of the races to discourage cooperation across color lines. However, rules against miscegenation extended to the northern colonies as well, especially since beliefs about race often were fused with religious sentiment. Massachusetts and Pennsylvania, with their strong religious foundations, also had very strict rules against interracial sex and marriage. Free blacks or mulattoes who were caught having sex with whites could be sold into slavery.

Although intermarriage was frowned upon and often prohibited, interracial sex was nevertheless fairly common, occurring both as everyday transgressions of community norms and as one aspect of masters' abuse of slaves in a slave society. As many as one in three black Americans living today have a male ancestor of European descent, largely because of such liaisons between slave women and their owners. However, being of mixed race did not qualify an individual for an intermediate status in British colonial society. On the contrary, most offspring of black-and-white unions were and remained slaves throughout the colonial period.

The abundance of land, a shortage of indentured servants, the lack of an effective means to enslave native peoples, and the growing European demand for colonial goods led to the emergence of the Atlantic slave trade.

One of the big problems confronting planters in the British colonies was that both white and Indian laborers had options and could be difficult to control. White indentured servants could run away and blend into the population, or even band together and demand government intervention on their behalf. Easy access to land ownership in the colonies also made the idea of doing backbreaking, poorly paid work for others unappealing to Europeans. Similarly, if Indians were forced to do plantation labor, they could use their local knowledge and connections to disappear.

At the same time, Indians were very vulnerable to Old World diseases, while Europeans succumbed to malaria more easily than Africans. Thus, if Africans could be subjected to the harsh slave codes of the Caribbean, mainland planters could have a more reliable source of labor. This facilitated the export of tobacco from the Chesapeake area and rice from South Carolina and enriched a planter aristocracy at tremendous human cost.

Depiction of a tobacco wharf in colonial America

The slave trade expanded rapidly to absorb the demand for new slaves to work on the plantations and farms and in the households and shops of whites in British North America. In all, about 500,000 Africans were brought from Africa and the Caribbean to what is now the United States before the end of the transatlantic trade in 1807. This was only 6 percent of the total number of slaves brought from Africa to the Americas. However, slaves on the North American mainland reproduced at much higher rates than elsewhere, which in turn led to the development of a sizable internal trade in slaves.

Reinforced by a strong belief in British racial and cultural superiority, the British system enslaved black people in perpetuity, altered African gender and kinship relationships in the colonies, and was one factor that led the British colonists into violent confrontations with native peoples.

While slavery and the slave trade expanded, Europeans elaborated on racial ideas which served to legitimize the unprecedented use of fellow humans in new and more brutal forms of slavery. Blacks were typically portrayed as not only inferior and savage but often as subhuman or a different species of human altogether. These notions were thought to justify the introduction of chattel slavery, in which slaves were treated entirely as property. Although these ideas evolved partially in response to economic developments, the English had often associated blackness with wickedness and death even before interactions with the African continent became common. Historically, the English had fewer connections with Africa than Mediterranean peoples such as the Spanish and the French, and their ideas about black people were often rooted in legends and outrageous tales about demons and monsters rather than personal interaction.

Power and ideology allowed slave masters control of slave families. Slave owners often preferred to purchase male slaves, but since these were also in demand in the Caribbean, the mainland colonies ended up with a greater balance of women and men than elsewhere. Sometimes slave women were brought in to provide companionship for male slaves, or more strategically, to ensure reproduction of the slave population.

In slavery, Africans saw their accustomed gender roles and kinship structures challenged or fundamentally changed. Men were forced to hoe the fields, a task reserved for women in West Africa. Both men and women performed their work as part of the owner's commercial plan rather than to feed their families, to the extent they were even allowed to have families. Although masters often encouraged procreation, they viewed slaves as property, meaning their rights as spouses and parents were severely limited or even non-existent.

African women, who saw the role of mother as the most important of all, experienced tremendous physical and mental anguish from constant demands that they not only bear children at regular intervals but return to the fields quickly thereafter. Furthermore, the pregnancies were often the result of rape by the master or someone else in the household. Obligations toward children limited opportunities to resist or attempt to escape, and the breakup of families was a common form of disciplinary action against slaves who were considered unruly.

Slave auction

Notions of superiority and inferiority also affected the relationships between white settlers and indigenous people. The New England Puritans, for example, believed that the Indians had been lured into settling in the New World by Satan, in order to lead them away from God. When epidemics broke out among the Indians due to the introduction of European diseases, they took this as confirmation that God favored them and meant to punish the natives. Even brutal warfare and outright massacres were justified in the same way and seen as righteous actions in the name of the Lord.

Africans developed both overt and covert means to resist the dehumanizing aspects of slavery.

Despite the fear of violent retribution, slaves sometimes managed to demonstrate their agency by resisting slavery in various ways. These included "passive" acts of resistance: avoiding work, pretending to be sick and ignoring the commands of masters and overseers. More direct forms of resistance included destroying equipment, organizing slowdowns and even serious attempts to confront the power of owners such as arson, large-scale sabotage, and murder.

Another way of resisting was simply running away. Typically, running away was a negotiation tactic. Slaves hoped that by disappearing and avoiding their work, if only briefly, they might convince their owner to improve the terms and conditions of their enslavement. Although slave owners in principle had full control over their property, the humanity and agency of the slaves forced them to bargain about the pace and amount of work to be completed and many other aspects of slaves' lives.

Some slaves also attempted to run away for good. The slaves who ran away had often served in roles that allowed them to leave the plantation on occasion, providing them with more familiarity with the outside world. In colonial times, they often headed to cities with a free black population, or to swamps, forests and other inhospitable areas where they would be difficult to find. If there were numerous runaways in an area, they sometimes managed to form Maroon communities, which helped them elude capture or even violently confront search parties.

The most dramatic form of resistance, and one that was greatly feared by slaveholders, was rebellion, or armed uprising. Such conspiracies and insurrections were more common on the Caribbean islands where blacks often represented an overwhelming majority of the population and where large numbers of Africans with a common culture and language were sometimes brought in within a short period. However, they also occurred in both the northern and southern colonies on the North American mainland.

The largest colonial uprising was the Stono Rebellion of 1739. On the mainland, rebellions were usually doomed from the outset, as reinforcements could always be brought in to subdue the slaves and execute anyone believed to have been involved. In addition, slaveholders did their best to divide and conquer slave populations by differentiating between light and dark skin, house slaves and field slaves, plantation slaves, and family farm slaves and so on. This prevented slaves from building the kind of cohesion and unity required to carry out mass uprisings.

Along with other factors, environmental and geographical variations, including climate and natural resources, contributed to regional differences in what would become the British colonies.

The climate and natural resources of the British colonies affected settlement patterns and differences in long-term trajectories of development. The climate made New England less vulnerable to infectious diseases, but winters could be difficult, the growing season was relatively short, and the soil tended to be rocky. However, abundant timber resources were useful for the shipbuilding industry, which in turn supported the growth of fisheries and seaborne commerce. The Middle colonies farther south had a milder climate and good soil for farming, which lead to the development of prosperous agricultural communities. Grain, corn, and meat were sold to other colonies, and good ports and the central location of these colonies allowed for the rise of merchants and craftsmen in the two biggest cities of the colonial era, Philadelphia and New York.

Exploring northern Georgia

In the southern colonies, the warm climate allowed for a long growing season and the spread of plantations that grew export commodities. In Virginia, there was a mix of plantations and family farms and a mixed agriculture of cash commodities, food crops, and livestock. Planters dominated the tidewater areas, while the backcountry, as well as the less favorable land found in North Carolina, was settled mainly by small farmers. Subtropical South Carolina and Georgia more closely resembled the Caribbean colonies, with a strong focus on growing rice—and later indigo and cotton—by using slave labor.

The New England colonies, founded primarily by Puritans seeking to establish a community of like-minded religious believers, developed a close-knit, homogenous society and—aided by favorable environmental conditions—a thriving mixed economy of agriculture and commerce.

The founding of the New England colonies (Massachusetts, Connecticut, Rhode Island, and New Hampshire) was motivated by both economic and religious factors. Unlike the Spanish colonies—where missionaries set out to spread the official religion of the home country—the New England colonies were settled by religious dissenters. They were mostly Puritans, who had sought to purify the church at home but decided instead that they would have to create a new society across the Atlantic, taking on an "errand into the wilderness" to show the world a "city upon the hill," an ideal community for other Christians to observe and eventually emulate.

The Puritan settlement was remarkable in that a large number of people—20,000 in the 1630s alone—arrived there in a time when crossing the Atlantic was a major endeavor in terms of both cost and safety and the conditions in the promised land very uncertain. Before long, they had founded numerous towns and set up churches on their favored Congregationalist model, which, in contrast to the Church of England, allowed each church substantial autonomy. Attending church was mandatory, but only a select few, the "saints," were actually church members.

As Calvinists, the Puritans believed that every individual was predestined for either salvation or damnation, and they developed elaborate tests and procedures to make sure that only the former group was recognized as members of the church. This was important because Massachusetts was a theocratic society in which only church members could vote in elections, individual morality was heavily regulated and dissenting views could be punished by death or banishment from the colony.

One of those banished was Roger Williams, who considered religion a private matter and wanted to separate church and state and make church attendance voluntary. After being exiled, he founded Providence and was able to start a new colony in Rhode Island. Unlike the other New England colonies, Rhode Island became known as a land of religious freedom. Among the Puritan colonies, Connecticut was somewhat more open to religious diversity than Massachusetts, as it did not limit voting rights to church members.

Despite the hierarchical division of people based on religious factors, colonial New England was a fairly egalitarian society for its time. Most of the inhabitants lived on small farms where they produced much of what they needed for themselves. However, their religious beliefs indicated that God had called them to do hard work, and that material success was a sign of divine favor. For these reasons, the Puritans strove to improve their material lot and engaged in a variety of crafts and trades.

Roger Williams building his house

The colonial economy grew, and the average standard of living was quite high, even though New England crops such as barley, oats, and rye were also produced in Europe and not in high demand as exports. Growth was supported by active provincial and local governments that worked to improve the infrastructure of the region and even subsidized the building of mills and other early manufacturing works. The legal system was adapted to capitalist development by securing the sanctity of contracts and property rights. New England became famous for its entrepreneurial spirit.

The demographically, religiously and ethnically diverse middle colonies supported a flourishing export economy based on cereal crops, while the Chesapeake colonies and North Carolina relied on the cultivation of tobacco, a labor-intensive product based on white indentured servants and African chattel.

The middle colonies, including New York, New Jersey, Pennsylvania, and Delaware, were more diverse in terms of religion and ethnicity than New England, which was dominated by Puritans from the English low country. Both the Netherlands and Sweden had tried to establish colonies in this region, and the vast tracts of fertile land soon attracted immigrants from Germany, France, Scotland, Ireland and other places in Europe. Some came as indentured servants but ended up as successful craftsmen or farmers. Pennsylvania, founded by Quakers, offered religious freedom to a wide variety of sects and denominations, and New York offered citizenship to anyone who embraced Christianity. Quakers, Baptists, Methodists, Episcopalians, Lutherans, Amish and Mennonites flocked to the middle colonies from other colonies and Europe.

Quaker woman preaching in New Amsterdam

The fertile soil allowed farmers in the middle colonies to grow a big surplus of grains for export. Pennsylvania became the largest producer of food on the continent. The rivers of the area offered useful connections between port cities and a hinterland that supplied fur and lumber. These rivers also supplied energy for mills and other manufacturing enterprises. The economy flourished, but not everyone benefited equally. In some areas, land ownership was controlled by the Dutch *patroons* and Englishmen favored by the Crown, and the riches of the cities tended to be concentrated among a few prosperous merchants. Although there was a sizable middle class of farmers, artisans, and shopkeepers, there was also a large underclass of tenants, laborers, servants and slaves.

While the economy of the middle colonies was diverse and encompassed hunting, trapping, fishing, farming, crafts, mining, metalworking, manufacturing, shipping and trade, the economy of the Chesapeake colonies, Virginia and Maryland, relied to a great extent on tobacco. Large plantations were the centers of economic activity, to the detriment of urban development. Planters brought in indentured servants and slaves to work the land, secured the best farmland and organized most of the shipping themselves. Population growth was slow, as there were limited opportunities for poor European immigrants, and the mortality rate was high due to widespread epidemics.

The rebellion of Nathaniel Bacon in 1676–77 appealed to disempowered whites by attacking both Indians and local authorities in Virginia but was soon struck down by the power of the Crown and the planter class. The rebellion was spurred by a decline in tobacco prices which caused economic hardship. In the 18th century, Chesapeake farmers and planters chose to reduce their risk of failure by diversifying crops, and they began producing more grains, flax, and meat.

The colonies along the southernmost Atlantic coast and the British islands in the West Indies took advantage of long growing seasons by using slave labor to develop economies based on staple crops; in some cases, enslaved Africans constituted the majority of the population.

While the development of the British West Indies and the mainland colonies were intimately connected politically, culturally and economically, the Caribbean islands had their own unique characteristics. Their intense focus on producing sugar and their dependence on trade for virtually everything else gave them little of the semblance of self-sufficiency found in some mainland colonies. The vast estates, plantations worked by hundreds of slaves and often owned by wealthy men who did not even live on the islands, were another distinguishing characteristic.

Barbados, for example, had been founded as a colony for growing tobacco, but soon shifted to sugar as competition from the Chesapeake colonies intensified. Slaves—and, at first, convict laborers from Ireland—cut down tropical forests all over the island to grow sugarcane. Almost 400,000 slaves were brought to the island, but death rates were high, and many were resold in other American markets. Nevertheless, by the 18th century, blacks outnumbered whites by three to one. Yet this was a relatively low ratio compared to many of the other colonies.

The colony of Carolina, split into North and South Carolina in 1729, had its twin origins in the cultures of Barbados and the Virginia backcountry. The northern part of the colony, settled by Virginians, lacked land suitable for plantations and natural ports facilitating international trade. The southern part, on the other hand, became a colony in the Caribbean mold, featuring large plantations, a slave majority, and a monocultural focus after rice became the predominant crop early in the 18th century. South Carolina was also a center for trade in Indian slaves. Eventually, the colony began efforts to attract European immigrants to the backcountry, partially as a defense against potential slave rebellions.

Georgia, established much later than the Carolinas, had a stunted development due to the original prohibition of slavery in the colony. Only a few Europeans settled there before slavery became legal in 1749. For that reason, the early history of Georgia was similar to that of North Carolina. However, with the advent of plantation slavery, Georgia was on its way to becoming like South Carolina and, by extension, the Caribbean possessions.

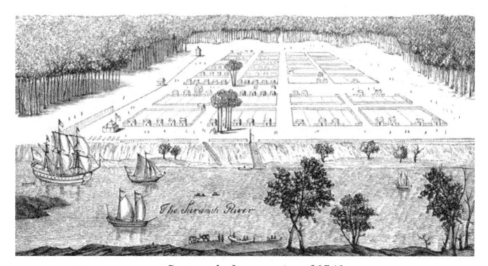

Savannah, from a print of 1741

> **KEY CONCEPT 2.2:** European colonization efforts in North America stimulated intercultural contact and intensified conflict between the various groups of colonizers and native peoples.

Indian trade with the Europeans, and with it, access to European goods and technologies, offered new lifestyles, new status symbols, and new ways of waging war. Better tools, weapons and household goods were great advantages that could tilt the balance of a preexisting rivalry between tribes in favor of those most closely connected to the white newcomers. These opportunities also induced indigenous people in French, English and Dutch territories to increase their trapping activities, as furs were highly sought after in Europe.

For these reasons, Indians often thought it beneficial to maintain a working relationship with European settlers, despite the disruptive effects of disease, the introduction of new flora and fauna and the outright expropriation of land. Thus, early colonial relations were often a mix of cooperation and intermittent conflict. However, the rapid and continuous increase of the white population and the corresponding quest to control land and other natural resources inevitably created tensions that at times erupted into murder, massacre, skirmishes, and war. In the long run, Indian resistance tended to be futile, as wars typically ended in defeat and the surrender of rights and land. As white settlement moved beyond the coastline, conflicts intensified and multiplied as both Indian refugees and European colonists encountered and confronted the tribes of the interior.

Competition over resources between European rivals led to conflict within and between North American colonial possessions and American Indians.

As the power of Spain began to decline in the early 17th century, the Dutch, who were at that time fighting for their independence from Spain, began to challenge Spanish hegemony in the Americas. France and England followed suit. Due to the continuing decline of Spain and the eventual defeat of the Dutch in several wars with the English, the rivalry between France and Britain eventually became the central conflict in 18th-century North America. The various colonial powers also had Indian allies who played important roles. In many cases, the Indians favored the more accommodating and less land-hungry French and Spanish rather than the increasingly populous and aggressive English colonies.

Between 1688 and 1748, the colonial powers were embroiled in three major wars that could arguably be classified as world wars. The first of these was King William's War (1688–97), known as the Nine Years' War in Europe, which was fought to prevent France, the major power on the continent, from becoming too dominant. In North America, the war was fought for different purposes, as the French were few and seemingly weak there, trying to hold on to vast territorial claims on the Hudson Bay region and the St. Lawrence and Mississippi Rivers with a very limited settler population.

The French, however, were able to inflict numerous defeats on the English colonists, partially because of the effective combination of French, colonial and allied Indian troops. The French were also successful in North America because the English government chose to prioritize the West Indian colonies, as the profits from the sugar islands made them more valuable.

The arrival of the Indian allies at the French camp

Queen Anne's War (1702–13) was also part of a larger European conflict, the War of the Spanish Succession. Again, the goal was to limit the power of France, as a member of the French monarchy had inherited the throne in Spain. This meant that the British had to battle both Spanish and French forces in the Americas. Once again, the British clashed with the French and their allies to the north, but this time with greater success. By the end of the war, France was forced to cede Nova Scotia, Newfoundland, and the Hudson Bay region. Meanwhile, Spanish Florida had been completely devastated by the brutal raids of the British and their Indian allies, inflicting so much death and destruction that the Spanish colony never quite recovered.

A generation later, two other wars erupted in the Americas, and once again they were intertwined with a European conflict, the War of the Austrian Succession. In the War of Jenkins' Ear (1739–48), the main issue was the British monopoly on the slave trade to the Spanish colonies. Much of this war played out in South and Central America and the Caribbean, but in 1742 Spanish forces invaded Georgia. After this attack was repelled, the North American theater was relatively calm for some time.

By 1744, however, King George's War had broken out with renewed fighting between the French and the British. The British forces were able to capture the Fortress of Louisbourg in Nova Scotia, but this did not prevent French forces and their Indian allies from raiding frontier areas. The British settlements north of Albany had to be abandoned entirely until the war ended in 1748. The colonists in New York and especially those in Massachusetts suffered very heavy casualties during this war and were incensed when the peace treaty traded Louisbourg for a town in India.

Conflicts in Europe spread to North America as French, Dutch, British and Spanish colonies allied, traded with and armed American Indian groups, leading to continuing political instability.

Early modern Europe was a dangerous and violent place with numerous long, brutal wars. The continual conflicts between the great powers did not only take place at home but spread to include lengthy, costly and destructive colonial wars as well. For example, the Spanish settlements in Florida were often attacked by English and French forces and their respective Indian allies, and so much death, destruction and enslavement ensued that by the early 18th century the whole area was almost devoid of people. Other Spanish colonies faced fierce Indian uprisings, such as the Pueblo Rebellion of 1680 and the Pima Revolt of 1751.

The 17th-century Beaver Wars, also known as the Iroquois Wars, were a series of wars between the Iroquois tribes supported by the Dutch and English and the Algonquian tribes supported by the French. The imperialist Iroquois sought to extend their domains and control the fur trade in the Great Lakes region, expanding from their eastern strongholds into new, western lands. In wars increasingly marked by extreme brutality, the Iroquois enlarged their empire and destroyed or displaced many of the other Indian tribes. As enemy groupings disintegrated and fled to the west and south, large swaths of land in the Great Lakes region and the Ohio Valley became virtually depopulated. This strengthened the hand of England in colonial North America and even facilitated the settlement of this area by white Americans in the early United States.

The 18th-century Chickasaw Wars, although ostensibly a conflict between Indian tribes, had similar beneficial effects for British interests. The Choctaws, acting as proxies of the French in Louisiana, sought to defeat the Chickasaws, who were allied with the English and threatened French communications and trade along the Mississippi River. Even French efforts to wage European-style campaigns with heavy artillery proved futile, as did the decades-long Choctaw harassment consisting of raids, ambush attacks and failed sieges.

As European nations competed in North America, their colonies focused on gaining new sources of labor and on producing and acquiring commodities that were valued in Europe.

Since the main aims of colonization were to take control of land and resources and sell exports to Europe, the colonists had a pressing need for a labor force. Many workers were needed on the vast "new" lands to raise crops and livestock, labor in mines, mills, docks, shops, and workshops, or to work as craftsmen or servants. Because of this need, colonial elites worked tirelessly to find new labor sources, including both free and indentured immigrants, convicts, Indians, and Africans. Early labor forces were often a mix of African, Indian and European workers, but where large plantations dominated there was a tendency to eventually rely almost exclusively on slaves of African descent.

Scene on a plantation

These large plantations in the South produced many of the main export commodities that North America had to offer, primarily tobacco, rice, and indigo. In addition, the northern colonies exported wheat and wheat flour, corn, fish, livestock and horses, and some lumber and metal products. Foodstuffs were often sold to the planters on the Caribbean islands where sugar was by far the dominant export, integrating the mainland colonies into the sugar economy.

The French colonies on the mainland, however, exported little of value except for large numbers of furs. New Spain (present-day Mexico and southwestern United States) had an economy long focused on mining, but by the 18th century, silver exports were supplemented by other colonial exports like sugar, tobacco, cocoa, cotton, and dyes. However, the failure to distribute water resources in an equitable manner was a disaster for agriculture, which in turn meant that the Indian population that provided most labor continued to decline.

Carolina rice field

The goals and interests of European leaders at times diverged from those of colonial citizens, leading to growing mistrust on both sides of the Atlantic, as settlers, especially in the English colonies, expressed dissatisfaction over territorial settlements, frontier defense, and other issues.

Colonial subjects were often dissatisfied with their European rulers, who saw the colonies primarily as a source of resources and revenues for the mother country. They especially complained about the distribution of lands and occasional failures to protect vulnerable settlements against European rivals or hostile indigenous people. In addition, they often circumvented laws and taxation by smuggling goods from one colony to another, thereby weakening the grip of the European powers.

The fur trade is an important example of this latter tendency because of its significance to Indians, colonists and European governments. While governments tried to control the fur trade and introduce monopolies, widespread smuggling occurred in and between the English, French and Dutch colonies. The same thing happened with tobacco from the Chesapeake colonies; it is sometimes suggested that the amount of tobacco smuggled was at least equal to the amount of tobacco exported through approved channels. Some settlements in the Caribbean were created with smuggling as their main purpose.

European governments sought to limit colonial production of commodities that could be made in the home country. In England, the 1699 Wool Act prohibited American colonies from exporting wool or yarn and cloth made from wool to Britain, and it also restricted trade in wool between the colonies. At other times, governments could issue regulations that favored their own colonies over those of their rivals, or some colonies at the expense of others.

For example, the Molasses Act of 1733 was meant to favor planters in the British West Indies by taxing molasses imports from the colonies of other countries. This legislation favored sugar growers in the British colonies, but it was very harmful to the interests of New England and the middle colonies since they had grown accustomed to buying less expensive molasses from French, Spanish and Dutch possessions. This favoritism demonstrated that many British leaders considered the West Indian colonies more important to the imperial economy than the mainland colonies.

Clashes between European and American Indian social and economic values caused changes in both cultures.

Indian culture was forced to change by the advent of Europeans, at first simply by the force of disastrous epidemics and dramatic population decline. Later, the ways of the Europeans altered Indian practices at a deeper level. Indigenous people were encouraged to fight wars against each other to capture slaves for white buyers, and the goods they received in return, such as alcohol, caused not only cultural change but also dependence and social problems.

Indians were also encouraged to hunt animals such as deer for their pelts only, rather than focusing on food needs. This led to the overhunting of game. Similarly, European land use put vast tracts under monoculture, eliminating other uses for the area and exhausting the soil. Thus, European influence had a tremendous impact on the Indian way of life.

At the same time, Indian culture also influenced the European colonists. This is especially true of the Spanish colonies where widespread intermixing of races led to a parallel mixing of cultural, social and economic values. However, the British settlers also adopted aspects of Indian culture, most importantly the system for raising corn. Styles of artistic expression were also influenced both ways. Colonial officials expressed considerable concern about their subjects "going native" by adopting Indian lifestyles, especially in the case of whites who had been captured in raids or war. In many cases, long-time captives refused to return to what the colonists thought of as civilized life, instead running away from settlements to rejoin their captors.

Continuing contact with Europeans increased the flow of trade goods and diseases into and out of native communities, stimulating cultural and demographic changes.

There are many examples of the changes wrought by cultural contact. The Catawba people, once a formidable tribe in the Southeast, were so devastated by 18th-century smallpox epidemics that most of its members died, and the rest had to accept settlement on a small reservation in South Carolina. Similarly, the Huron tribes in present-day Ontario succumbed to epidemics in the 1630s and then in the 1640s came under attack by the Iroquois Confederacy, which was trying to secure control of new territories and replace members who had died from the European diseases. The Hurons, originally farmers who had been drawn into the fur trade by their French allies, were dispersed, some joining the Iroquois and others making desperate attempts to resettle in new lands. By that time, however, the overwhelming majority of the Huron population had died.

King Philip, or Metacomet

Like the Hurons, who divided into traditional and pro-colonist factions at the time of their collapse, the Wampanoags ended up devastated by disease and war and failed to preserve much of their identity and culture, which had been challenged by contact with Massachusetts colonists.

The Wampanoags, who eased the colonists' transition to America and are remembered in the celebration of Thanksgiving, initially forged peaceful relationships with the white settlers in order to access trade goods and win allies against their Indian enemies. Eventually, however, the leader of the Wampanoags, King Philip, came to the conclusion that the influence of the colonists—especially the spread of Christianity and the hunger for land—was detrimental to traditional Indian culture. King Philip initiated a bloody conflict with the English colonists in 1675. However, the consequences of the war mostly harmed the Wampanoags and allied tribes; despite heavy losses, the English successfully defended their settlements. Thousands of Indians were killed, died from disease, or were sold into slavery.

Spanish colonizing efforts in North America, particularly after the Pueblo Revolt, saw an accommodation with some aspects of American Indian culture; by contrast, conflict with American Indians tended to reinforce English colonists' worldviews on land and gender roles.

After the Pueblo Revolt, Spanish colonial officials used heavy-handed tactics to squelch new insurgencies, but their overall strategy was greater accommodation of Indian culture. The activities of the Franciscan missionaries were restrained, and the Pueblo were able to worship according to their tradition and perform their own rituals. They were also granted land, and a Spanish lawyer was sent to serve their interests in courts of law. Similarly, after a joint Spanish and Pueblo force were able to finally strike a decisive blow against nomadic Comanche raiders, the colonial government in New Mexico sought peaceful coexistence rather than the destruction of the tribe.

In contrast, the English colonists often failed to accommodate native interests, primarily because the English were so numerous and so eager to secure new lands for farming and other activities. Their entrenched view of their own superiority also made the English inclined to push their values and culture on neighboring peoples.

The "praying towns" instituted by the Puritans in New England were meant to convert Indians not only to Christianity but more broadly sought a full conversion to a European way of life. They insisted that Indians should be farmers rather than hunters and gatherers and should adjust their clothing, hairstyles, manners and family relations to a European norm. Women lost much of the stature and influence they previously possessed in traditional settings. This wholesale conversion to a new way of life was very different from the methods of the French Jesuits in Canada, who tolerated syncretism—a mix of Christian and native rituals and practices—in their conversion efforts.

By supplying American Indian allies with deadlier weapons and alcohol and by rewarding Indian military actions, Europeans helped increase the intensity and destructiveness of American Indian warfare.

Trade was an important aspect of relations between indigenous people and colonists in North America. The fur trade was especially important because furs were considered highly fashionable symbols of status in Europe. In return for furs, European traders offered iron knives and axes, textiles, blankets, utensils, cookware, and jewelry that Indians could use to improve their standard of living or display their social status.

Over time, the Indians became dependent on these items and often preferred them to traditional goods that could be made with local resources and indigenous knowledge. In addition, the traders introduced strong alcoholic beverages like rum and whiskey. Perhaps because many of the Indian tribes saw spiritual potential in trance- or dream-like states, alcohol quickly became incredibly popular. Social problems arose as a consequence, and some colonies made attempts to prohibit the sale of alcohol to Indians. However, high demand and correspondingly high profits made most of these laws ineffective.

The dependence on alcohol made several of the tribes dependent on furs, which in turn encouraged both ecological mismanagement and intermittent warfare with other tribes over hunting grounds. These wars were facilitated by and became bloodier as a result of another European trade good: firearms. The trade in weapons was on such a scale that the price of beaver pelts could be quoted in pistols or trade guns. The French and English also supplied their Indian allies with firearms as part of their efforts to limit each other's influence. Their encouragement of wars for territory and hunting grounds increased the prevalence and scale of conflicts in colonial North America.

Trading with Indians

> **KEY CONCEPT 2.3: The increasing political, economic and cultural exchanges within the "Atlantic World" had a profound impact on the development of colonial societies in North America.**

The concept of an "Atlantic World" is used to describe the complex exchanges between Western Europe, West Africa, and the colonies in the Americas. In numerous areas, including not only the political, military, legal and economic histories but also the demographic, social, cultural and intellectual histories of this megaregion, national boundaries were transcended by cross-cultural, international exchanges. The many connections between different points in the Atlantic World developed in a complicated web of exchanges that often transcended the scope of any national or colonial government's authority. The development of chattel slavery, religious awakenings, trade expansion, epidemics, environmental change, and even colonialism itself should be seen in this light.

Thousands of ships carried millions of men and women, including explorers, soldiers, officials, traders, farmers, preachers, laborers, servants, and slaves from Europe and Africa to the Americas. They brought precious metals, agricultural commodities, furs, pioneers and colonists, who may or may not have been successful, across the Atlantic. Every journey brought a new set of encounters and reshaped the cultures of both the Americas and the Old World continents, connecting millions of lives in time and space.

"Atlantic World" commercial, religious, philosophical and political interactions among Europeans, Africans and American native peoples stimulated economic growth, expanded social networks, and reshaped labor systems.

Europeans explorers, merchants, conquerors and settlers initiated much of the activity that eventually linked the Atlantic World together, although other groups played important roles as agents in this process as well. The creation of an Atlantic World contributed greatly to the creation of a world economy, promising great wealth for some, modest comforts for others and devastation, ruin and enslavement for many of the indigenous people of Africa and the Americas. American precious metals allowed a more dynamic, freer economy in Europe, and colonial stimulants, like tobacco, sugar, and cocoa, promoted harder work and a culture of mass consumption, paving the way for the Industrial Revolution. Labor systems were transformed as Indians and Africans were exploited as slave labor while European colonists could rise from subordinate positions to become independent farmers, traders, and craftsmen.

However, the Atlantic exchanges were not merely economic in nature. The crossings of people, books, habits, and customs spread new ideas and beliefs and forced both colonizers and colonized to adjust their views. Religious and political philosophies shaped how colonies were organized, especially in some of the English colonies purposely established as New World utopias. At the same time, the European encounter with America led to a new understanding of the world, forcing intellectuals and scientists to reconsider the ancient writers and the Bible as infallible sources of authority. The discovery of new lands and peoples opened up new intellectual worlds and brought old verities into question. The newly emboldened Europeans and Americans then set out to revolutionize the world through science, technology, and political transformation.

The growth of an Atlantic economy throughout the 18th century created a shared labor market and a wide exchange of New World and European goods, as seen in the African slave trade and the shipment of products from the Americas.

The labor systems of the New World drew upon the availability of conquered Indians and Africans who could be bought in the West African ports. European workers were also important; before 1700, most white immigrants came to the Americas as indentured servants rather than free men and women. Some of them were convicts, but most simply paid for the very expensive passage to the Americas with years of their lives. Like slaves, they received no wages but were provided with room, board and simple clothing. They were not allowed to marry or have children, and their working conditions were often miserable. At the end of their contract, they were free to leave and use whatever skills they had acquired to secure their financial independence.

However, this solution to the problem of securing labor was not particularly satisfactory to either the white elite or to the indentured servants themselves. Similarly, using Indians as slaves became controversial in the Spanish possessions, and their death rates and tendency to escape made African slaves a relatively favorable alternative, especially for plantation owners who needed a large labor force to grow sugar and other staples. On the other hand, slavery did not become equally widespread in areas without plantation agriculture, suggesting the role of practical considerations in developing new labor systems.

The success of plantation products, especially sugar and tobacco, both increased the demand for workers and enabled the planters to invest in more land and more slaves. Thus, the success of sugar and tobacco in Europe and the success of slavery in the Americas were tightly entwined and dependent on each other. At the same time, the flow of sugar and tobacco provided a stimulus to European workers, enabling them to work harder and encouraging them to enter labor markets to make the wages without which they could not procure colonial goods. While Africans and Indians became dependent on European wares, the Europeans grew equally dependent on colonial commodities. Entrepreneurs on both sides of the Atlantic consequently made great profits.

Sugar cane

Several factors promoted Anglicization in the British colonies: the growth of autonomous political communities based on English models, the development of commercial ties and legal structures, the emergence of a transatlantic print culture, Protestant evangelism, religious toleration and the spread of European Enlightenment ideas.

Starting in the late 17th century, the diversity and novelty of the individual British colonies on the North American mainland began to disappear in some ways. Colonists had adjusted to the climate and health risks and found ways to sustain growing populations with food. Families became more European in structure, and even warfare became more European, increasingly focused on colonial rivals rather than Indians. The Crown began to take a greater interest in the far-off colonies and imposed a more coherent legal and political structure on them. The colonies became increasingly anglicized, meaning that they came to resemble England to a greater degree.

The colonies also became more cosmopolitan as more urbanization was taking place, and information from the Old and New Worlds could be gathered from pamphlets and newspapers due to the spread of print culture. However, this was less prevalent in the South, home of the slave plantations, than in the North, home of colleges, seminaries and law schools. The southern elite outwardly emulated the English elite, but their way of life was fundamentally different. At the same time, they were still dependent on their commercial ties with England.

Across the colonies, the dominant elites were beginning to depart from their original projects, utopian or not, and express admiration for the workings of the British system of government. Colonial intellectuals absorbed the discourse of leading British writers on politics, law, and religion. They saw themselves as British patriots and fought wars against the Spanish and French with remarkable enthusiasm and imperial fervor. Even the religious revivals were inspired by European innovations in religious thought, and American thinkers familiarized themselves with the classical liberalism of John Locke as well as the great minds of the French and Scottish Enlightenment.

Even before the influence of Enlightenment freethinkers, some colonies began to expand religious toleration in a bid to welcome a variety of immigrants rather than trying to create a new society where everyone shared the same beliefs, as had been the case most prominently in Massachusetts. Rhode Island was founded in explicit opposition to the Puritans' zeal for persecuting dissenters, and the foundation of Maryland also coincided with an articulation of principles of religious tolerance. However, the Maryland Toleration Act did not go as far as Rhode Island, as only Christians who believed in the Trinity were accepted. The main purpose of religious toleration in Maryland was to secure a safe haven for English Catholics in the New World.

In Pennsylvania, founder William Penn allowed migrants of all faiths to settle. He and his fellow Quakers were convinced that people should find God in their own way, and unlike the other colonies, no official church was established in Pennsylvania. Penn believed that religious toleration would ensure peace and prosperity in the new colony and invited persecuted groups to leave Europe behind and find freedom in the New World. However, religious freedom did not mean religious equality. Only Christians were allowed to participate in politics as voters or officeholders.

William Penn

The presence of slavery and the impact of colonial wars stimulated the growth of ideas on race in this Atlantic system, leading to the emergence of racial stereotyping and the development of strict racial categories among British colonists, which contrasted with Spanish and French acceptance of racial gradations.

In the 18th century, the difference in racial ideas between Spanish, French and British colonizers persisted. The Spanish continued to rely on complex hierarchies of status and power where mixed-race individuals such as mulattoes and mestizos were viewed differently from blacks and Indians. A caste system was meant to provide each person with a social status depending on their specific mix of European, African and indigenous descent. Such subtleties did not exist in the British colonies, where mulattoes were seen as essentially the same as blacks, and mestizos were rare and lacked the special status of intermediaries between colonists and natives.

French Métis

In the French model, Indians and Métis could even be seen as "natural" subjects of France and part of that community. This reflected the lack of French settlement in New France and the corresponding dependence on Indian or mixed-race intermediaries in building commercial ties and brokering alliances.

Race became extraordinarily important in the version of slavery that evolved in British North America. In other times and places, slaves and masters had often come from the same racial background. This meant that some slaves could be freed and become integrated into society on equal terms, but this was not really possible in the colonies. There, slavery became intimately tied to differences in racial characteristics, leading to lasting segregation and inequality. Since black slaves were "chattel," the law in practice defined white people as human beings and black people as things or property.

Britain's desire to maintain a viable North American empire in the face of growing internal challenges and external competition inspired efforts to strengthen its imperial control, stimulating increasing resistance from colonists who had grown accustomed to a large measure of autonomy.

As the British colonies grew in population and productivity, the home government began to take more of an interest in their development. Whereas the colonies had emerged out of a variety of commercial ventures, idealistic projects, and personal ambitions and had practiced considerable autonomy in the early years, the government now tried to impose its authority on the American subjects of the Crown. Many proprietary colonies became royal colonies with royal governors who wielded considerable power that tended to increase over time.

However, the colonies typically had two other organs of government: the council appointed by the Crown and the assembly elected by voters. Although the power of the assembly was limited in some ways, it had the very important prerogative of controlling taxation. Agents of the assemblies also cooperated with the British Board of Trade, which wielded a lot of power in colonial matters. Through measured protests against overzealous governors, the colonists were usually able to maintain considerable autonomy without engaging in outright conflict with the British government.

One example of the government's efforts to standardize legislation and impose imperial control on colonial matters it had long neglected was the Debt Recovery Act of 1732. This new law was meant to introduce uniformity throughout the empire in the treatment of people who were unable to pay their debts. It stipulated that houses and slaves should be treated as equivalent to land in the collection of debts, meaning that slaves, buildings and real estate could be sold at auction if debtors could not satisfy their creditors otherwise. In Virginia, the assembly, called the House of Burgesses, passed a new law in the 1740s to counteract this law, making it more difficult for British merchants to collect on the debts of the powerful Virginia planters.

The Hat Act, also passed in 1732, was a more direct attempt to extend mercantilism by means of very specific regulation aimed to limit colonial manufacturing so as to avoid any undesirable competition for manufacturers back in Britain. The Hat Act not only limited the numbers of hats that could be made, sold or exported by American hatters, it even specified how many workers and apprentices hatmakers could employ. The point of this legislation was to force colonists to buy more expensive hats imported from Britain and consequently fostered a lot of resentment of a seemingly arbitrary power play on the side of the Crown.

As regional distinctiveness among the British colonies diminished over time, they developed largely similar patterns of culture, laws, institutions, and governance within the context of the British imperial system.

Colonization involved adaptation to a new environment, a process of building new institutions and creative transformations of cultural practices. The simple and in many ways dissimilar colonial societies of the 17th century became more complex and similar in the 18th century. Subject to many of the same regulations, political institutions, and laws, the colonies found commonalities that they could eventually use to present a more united front against the

British government. This happened despite the lack of any real movement away from British culture and political thought in the colonies. Rather it was the common experience within the imperial system that made understanding and cooperation possible.

One of the main reasons for cultural convergence was the spread of print culture. The printing presses in the colonies, along with materials imported from Britain, supplied both literary and more popular written works in vast numbers at very reasonable prices. Poems, sheets of music, chapbooks and stories about robbers and pirates were exceedingly popular. At the same time, the rapid spread of literacy meant that colonial Americans were also reading about politics, history, and religion, coming together as a kind of unified reading public.

Puritan

The educational system that taught people how to read also created a sense of uniformity, even though there were significant differences between the various colonies. In New England, education was especially valued, as the Puritans saw illiteracy and ignorance as the work of the devil. In the middle colonies, education involved more practical considerations, teaching boys work-related skills in addition to reading, math, and religious subjects. In the South, schooling was more rudimentary, except for the children of aristocrats who could afford to hire tutors and governesses.

However, education equipped most white males in the colonies with the tools needed to stay informed about outside events and develop a sense of identity transcending the family and local community, thus facilitating communication with like-minded people elsewhere in the vast colonial empire.

Late 17th-century efforts to integrate Britain's colonies into a coherent, hierarchical, imperial structure and pursue mercantilist economic aims met with scant success, due largely to varied forms of colonial resistance and conflicts with American Indian groups, and were followed by nearly a half-century of the British government's relative indifference to colonial governance.

The move from autonomy or neglect to stricter control by the royal government was especially tied to trade policies. The British Empire was set up to follow a mercantilistic model of political economy, which in practice meant a desire to control or even monopolize both exports to and imports from the American colonies, regulating and often limiting the colonies' trade with other countries or even with other colonies within the empire. In addition, the Navigation Acts specified that shipping to and from Britain and the colonies could only be handled by English ships, an effort to deprive the Dutch of their maritime supremacy. Eventually, Americans were even barred from producing finished iron goods—everything was to be imported from Britain.

In 1686, the royal government made an attempt at centralization by revoking the old charters of the northeastern colonies and introducing a new administrative structure, the Dominion of New England. The government had become concerned that the northern colonies were beginning to deviate from mercantilism by developing their own trade and manufacturing, in effect competing with the home country. The proposal was intended to impose a system more similar to the Spanish colonies in the Americas. However, this structure collapsed only three years later in the wake of the so-called Glorious Revolution in England. More generally, mercantilist policies were not particularly successful in preventing the development of a mixed economy of agriculture, commerce, and manufacturing in the colonies, or in convincing the colonists that their role was simply to make the home country rich.

One of the main reasons why mercantilism remained less than effective was a lack of sincere efforts to enforce the laws on the books. Instead, Britain preferred to look the other way and continued to allow the colonies to develop in accordance with the wishes of local white men with property. The government was so concerned with their rivalry with the French that they thought it would be imprudent to alienate the colonists, especially as the French were often more successful in recruiting Indian allies than the British.

Resistance to imperial control in the British colonies drew on colonial experiences of self-government, evolving local ideas of liberty, the political thought of the Enlightenment, greater religious independence and diversity, and an ideology critical of perceived corruption in the imperial system.

In addition to the long history of salutary neglect on the part of the Crown, leading to a long-standing tradition of self-government and relative autonomy in the colonies, colonial thinkers also applied Enlightenment ideas to the question of colonists' rights against the king. They were suspicious of authority, and often embraced the notion of popular sovereignty—the people as the source of authority—proposed by John Locke. Locke, writing in the late 17th century, believed that government was a result of a contract between the people and those in power, a social contract that created and maintained society. Unlike some previous writers, Locke held that such social contracts always had limits because some of the rights of the people, such as life and liberty, were "inalienable rights" and could not be given away.

Portrait of John Locke

The doctrine of the divine right of kings, on the other hand, suggested that the monarch could not be subjected to any authority on earth and answered only to God. Power, according to this theory, came from God, and the people had no right to judge or depose the king, no matter how disappointed they might be with his decisions or how many travesties were committed by his representatives. Any attempt to do so would be turning away from God since the king ruled by God's grace. However, in 18th-century America, the government was coming to be seen as something created by man rather than ordained by God. The king had no divine right to rule, and his true role was to serve the people and preserve their liberties—not only in the home country but in the colonies as well.

In addition to the influence of new political ideas came the complex religious situation in America. The colonies represented a variety of religious projects and a spirit of denominational competition. This, too, drew on a long tradition of questioning the authority of established churches and of dissent in matters of thought and belief. This contributed to the general anti-authoritarian mindset of the mid-18th century, especially after the tremendous success of the evangelical Great Awakening.

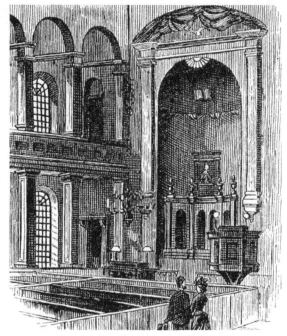
Interior of Christ Church, Boston

The Great Awakening was an outburst of emotionally charged revivals across many of the British colonies in North America in the 1730s and 1740s. It broke away from the theological boundaries, social hierarchies and traditional rituals of Protestant Christianity by introducing a new brand of much more individualistic and personal faith. This personal faith was based on stirring sermons, strongly felt belief and a deep need for salvation and redemption, leading in turn to further quests for introspection, moral improvement, and powerful religious experiences. The Great Awakening had a lasting impact not only on religious affairs but stimulated new ways of thinking about politics and social issues as well.

Resistance to perceived excesses on the part of the British government also drew on the ideology of republicanism. Republican thought, originating in the ancient world and the Renaissance, came to America through English Republicans who saw the virtue of the citizenry rather than the judgment of the king as the best guarantee for a prosperous and free commonwealth. Republicans saw power as essentially corruptible and feared the tendency of all governments to culminate in tyranny unless they were watched by vigilant citizens. While placing a new emphasis on freedom and civic virtue, this line of thinking also instilled Republicans with a certain paranoia and a tendency to develop conspiracy theories.

According to American Republicans of the 18th century, politics must be seen as a continuing struggle between freedom and power. Power must always be kept in check for the people to maintain their liberties because it would otherwise be prone to aggression and corruption. This is why any just and virtuous society is dependent on the civic engagement of engaged citizens. In extreme cases, virtue would have to mean not only opposition and protest but also an armed revolution against the ruling government. Every man of substance, that is to say, every property owner, should be able to carry arms if necessary, to stave off the abuses of ambitious kings. Republicans were especially concerned about the use of military force and taxes as instruments of royal aggrandizement.

PERIOD 3

1754-1800

Birth of a new American republic as the reaction to British imperial attempts to reassert control over its colonies. New nation's struggles over its social, political, and economic identity.

Major historical events of the period:

1754-1763 – French and Indian War

1754 – Albany Congress

1763 – Chief Pontiac's rebellion

1770 – Boston Massacre

1773 – Boston Tea Party

1775-1783 – American Revolutionary War

1776 – Colonies declare independence from Great Britain

1777 –Articles of Confederation

1785-1795 – Northwest Indian War (Little Turtle's War)

1787 – Constitutional Convention

1787 – The Northwest Ordinance is formed

PERIOD 3: 1754-1800

> **KEY CONCEPT 3.1:** Britain's victory over France in the imperial struggle for North America led to new conflicts among the British government, the North American colonists and American Indians, culminating in the creation of a new nation, the United States.

The continuing conflicts between Britain and France finally ended in a decisive British victory in the French and Indian War, forcing France to give up virtually all of its possessions in North America. However, disputes over who should bear the costs of the lengthy war, as well as other matters that divided colonists and the imperial government, brought new tensions into play. Both Brits and colonial Americans increasingly feared conspiracies on the other side, and the Crown's efforts to reassert control over the colonies after a long period of salutary neglect eventually prompted an armed rebellion and the Declaration of Independence for the thirteen colonies.

First shot in the French and Indian War

Throughout the second half of the 18th century, various American Indian groups repeatedly evaluated and adjusted their alliances with Europeans, other tribes and the new U.S. government.

The French and Indian War (1754–1763) was the fourth in a series of conflicts between the British and the French in North America, all with significant participation by indigenous tribes. Before the war broke out, much of the territory claimed by the two European powers was in effect controlled by Indians: the Mi'kmaq and the Abenaki in what are now the borderlands between Canada and the eastern parts of the United States; the Iroquois along the Great Lakes and the Ohio River; Creeks, Choctaws and Cherokees in the South; the Huron, Ojibwa and other tribes in the Northwest, and so on.

The French and Indian War got its name because many of these tribes sided with the French. French allies included most of the Algonquian peoples to the north, as well as many other tribes in what is now the United States, while the main Indian ally of the British was the Iroquois Confederacy. The Indians tended to favor the French because the much smaller French population constituted less of a threat to Indian livelihoods and behaved less aggressively toward Indian neighbors. However, some of the tribes were eventually convinced to remain neutral, following British promises that white settlement in the interior would be limited after the war. These promises would later lead to increased tension between the British government and ambitious colonists who wanted to make use of these lands for their own purposes.

English population growth and expansion into the interior disrupted existing French–Indian fur trade networks and caused various Indian nations to shift alliances among competing European powers.

Britain had been trying to tap into the fur trade in the French territories in North America since the 17th century. In the 1740s, tension intensified as traders from the British colonies crossed into the interior to trade with Indians in the Ohio Country, land which was claimed by France. During King George's War, Britain imposed a fairly successful blockade on French trade to and from North America. As French traders lacked manufactured goods with which to purchase furs, British traders soon became dominant in the Ohio Valley. An expedition into this area, led by Pierre-Joseph Céloron, failed to reassert French dominance.

In the early 1750s, new French military and diplomatic expeditions were sent into the area in response to Indian recalcitrance and the British decision to assign lands in the West to an Ohio company. The French and Indian War began when George Washington, leading colonial troops and Indian allies, attacked a small scouting party under the leadership of Joseph Coulon de Jumonville.

By that time, the long-standing relationship between the Iroquois and British had become increasingly strained as a consequence of British claims to Indian lands. The Mohawk, one of the Iroquois tribes, had declared the "Covenant Chain" broken, leading to the Albany Congress in 1754 where representatives from several of the colonies tried to establish some form of cooperation to improve relationships with the Indians. However, it was only the 1758 Treaty of Easton that succeeded in satisfying the Iroquois and other tribes under their suzerainty by establishing the Allegheny Mountains as a boundary for white settlement.

Sir William Johnson in treaty with the Mohawks

The Cherokees, long-standing allies of the British, rose up against the governments of Virginia and the Carolinas in 1758, after a long series of disappointments and misunderstandings. The Cherokees were not allies of the French, but fought their own war, drawing thousands of British soldiers away from the northern theater. This war lasted until 1761.

After the British defeat of the French, white–Indian conflicts continued to erupt as native groups sought both to continue trading with Europeans and to resist the encroachment of British colonists on traditional tribal lands.

At the end of the French and Indian War, the British took over the forts in the Great Lakes area and the Ohio country surrendered and abandoned by the French. The Indians in the region, especially those who had allied with the French, were treated as conquered people who had no say in the future development of the region. This was true of the Algonquian tribes around the Great Lakes and the Huron, Illinois country tribes, such as the Miami and Kickapoo, and even some of the Ohio country tribes who had signed the Treaty of Easton. In addition, one of the Iroquois tribes, the Seneca, had become unhappy with their alliance with the British.

Jeffrey Amherst, the British commander-in-chief in North America at the time, felt that the Indians were unlikely to be able to resist the British without the support of the French. Consequently, he treated them with contempt, cut back on gift-giving and gunpowder sales and left only very small garrisons to defend the forts. At the same time, a religious awakening broke out among the Indians, with the prophet Neolin urging indigenous people to avoid the bad habits and corrupting influence of Europeans altogether.

Pontiac's attack on Fort Detroit

In 1763, when these tribes learned that France was prepared to give up their territorial claims in the region, widespread uprisings broke out, starting with the attack on Detroit by the Ottawa Chief Pontiac. The Indians failed to capture Fort Detroit and Fort Pitt (Pittsburgh), but took control of eight other forts in the next several months. Although the conflict only lasted until the next year and ended in diplomatic accommodation, the relationship between colonists and Indians reached a new low as massacres were perpetrated and hatred stoked on both sides.

The Royal Proclamation of 1763, reiterating the British government's commitment to keeping white settlement east of the mountains, had already been underway before Pontiac's Rebellion. However, the massive uprising created a new sense of urgency as officials scrambled to appease the Indians. The idea was to (at least temporarily) separate colonists in the East from Indians west of the Appalachians, establishing what was termed an Indian reserve. Colonists now faced prohibitions against making private purchases of land west of the mountains; all land had to be purchased by the Crown after negotiations with indigenous leaders.

Both speculators and prospective settlers among the colonists were disappointed with the proclamation, and some whites were already living beyond the boundaries established by the Crown. There was pressure on the British government to enter into new negotiations with the Indians, and in 1768, treaties with the Cherokee and Iroquois granted the colonists access to lands in what is now Kentucky and West Virginia.

During and after the colonial war for independence, various tribes attempted to forge advantageous political alliances with one another and with European powers to protect their interests, limit migration of white settlers and maintain their tribal lands.

The Revolutionary War offered stark alternatives to the Indian tribes as they typically had to choose sides between land-hungry colonists eager to settle their lands or a distant British government with a mixed track record. The Iroquois Confederacy, long a powerful united force with strong ties to Britain, was torn apart as some of the constituent tribes supported the revolutionaries and others remained loyal to Britain. In general, the victory of the colonists did not bode well for the Indians as the British government gave up its claims to the Indian Reserve west of the Appalachian Mountains, essentially leaving it as spoils of victory for the Americans. Iroquois and Cherokee offensives against the Patriots had already been met by ferocious counteroffensives employing scorched earth tactics.

While the British had been decisively defeated at Yorktown, there had not been any similar event to end the war between the newly formed United States and the Indians of the Northwest. Since those tribes were not party to the Treaty of Paris that officially ended the war, they refused to accept American rights to the region. At the same time, the forts in the region were also occupied by the British, who continued to provide the Indians with weapons and gunpowder in exchange for furs.

The new American government nevertheless made provisions for taking over the land and distributing it among white settlers. The Land Ordinance of 1785 and the Northwestern Ordinance of 1787 outlined the rules of this process, but both Indians and settlers often refused to follow these rules. As a result, tensions mounted, and violence was common.

As early as 1785, the Western Confederacy was forming to unite the Indians in the region against white encroachment. Among the many tribes involved were the Huron, the Shawnee, and the Miami. Raids against white settlements became common and were sporadically met by military action. In 1790–1791, allied Indian forces led by Little Turtle and other war chiefs inflicted devastating losses on American military expeditions, including the troops of Arthur St. Clair. St. Clair, the governor of the Northwest Territory, lost more than 600 men and 200 civilian followers in one battle.

After this setback, the American government had to change its thinking about military operations against the Indians. Instead of relying on local militias, General Anthony Wayne built a legion of well-prepared soldiers and finally handed the United States a decisive victory over the Western Confederacy at the 1794 Battle of Fallen Timbers. Shortly thereafter, the war ended with a treaty in which the Indians recognized American sovereignty in the Old Northwest and surrendered massive tracts of land in Ohio and Indiana.

During and after the imperial struggles of the mid-18th century, new pressures began to unite the British colonies against perceived and real constraints on their economic activities and political rights, sparking a colonial independence movement and war with Britain.

Starting in the mid-1760s, some colonists began to express serious concerns about the rule of the British in America. They rejected Parliament's authority to tax the colonies since the colonies were not represented in Parliament. They also resisted British efforts to collect duties and impose new laws that they perceived as detrimental to their economic well-being and political autonomy. Following the Boston Tea Party and the British response, known collectively as the Coercive or Intolerable Acts, colonial subjects divided into Loyalists, who supported the Crown, and Patriots, who felt that loyalty to the Crown was no longer possible.

Boston Tea Party, throwing tea overboard

By 1775, fighting broke out between Patriots and British soldiers in Massachusetts and the conflict between the colonies and the metropole (colonial power) escalated into a full-fledged war. Representatives of the thirteen colonies declared independence from Britain in 1776, claiming that King George III had become a tyrant and no longer had any right to rule in America. These founding fathers of the United States espoused ideologies of republicanism and classical liberalism and insisted on a new understanding of social relations based on equality.

Great Britain's massive debt from the Seven Years' War resulted in renewed efforts to consolidate imperial control over North American markets, taxes and political institutions—actions that were supported by some colonists but resisted by others.

When the war with France ended in 1763, Britain was left with great debts incurred in the protection of the colonies and the conquest of Lower Canada. Part of the reason for the proclamation limiting white settlement on the continent was the cost of administration and war connected with further expansion. In addition to limiting costs, the government also wanted to increase revenue. The British sought to accomplish this by making the collection of existing duties more effective and by imposing new duties on the colonies. Part of the rationale was that Americans should pay for their own defense. However, many colonists argued that in the absence of any French threat, there was little need for a standing army of British soldiers in the colonies.

The 1764 Sugar Act imposed duties on molasses and other goods, but these were still indirect or external taxes. The 1765 Stamp Act, on the other hand, was a direct or internal tax on many kinds of printed materials. Although the British argued that the level of taxation was quite low, the colonists protested on the grounds that they were not represented in Parliament. They believed that as English subjects they could not be taxed without representation and pointed out that they also paid local taxes which had contributed greatly to the war effort.

Opponents of taxation without representation formed the Sons of Liberty and worked to make the new laws difficult to enforce. Parliament meanwhile argued that the colonies technically were mere corporations subject to British authority and that the interests of the American colonists were considered by the government in a kind of virtual representation. Still, in 1766 Parliament repealed the Stamp Act, while sticking to the principle that Britain had every right to legislate for the colonies.

Reading the Stamp Act

The next year a new set of laws, the Townshend Acts, were passed to impose duties on a variety of goods and to follow up on existing trade regulations. These laws were met with new protests and boycotts, and tensions escalated, especially in Boston, where riots ensued when a smuggler's vessel was seized by the authorities. In 1770, a mob confronted British soldiers, resulting in five deaths. Although the soldiers involved in the shooting were acquitted, the incident became known as the Boston Massacre and added to the outrage of many colonial dissidents. Later that year, all the taxes were withdrawn with the exception of a tax on tea.

Despite the concessions of the government, tensions continued to mount. Between 1772 and 1774, disgruntled community leaders in the thirteen colonies formed the Committees of Correspondence in order to coordinate action and provide information against what they considered to be the outrages of the government in Britain. The Tea Act, passed by British Parliament in 1773, was intended to ensure that the East India Company would be able to sell its tea in the American colonies at a lower price than colonial merchants and smugglers with access to Dutch tea. Since the act harmed the interests of many American merchants and smugglers while also violating the principle of no taxation without representation, opposition was widespread. The Boston Tea Party was a result of this opposition to the new legislation.

The response to the Boston Tea Party was four new laws: the Coercive Acts. Known among Patriots as the Intolerable Acts, they altered the Massachusetts charter, changed rules regarding the trials and quartering of British soldiers serving in the colonies, and shut down the port of Boston until the vast sums destroyed by the Tea Party had been compensated. Another new law extended the territory of Quebec to include the land beyond the Appalachians, thus limiting the thirteen colonies' opportunities for westward expansion.

The government saw these acts as a way of making an example out of Massachusetts, but many Patriots saw them as arbitrary and tyrannical. Corresponding committees began to function as shadow governments, and Patriots in Massachusetts formed the Massachusetts Provincial Congress and started training military recruits for battle against the British authorities. Eventually, the Continental Congress was formed and called for a general boycott of all British imports.

The resulting independence movement was fueled by established colonial elites, as well as by grassroots movements that included newly mobilized laborers, artisans, and women, and rested on arguments over the rights of British subjects, the rights of the individual and the ideas of the Enlightenment.

The leaders among both Patriots and Loyalists were typically educated men who owned property. For example, many of the leaders of the Revolution were prominent planters from the South, especially Virginia. In general, however, Loyalists were more often well-connected, with close ties to British trade, finance, and official life. Rich merchants, fur traders, government officials and people associated with these groups, were often Loyalists. Although a fair number of colonial elite men were Patriots, the main support for colonial protests came from backcountry farmers, craftsmen, shopkeepers and so on. Even common laborers were able to make their support for the revolution known, sometimes in rowdy mob actions.

Women also contributed to the resistance against Britain. They did their share by boycotting British imports and by supporting Patriot soldiers and spying on the enemy. Mercy Otis Warren used literature to attack the Loyalists and also organized meetings in her home. At the same time, many women were Loyalists and worked to secure British victory. On either side, everyday activities became infused with political meaning. To avoid buying British textiles, Patriot women were forced to relearn the skills of spinning and weaving. The thinking behind the Revolution was heavily influenced by certain strains in English thought, especially that of liberals like John Locke and republicans like James Harrington.

Portrait of Mercy Otis Warren

Locke believed that all men were born free and equal and that the origin of rightful government could only be a social contract where citizens retained some God-given rights such as life, liberty, and property. Thus, the government should be limited in its activities and rely on the consent of the governed while protecting their natural rights. American Patriots also believed that governments, whether at a state or federal level, should rely on checks and balances to ensure that no branch of government got the upper hand, a way of thinking heavily influenced by the French Enlightenment thinker Montesquieu.

Even though Montesquieu had used the English system of government as an example of a suitably mixed constitution with an appropriate balance of powers, the American founding fathers were skeptical of monarchy and aristocracy in the British tradition. In the tradition of Harrington and other Republicans, they viewed the British government with great suspicion, focusing on the corruption of the royal court and the dangers of standing armies and public debts.

One of the most prominent prerevolutionary writers was John Dickinson, who authored the *Letters from a Pennsylvania Farmer* in response to the Townshend Acts. Dickinson exemplifies another strain of thinking about colonial politics and governance little influenced by liberalism, republicanism or the Enlightenment. Instead, Dickinson was a constitutionalist with a legal background. As a lawyer and property owner, he argued that there could be no legitimate taxation without representation and that there could not be such a thing as "virtual representation." He fully acknowledged the British right to control and regulate trade, to impose import and export duties, and even to rig the whole system in favor of British merchants, but the principle that property owners had to be involved in the political process before paying taxes was, in Dickinson's view, inviolable.

Despite considerable loyalist opposition, as well as Great Britain's apparently overwhelming military and financial advantages, the patriot cause succeeded because of the colonists' greater familiarity with the land, their resilient military and political leadership, their ideological commitment and their support from European allies.

The victory of the United States in the Revolutionary War was by no means a foregone conclusion, given the considerable human and financial resources available to the vast British Empire. At the high point, the royal army was made up of almost 80,000 troops, whereas Washington only had 20,000 under his command.

However, taking the colonies against the will of many of the inhabitants was very difficult. The areas involved were vast, and it was difficult for the British to control rural areas or even protect Loyalists from the wrath of Patriots. Even though the Loyalists formed a significant minority among the colonists, they were rarely utilized by the British generals and often treated with mistrust. This contributed to the failure to win the hearts and minds of the very large part of the population that did not take a clear standpoint at the outset of the conflict. Similarly, the British promise of freedom to slaves who would fight for the Crown helped recruit some soldiers seeking emancipation but alienated the powerful planters in the South.

The Americans had the advantage of being more familiar with the land than British regulars and German mercenaries. They had also learned tactics from the Indian wars that made it possible to keep an insurgency going, disappearing into the woods after quick ambush-style attacks. Washington mostly avoided big battles, which made it impossible for the British to inflict a decisive defeat on his army.

General George Washington

Most importantly, France, Spain, and the Netherlands intervened in the war on the side of the rebels. The French especially spent enormous sums of money supplying the war effort and contributed soldiers and naval support as well. The involvement of other maritime powers also forced Britain to shift its focus to the defense of other colonies, including the lucrative sugar islands in the Caribbean.

Another very important factor was the support of many, if not most, colonists for the revolution. Thousands of ordinary people were committed to the cause and the ideology behind it and were willing to risk their lives or otherwise sacrifice for the cause. They had become motivated and engaged by the many high-profile conflicts in the years preceding the American War of Independence, and participated in town meetings, Sons of Liberty protests and more violent forms of agitation. During the Revolutionary War, as many as 400,000 Americans took up arms against what they considered to be a tyrannical government.

In response to domestic and international tensions, the new United States debated and formulated foreign policy initiatives and asserted an international presence.

The great breakthrough for American diplomacy was the alliance with France, entered upon in 1778. Alliances with Spain and the Netherlands soon followed and turned the Revolutionary War into a war of great international significance. The efforts of founding fathers Benjamin Franklin, Thomas Jefferson and John Adams as diplomats were key to international recognition of the United States and securing financial and military support for the war effort. In 1789, Jefferson became the first secretary of state under the new constitution. The need for coordinated and effective foreign policy was one of the reasons for creating a new constitution to replace the more decentralized Articles of Confederation.

The outbreak of the French Revolution in 1789 caused both international tensions and extensive debate within the United States. Many Americans were hoping for France to turn into a republic similar to the United States, and thus a natural ally against the monarchy in Britain. However, the revolution in France was considerably more radical than in America. It entailed so much violence and demanded such drastic changes that some Americans were frightened. A split occurred within the political elite, with Republicans taking the French side and Federalists supporting the British. President George Washington sought to maintain a balance and was very wary of entangling the United States in European affairs.

By 1793, Britain had entered into the international wars of revolutionary France. The United States remained neutral and managed to sign a treaty with the British which strengthened commercial ties while securing the withdrawal of British forces from the forts in the Old Northwest. This treaty was designed by federalist leader Alexander Hamilton and vehemently opposed by the Jeffersonian Republicans.

Thomas Jefferson (left) and Alexander Hamilton (right)

While relations with Britain were improving, relations with France were increasingly hostile. The United States refused to make payments on its war debts, arguing that the debts were owed to the Kingdom of France and not to any Republican state. As a consequence, France allowed privateers to begin seizing American ships. Since the United States did not have a navy, hundreds of ships were taken without any effective response. By 1798, the Adams administration decided to seek congressional authorization to revive the Navy and the Marine Corps, break off all treaties with France, and fight the French navy. The so-called Quasi-War of 1798–1800 followed.

The war consisted of a series of naval engagements, and by 1800 the activity of French privateers and warships along the American seaboard had declined significantly. Nevertheless, the Federalist administration of John Adams became increasingly popular due to the passage of the Alien and Sedition Acts, introduced to silence dissenters and limit the rights of immigrants during the war.

The continued presence of European powers in North America challenged the United States to find ways to safeguard its borders, maintain neutral trading rights and promote its economic interests.

Independence brought a number of foreign policy problems to bear on the American experiment. American ships were no longer sailing under British flags, and until the Jay Treaty of 1795, they were restricted from selling their goods in the British West Indies, an important market for foodstuffs and other agricultural products for southern planters and farmers. American sailors even risked being taken as slaves by North African pirates.

On the mainland, Britain and Spain retained large territories in North America and often acted in a hostile fashion. The British refused to vacate the forts in the Old Northwest for more than ten years after the end of the Revolutionary War, citing the failure of the new republic to compensate Loyalists for losses due to confiscation during the revolution. This problem was also resolved by the Jay Treaty. Similarly, Spanish authorities refused to accept American sovereignty south of the Ohio River and closed the Mississippi River to American traders. They even got involved in secret conspiracies with prominent Americans in an effort to secure the Old Southwest for Spain. However, Florida and Louisiana were peripheral parts of the sprawling Spanish Empire in the Americas, and the differences over borders and trade were eventually settled in Pinckney's Treaty, signed in 1795.

The French Revolution's spread throughout Europe and beyond helped fuel America's debate not only about the nature of the United States' domestic order but also about its proper role in the world.

The French Revolution threatened the old order in Europe, which had been similarly challenged by the revolution in America. Thus, Americans at first viewed the Revolution with delight, hoping that it would usher in a new era of liberty and equality. The introduction of a constitution limiting the king's power was looked upon favorably.

However, the Revolution went much further than this. Soon France was embroiled in war, a republic was declared, the king was executed, and a reign of terror set in. The radicalism of the French Revolution even entailed the emancipation of slaves in the West Indian colonies. These new developments stirred debate and vigorous arguments between supporters and opponents of the Revolution across the Atlantic.

Federalists tended to support Britain, while Republicans preferred republican France in the ferocious war going on in Europe. Republicans like Jefferson saw what was happening in France as part of a wider struggle against the old order, while Federalists believed that the radical tendencies of the French revolutionaries jeopardized the concept of social order altogether. These developments brought many Americans to believe that some of their own countrymen held opinions that were not only wrong but evil, and that such opinions had to be suppressed, as in fact they were by the Alien and Sedition Acts. Each side began to see the other as a threat to what they thought the United States should be.

Illustration of an execution, Revolution Square, France

Although George Washington's Farewell Address warned about the dangers of divisive political parties and permanent foreign alliances, European conflict and tensions with Britain and France fueled increasingly bitter partisan debates throughout the 1790s.

The revolutionary wars in Europe created tensions between pro-French and pro-British factions in American politics. As such, international politics and questions of foreign policy played an important role in dividing the American political elite into two camps and thereby constituting the first party system in the United States. By 1796, political contests were no longer personal but rooted in organized efforts to further certain principles and promote certain interests. The political climate became more unpleasant, and several politicians and newspaper men were arrested under new laws limiting the right to dissent. However, the election of 1800 showed the solidarity of the political system, as power passed peacefully from Federalist to Republican hands. Upon being elected president, Thomas Jefferson called for unity and reconciliation.

> **KEY CONCEPT 3.2: In the late 18th century, new experiments with democratic ideas and republican forms of government, as well as other new religious, economic and cultural ideas, challenged traditional imperial systems across the Atlantic World.**

The late 18th and early 19th centuries saw outbreaks of revolutions on both sides of the Atlantic Ocean, with profound and long-lasting consequences both in the Americas and in Europe. The American Revolution occurred and was secondary in importance only to the French Revolution, which had the greatest effects due to the status of France at that time and the fact that the influence of France spread with its military expansion during the Revolutionary and Napoleonic Wars. In the Americas, Haiti was affected early on and Spanish America somewhat later.

The timing of these events was not coincidental; the revolutionaries in different countries and colonies knew about each other and emulated each other. The ideals of republicanism, democracy, and human rights spread widely, threatening existing institutions such as monarchies, aristocracies and powerful state churches. The revolutionaries professed Enlightenment beliefs, fighting for freedom, equality and expanded opportunities for political participation and the rule of law. Their success demonstrated that starting from scratch with a brand new system of government was possible and in some cases both effective and popular.

During the 18th century, new ideas about politics and society led to debates about religion and governance and ultimately inspired experiments with new governmental structures.

By the 18th century, science had begun to vastly increase human understanding of nature, which led Enlightenment thinkers to conceive of the idea that the social and political world could also be understood, explained and improved with the use of rational thought. Increasingly, intellectuals and activists questioned authority and doubted the legitimacy of existing social arrangements, including government structures. Along with this new, more critical mode of thinking came suggestions for new models of government and society. Enlightenment thinkers tended to favor systems based on freedom, toleration, equality, and consent. However, opponents often argued that reason alone could not build a better society than the wisdom of the ages and saw in some of the excesses of the French Revolution a confirmation of the dangers of a political system based on reason rather than tradition.

Protestant evangelical religious fervor strengthened many British colonists' understandings of themselves as a chosen people blessed with liberty, while Enlightenment philosophers and ideas inspired many American political thinkers to emphasize individual talent over hereditary privilege.

The Puritans had always tended to see themselves as a chosen people sent to the New World on a divine errand. However, social and political changes had transformed Puritan thinking by the 18th century. Some conservatives, called Old Calvinists, continued to cling to old beliefs and practices, but a number of influential clergymen, called the Old Lights, were eager to increase the appeal of the church to the population at large, opening up membership and preaching a more liberal doctrine. The Great Awakening of the 1730s and 1740s brought a new development, the evangelical New Lights, who built on old-fashioned Puritanism but set out to bring powerful, individual experiences of salvation to people throughout the colonies.

The Protestant clergy played a key role in preparing the colonial population for war against Britain, responding to British policies with severe denunciations and suggesting that Britain was doing the work of Satan and referring to the king as the "Whore of Babylon." In retrospect, some Loyalists even claimed that the fervor and influence of Protestant preachers was the main reason behind the success of the Patriots.

Profile of Adam Smith

At the same time, Enlightenment philosophers also influenced American political thought. Social contract theorists like John Locke and Jean-Jacques Rousseau based their notion of political legitimacy on the idea that men were naturally free and equal, suggesting that differentials in power and status should be based on talent, character, and merit rather than traditional and hereditary privileges that had previously been ascribed to divine providence. Similarly, Adam Smith argued that economic privileges and monopolies should be abandoned in favor of free competition on open markets, allowing skilled individuals of any background to pursue their economic interests. He argued that market mechanisms would ensure that this pursuit of individual enrichment would also lead to better allocation of resources and a more successful economy.

The colonists' belief in the superiority of republican self-government based on the natural rights of the people found its clearest American expression in Thomas Paine's *Common Sense* and in the Declaration of Independence.

Thomas Paine was an important intellectual figure during the American Revolution. His pamphlet *Common Sense* offered a blistering attack on the king and the concept of monarchy, suggesting that the people of the colonies had been forced to rise up against the king to preserve their natural right to freedom. In Paine's opinion, government was a necessary evil at the best of times, always impinging on the rights of men. Only a republican government based on consent could avoid the kind of tyranny King George was trying to impose, so a complete break with history and tradition was necessary. Paine's style of writing was so simple and direct that it gained widespread circulation in virtually every class of society, reaching anyone interested in political ideas and not just the educated elite.

In breaking with the established rule of tradition and monarchy, the founders who penned the Declaration of Independence wanted to go beyond the ancient rights of Englishmen and the existing constitution. They made the natural rights of men to life, liberty and the pursuit of happiness a new foundation of political legitimacy and explained that when a government

such as the British threatened these rights, the inhabitants of the colonies had every right to resist and even overthrow the authorities. Instead of conceiving of rights as something dependent on a given political system, Jefferson, the main author of the Declaration, thought of these rights as natural and "unalienable," and insisted that any legitimate political system must be set up to preserve those rights.

Many new state constitutions and the national Articles of Confederation, reflecting Republican fears of both centralized power and excessive popular influence, placed power in the hands of the legislative branch and maintained property qualifications for voting and citizenship.

The Articles of Confederation, adopted by the Continental Congress in 1777 and ratified by all thirteen states by 1781, created a U.S. government composed simply of a legislature. The legislature only had one chamber, and there was no executive or judiciary branch. Members of the legislature were appointed, rather than elected, and each state had one delegate regardless of its population. This reflected the belief that the United States should be a decentralized confederation of states with limited powers, and that all other powers should belong to state governments. The appointment of delegates by state legislatures rather than election by the populace similarly reflected that the founders had limited faith in democratic electoral politics.

At the same time, state constitutions moved power from the executive branch to the legislative branch, due in large part to the bad experiences dissident Americans had had with British-appointed governors. Pennsylvania went so far as to abolish the office of governor and the upper house of the legislature, leaving only a unicameral legislature elected by all adult men who paid taxes.

However, the Pennsylvania constitution was far from typical, as most states placed significant restrictions on voting rights even for adult white men and even stricter restrictions on eligibility to hold elected office. In most cases, voter qualifications were similar to those known from the British system, meaning that voters had to be free adult males who owned property and belonged to the established church in that state (in some states, there was no established church). The limitation of voting rights to property owners was justified by the claim that only those who owned property were independent men with a true stake in society.

After experiencing the limitations of the Articles of Confederation, American political leaders wrote a new Constitution based on the principles of federalism and the separation of powers, crafted a Bill of Rights, and continued their debates about the proper balance between liberty and order.

The Articles of Confederation had limitations that in the view of many critics inhibited the development of effective governance and credible defense. The army was tiny and unpaid and there was no navy. In the case of foreign threats, Congress neither had sufficient money which was voluntarily donated nor the authority to tax the citizenry, which meant that no real preparations for war could be made. In addition, many of the states failed to honor the Articles, developing their own foreign policies and in some cases violating the terms of the peace treaty with Britain.

The money problem was exacerbated by two factors. The currency had become practically worthless, and the states failed to pay their taxes, meaning that the national government was unable to pay foreign debts. By 1786, the United States was practically bankrupt.

In 1787, the Constitutional Convention assembled to solve the many outstanding problems of creating a viable federal government. Federal executive and judiciary branches were introduced, with a plethora of checks and balances to ensure that no branch of government would be able to overpower the rest. At the same time, the Constitution was an attempt to strike a balance between the rights of the states and the need for centralization and leadership. The new legislature was bicameral, with one popularly elected chamber where the states were represented according to population. The members of the other chamber, the Senate, would be elected by state legislatures, and all of the states would have the same number of senators. The Constitution was made the supreme law of the land, and the United State Supreme Court was given the authority to hear appeals in cases originating in state courts.

The Convention at Philadelphia, 1787

As some skeptics were critical of the new Constitution, especially the danger that a strengthened federal government might infringe on the rights of states and individuals, a series of amendments were later added. These first ten amendments to the Constitution became the Bill of Rights, which secured for American citizens a variety of specific freedoms and protections important in everyday life, the development of civil society and legal proceedings.

Difficulties over trade, finances, and interstate and foreign relations, as well as internal unrest, led to calls for significant revisions to the Articles of Confederation and a stronger central government.

The Articles of Confederation limited the U.S. government to powers over diplomacy and Indian affairs, issuing currency, handling the mail and controlling a virtually nonexistent army. With no executive or judicial branch, there was no system to enforce the limits placed on the power of individual states. Thus, the problem of creating a unified and viable government was a serious one, especially due to the lack of resources and the difficulty of making decisions, as all thirteen states had to agree on vital decisions.

Congress lacked the power to tax and received little from the states, who in many cases preferred to issue their own currencies and build their own armies. They even imposed their own tariff regimes, placing tariffs on imports from other states. Both economic and foreign policy suffered from inconsistency and a lack of coherence. When Spain restricted American navigation on the Mississippi River, the government lacked the means to do anything other than protest.

At last, the government even failed to defend itself. When Shays' Rebellion (discussed in more detail further in this chapter) broke out in Massachusetts in 1786, it was struck down by mercenaries rather than the United States army. This embarrassment finally convinced political leaders that a new and more centralized constitution had to be put in place.

Delegates from the states worked through a series of compromises to form the Constitution for a new national government while providing limits on federal power.

The new Constitution emerged from a number of compromises between the states. The first and most important was the so-called Connecticut Compromise, which combined two original proposals, the Virginia Plan and the New Jersey Plan. The Virginia Plan suggested that population in Congress should be proportional to each state's population, while the New Jersey Plan called for equal representation as in the system put in place by the Articles of Confederation. The Connecticut Compromise combined the two by proposing a bicameral solution where representation in one chamber was equal for all states and in the other corresponded with the population.

However, this solution then raised the question of the extent to which slave populations should be taken into consideration. The southern states insisted that slaves should be taken into consideration when calculating state populations, while the northern states rejected this proposal. In the end, a compromise was made in the form of the three-fifths rule: one slave would count as three-fifths of a free person.

The southern and northern states clashed again over trade regulation. Southern elites were fearful that northerners might seek to abolish the slave trade and impose tariffs that would hurt southern export business. They wanted states, rather than the federal government, to regulate trade. The northern states, on the other hand, thought that trade regulation should be a federal responsibility. The Commerce Compromise meant that states would continue to regulate intrastate trade, but the federal government would regulate interstate trade. The case for import duties was accepted, but it was stipulated that there would be no export duties and no ban on the slave trade for the next twenty years.

Calls for greater guarantees of rights during the ratification process resulted in the addition of the Bill of Rights shortly after the Constitution was adopted.

During the ratification process, some critics argued that the Constitution did not adequately enumerate the rights of people as a protection against government abuses. They felt that the federal Constitution should have a Bill of Rights attached to it, just like several of the state constitutions already in existence. James Madison, who had been the main formative influence on the original Constitution, initially felt that such an enumeration of rights might suggest that rights not enumerated were not protected.

The Bill of Rights 175th anniversary

James Madison Bill of Rights $5 commemorative gold coin

However, due to popular skepticism, he finally proposed a series of amendments to the Constitution, of which ten eventually were adopted and became known as the Bill of Rights. These amendments barred the federal government (but not necessarily the states) from interfering with rights to free speech, free religion and the right to bear arms. It also offered protection from illegal seizures, cruel and unjust punishment and unfair trials, among many other rights. In keeping with the concept of natural rights, the Ninth Amendment specified that even rights not mentioned in the Bill of Rights are retained by the people.

As the first national administrations began to govern under the Constitution, continued debates about issues such as the relationship between the national government and the states, economic policy and the conduct of foreign affairs led to the creation of political parties.

The relationship between the federal and state governments continued to be the subject of important and heated debates in the late 18th century. When the Alien and Sedition Acts were passed during the undeclared war with France, legislatures in Kentucky and Virginia passed resolutions that held these laws to be unconstitutional, as they allowed the federal government to exercise powers not mentioned in the Constitution.

The Virginia version authored by Madison argued that the government's efforts to clamp down on free speech and free press were extremely dangerous, as these were notably the basic foundation for the defense of republican liberty and natural rights in general. According to Madison, Congress had not given the national government the power to infringe on these rights. Jefferson, who drafted the Kentucky Resolutions, went even further, arguing that the states had the power to nullify (i.e. invalidate) laws that were passed by Congress which the states found unconstitutional.

Before the outbreak of the Quasi-War with France, Madison and Jefferson took issue with the Proclamation of Neutrality issued by President Washington when war broke out between France and Britain in 1793. Alexander Hamilton offered arguments in favor of the proclamation on the basis of constitutionality, international law, and political expediency. Madison countered that a strict reading of the Constitution implied that Congress, not the president, should be responsible for foreign policy, and suggested that supporters of the Proclamation represented anti-revolutionary and anti-republican sentiments.

James Madison

In general, these conflicts over foreign policy and constitutional matters contributed greatly to the development of two parties, with Republicans like Jefferson and Madison distancing themselves from leading Federalists like Adams and Hamilton. Another aspect of this conflict was disagreements over economic policy. Hamilton presented ambitious centralizing financial plans that involved paying off debts incurred in the revolution by borrowing from the public in the form of issuing securities and suggested that only a central bank should be issuing currency. In this way, he sought to give the federal government financial credibility and make money available for investment in infrastructure projects.

However, Madison and Jefferson argued that this scheme was unconstitutional. Hamilton argued that the good of the nation depended on using any means necessary to further its interests, as long as a policy was not specifically prohibited by the Constitution. Madison, taking a much more narrow view of constitutionality, suggested that the federal government did not have the right to do anything that was not specifically mentioned as one of its responsibilities in the Constitution.

While the new governments continued to limit rights to some groups, ideas promoting self-government and personal liberty reverberated around the world.

Although the United States was a sparsely populated country very far away, Europeans were impressed and heavily influenced by developments in North American during and after the American Revolution. The Declaration of Independence codified a new way of discussing human rights, and many in Europe adopted the language and ideas of American revolutionaries. The French Revolution, for example, was in part inspired by the American precedent.

The United States was the "first new nation," created, as it seemed, by the application of philosophy and principle rather than justified by tradition and heredity. The notions that government should be based on the consent of the governed and the preservation of liberty, and that monarchs who failed to do so could be disposed of, were powerful ideas that inspired enthusiasm in some and animosity in others. Meanwhile, the language of freedom and equality did not actually grant freedom and equality for all in the United States. Women did not have the same rights as men, and slavery and the removal of Indians from their territories remained key elements of the new American reality.

During and after the American Revolution, an increased awareness of the inequalities in society motivated some individuals and groups to call for the abolition of slavery and greater political democracy in the new state and national governments.

During the revolution, critiques of British governance often referred to the situation of American colonists as a form of slavery. This way of speaking, along with the universalist language of freedom and equality for all, caused some Americans to reconsider the institution of slavery as it existed within farms, plantations, households and shops around the country. Many began to doubt that differences in skin color alone could justify keeping an entire people in slavery. Soon organizations working for the abolition of slavery were established, such as the Pennsylvania Abolition Society and the New York Manumission Society. In 1780, the Pennsylvania legislature passed a law that would allow "gradual emancipation" by declaring all children born of slaves free. The same act also banned the trade of slaves.

Abigail Adams

By 1788, eight states had abolished or suspended the slave trade. In the following decades, the northern states enacted laws of either gradual or immediate emancipation, but the southern states—where slavery was more prevalent—did not follow the northern states' lead. This led to mutual suspicion between the two sections, as when Abigail Adams questioned whether Virginians with their propensity to own slaves could really love liberty as much as the people of New England. While Martha Washington relied on slaves in the presidential household, Adams helped a young black man learn how to read and write.

The constitutional framers postponed a solution to the problems of slavery and the slave trade, setting the stage for recurring conflicts over these issues in later years.

Slavery was a serious problem for a country founded on ideals of freedom and equality. Founders like Washington, Jefferson and Madison found slavery repugnant but nevertheless held large numbers of slaves themselves. They did not see any practical way to end slavery. The Articles of Confederation did not mention slavery, and the Constitution failed to deal with slavery because of the divergent interests of the northern and southern elites. In exchange for concessions in other areas, the southern founders even forced the representatives of the northern states to accept a clause about fugitive slaves in the Constitution. Northern states were obliged to track down fugitive slaves and return them to their owners. Over the years, the question of slavery would reappear intermittently and create significant tensions between the North and the South.

The American Revolution and the ideals set forth in the Declaration of Independence had reverberations in France, Haiti and Latin America, inspiring future rebellions.

The American Revolution inspired liberals, republicans, and nationalists in Europe and throughout the Americas. They saw the United States as an example of putting Enlightenment ideas into practice in the name of liberty and equality. The Revolution encouraged the Irish to seek more freedoms from the British, and the Belgians to seek independence from Austria. The French Revolution became another example of a fight against privilege and tyranny in support of universal human rights.

However, when slaves in Haiti rebelled against their owners, the United States was not especially supportive. The American government cooperated with the Haitian revolutionaries when vocal slavery opponent John Adams was president, but the tide turned when Jefferson became president in 1800. Southern slave owners found the spectacle of a slave rebellion and a republic led by blacks terrifying, and the United States did not recognize the independence of Haiti until 1862, long after France had done so.

When the Spanish colonies in South America sought independence in the early 19th century, they were keenly aware of the examples of both the United States and Haiti. They rallied around ideals of freedom and national independence while fearing that the government of Spain could not protect them against slave rebellions. The disorganized state of the Spanish government during the lengthy revolutionary wars and Napoleonic Wars in Europe made Latin American separation and independence possible.

> **KEY CONCEPT 3.3: Migration within North America, cooperative interaction and competition for resources raised questions about boundaries and policies, intensified conflicts among peoples and nations, and led to contests over the creation of a multiethnic, multiracial national identity.**

After the revolution, Americans tried to create a unified national identity founded on ideas of equality, civic virtue, and commercial success. At the same time, the country was deeply divided along cultural, geographic, economic and racial lines. To some extent, the identity of Americans, or rather white property-owning male Americans, came to rely on subjugating and demonizing others, including women, Indians, blacks and poor whites. The evolution of the media facilitated this process by allowing a broad audience to seek an understanding of their own superiority that was rooted in guilt, fear, paranoia, and violence.

As migrants streamed westward from the British colonies along the Atlantic seaboard, interactions among different groups that would continue under an independent United States resulted in competition for resources, shifting alliances and cultural blending.

Even in colonial times, white settlers were trickling through the mountain passes and into what is now Kentucky and Tennessee as well as deeper into the South and the Ohio Valley. The viability of their settlements was threatened by the Proclamation of 1763, by Spanish and French designs on the area and by Indian resistance to their occupation of the land. These areas were characterized by instability, overlapping authority, conflicts, and cultural mixing. Due to the brutality of military action and massacres both during and after the Revolutionary War, they were also marked by hatred between peoples.

The French withdrawal from North America and the subsequent attempt of various native groups to reassert their power over the interior of the continent resulted in new white–Indian conflicts along the western borders of British—and later U.S.—colonial settlements and settlers looking to assert more power in interior regions.

The French withdrawal from North America created something of a power vacuum in the borderlands between the British colonies and the territories previously claimed by the French. The backcountry was only sparsely settled and conflicts between settlers and Indians multiplied as more whites sought lands in these areas. The Paxton Boys of Pennsylvania who became famous for their atrocities against local Indians turned to put pressure on the colonial assembly, demanding that more be done to protect the settlers against Indians. The Paxton Boys murdered and scalped peaceful women, children and old men to achieve their goals. This was only one example of the increasingly violent and brutal confrontation between whites and Indians as the rise in the European population encouraged migration into the interior.

Paxton Boys' massacre of the Indians at Lancaster

These confrontations continued to take place throughout the revolutionary period and into the national period. From the mid-1780s to the mid-1790s, a series of wars against the Indians played out in the areas to the west of the original thirteen colonies. The 1794 Battle of Fallen Timbers was the turning point, a decisive victory for a professionally trained American army that was followed by major Indian concessions in the Old Northwest.

Migrants from within North America and around the world continued to launch new settlements in the West, creating new distinctive backcountry cultures and fueling social and ethnic tensions.

Large numbers of colonists in the British colonies were not of English origin but rather hailed from other parts of Europe. Thus, white culture in North America was diverse from the beginning. One important cultural influence was that of the Scotch-Irish Protestants from Northern Ireland. Many of these immigrants settled in western Pennsylvania and later traveled along the Appalachians into the southern backcountry. Their emphasis on herding cattle and pigs, and on isolation, leisure and hunting, rather than community, hard work and farming differentiated them from English colonists. They were also significantly different in their other habits and values which, along with the deep class divide of southern society, often led to conflict with other segments of the white population.

Differences between the coastal areas and the backcountry prevailed in the North as well. In rural New England, the economy was still based on subsistence agriculture after the Revolutionary War. When merchants and tax collectors began to demand that debts and taxes be paid in hard currency, many farmers in the hill country were unable to pay and ended up losing their land and other valuables.

In 1786, armed groups of men in Massachusetts began to close down courts to stop creditors from enforcing judgments against debtors. When the legislature answered by passing laws to prevent further mob actions and even suspended habeas corpus, organizers in western Massachusetts began to mobilize to overthrow the government. They were led by Daniel Shays, a veteran of the Revolutionary War. In the absence of an army, the state's merchant elite organized mercenaries to defeat the rebellion.

Since thousands of people had taken up arms against the state government, Shays' Rebellion was an important factor to convince members of the political elite that a more centralized and powerful federal government was necessary.

Portraits of Daniel Shays and Job Shattuck, leaders of the Massachusetts Regulators

The Spanish, supported by the bonded labor of the local Indians, expanded their mission settlements into California, providing opportunities for social mobility among enterprising soldiers and settlers that led to new cultural blending.

In the 1770s, the Spanish sent explorers into California, and by 1776 they established San Francisco. However, the fierce resistance of the Yuma Indians closed the overland route to California from the 1780s to the mid-19th century, forcing colonists to arrive by sea. Nevertheless, the Spanish established more than twenty settlements along the coast from San Diego to San Francisco. There was essentially no white settlement in the interior.

The mission towns, located about a day's ride apart, were usually manned by a couple of friars and a handful of soldiers. The labor in the settlements was done by Indians who were either forced or persuaded to join the missions and hunted down if they tried to run away. The Indians were treated more or less as slaves, even though they were not slaves in a legal sense.

Mission Indians of Southern California

Eventually, the missions claimed vast lands—as much as one million acres per settlement. Soldiers and ambitious colonists could receive huge land grants virtually for free, and even foreigners could be granted lands provided that they were determined to become Spanish and Catholic. Despite these opportunities, the number of migrants to California remained low. As a consequence, the culture of the area was heavily influenced by the Indians.

Even the architecture of the Spanish missions was constrained by the dependence on local materials, and artistic renderings in the churches show the influence of Indian styles. California also developed its own version of the Spanish vaquero, or cowboy, with his own particular way of training horses and a unique way of life.

The policies of the United States that encouraged western migration and the orderly incorporation of new territories into the nation both extended republican institutions and intensified conflicts among American Indians and Europeans in the trans-Appalachian West.

Under the Articles of Confederation, the United States was unable to tax its citizens directly. In order to raise money, the Land Ordinance was passed in 1785. The Land Ordinance regulated the sale of western lands by the federal government and created a system for surveying public lands. Land was divided into townships that were six square miles, and these were in turn divided into thirty-six square sections.

Once townships and sections had been surveyed, they could be sold to settlers and speculators (the two were not entirely distinct categories, as most settlers also speculated in the long-term increase in land values). One section in each township was to be used to fund public schools in the area. Once the land had been sold, authority devolved from the federal government to local inhabitants, encouraging a strong sense of local autonomy in western development. At the same time, local autonomy sometimes intensified conflicts between Indians and whites due to the lack of coherent and consistent policies toward the indigenous population.

Surveying the Northwest Territory

As settlers moved westward during the 1780s, Congress enacted the Northwest Ordinance for admitting new states and sought to promote public education, the protection of private property and the restriction of slavery in the Northwest Territory.

The Northwest Ordinance of 1787 was of utmost importance because it defined the process of westward expansion of the United States. It determined that the new nation would expand westward by creating new states, not by the extension of old states. It gave Congress the power to create new states out of federal lands and outlined the political development of these states-to-be: when they had 5,000 adult males, they would have a territorial legislature but a federally appointed governor; once the free population surpassed 60,000, they could apply to become states.

The Northwest Ordinance followed the Land Ordinance in emphasizing the importance of public education. It also secured religious freedom and private property. More controversially, it also prohibited slavery in the area. In some areas, notably southern Illinois and Indiana, settlers still brought in slaves and fought to legalize slavery.

The Constitution's failure to precisely define the relationship between American Indian tribes and the national government led to problems regarding treaties and Indian legal claims relating to the seizure of Indian lands.

The Constitution did not deal directly with the question of how the relationship between the federal government and the Indians should be managed. However, an ordinance had already been passed in 1786, dividing U.S. lands into three districts with a superintendent for Indian affairs in each. In 1790, this was followed by the Trade and Intercourse Act, which described the process of licensing traders who ventured into Indian areas. It sought to define the terms of land acquisition by prohibiting white settlers from direct purchase of Indian lands. All land purchases had to go through the federal government. In addition, the Trade and Intercourse Act stipulated penalties for Americans who committed crimes in Indian country. This law was followed by several other trade and intercourse acts in the years that followed, meant to strengthen the protection of Indians against criminal whites attacking them and taking their lands.

As western settlers sought free navigation of the Mississippi River, the United States forged diplomatic initiatives to manage the conflict with Spain and to deal with the continued British presence on the American continent.

The Jay Treaty, signed by the United States and Britain in 1794, resolved some of the outstanding issues of contention that had lingered since the end of the Revolutionary War. The architect behind the treaty was Federalist Alexander Hamilton, who sought rapprochement with the British and an expansion of American trade. To Hamilton, the moment seemed opportune, as Britain had become involved in a new war with France.

The treaty was a victory for the United States because it finally ended the British occupation of the forts in the Old Northwest. The departure of the British was especially significant because it demoralized Indians who had hoped to stop American expansion into their lands. At the same time, the treaty was a consequence of the defeat of the Western Confederacy of tribes at the Battle of Fallen Timbers. As the Indians seemed unable to resist the American military, the British no longer had any real role to play in the area. The British justification for holding on to the forts had been unpaid wartime debts related to the confiscation of Loyalist property; both parties now agreed to send this matter to arbitration.

The Battle of Fallen Timbers

The Jay Treaty made the Spanish fear a future alliance between the United States and Britain. Spain had closed navigation on the Mississippi to Americans, but now agreed to reopen commercial channels and negotiate boundaries. By 1795, this resulted in Pinckney's Treaty, where Spain ceded control of most of what is now Mississippi and Alabama to the United States. Navigation rights were restored, and the Spanish pledged not to incite and arm the Indians against the United States. Thus, by playing the European powers against each other, the Washington administration managed to tighten the country's grip on frontier territories and reduce the risk of outside powers intervening in its dealings with the Indians. This facilitated the ongoing westward expansion of the United States.

New voices for national identity challenged tendencies to cling to regional identities, contributing to the emergence of distinctly American cultural expressions.

Having secured independence from Britain, some Americans were eager to define their new national identity as Americans. Especially among the elite, many saw this as a necessary condition for building a united and cohesive nation across a vast geographical expanse. It was important that this new culture be a republican culture and that American art and architecture have a distinctly republican flavor.

The image of George Washington became especially popular as Washington was considered the greatest American and a prime example of the virtuous republican citizen. His image appeared not only in paintings but on china and in various engravings. After his death, authors also began to publish biographies of Washington.

In addition to visual artists and literary figures, American inventors, architects, scientists, and philosophers also contributed to the new American culture. Education was especially important in shaping a national, republican identity. In this case, education did not just mean schooling, but more generally being exposed to art, culture, and knowledge in specific ways that promoted civic virtue.

Engraving of George Washington

As national political institutions developed in the new United States, varying regionally based positions on economic, political, social and foreign policy issues promoted the development of political parties.

Even during the Revolutionary War, Americans had been divided between Patriots, Loyalists and those who remained largely aloof. After the war ended, divisions remained as some of the founders were highly skeptical of the new Constitution, becoming known as Anti-Federalists. In the 1790s, political conflict in the United States intensified and became partisan. The Revolution in France and the continuing threat of war against either France or Britain put a great strain on citizens and members of the elite, with differing feelings about radical republicanism and different interests to preserve in terms of foreign policy. Disagreements over economic and financial policy were equally vehement, pitting proponents of a commercial, manufacturing civilization against those who relied on the civic virtue of the independent yeoman farmer in a predominantly rural republic.

All these conflicts to some extent reflected the need to come to terms with the legacy of the American Revolution. The radical and violent example of the French Revolution and the general instability of politics at home and abroad made this discussion increasingly necessary and difficult. It was apparent that the United States remained a tentative, experimental form of the republic that could not count on being left alone by the European powers. To some extent, this introduced an element of fear and apprehension into American political debate.

Although the father of the Constitution, James Madison, was an exception, most politicians, and Americans in general, did not believe that there was room for more than one legitimate political body in public life. As Patriots, they had assumed that all good people would be on the same side politically. This made the development of a party system especially painful for the new republic, and opinions on both sides tended to be strong and unyielding.

Newspapers added to this by being overtly political and highly critical of opponents. The great hero of the American Revolution, president and father of his country, George

Washington, was even attacked, vilified and ridiculed by the opposition press, sometimes seen as an enemy out to destroy liberty and the republic. Even worse abuse was heaped on the main protagonists of the party struggle, such as Hamilton and Adams on the Federalist side and Jefferson and Madison on the Republican side.

By the time of the 1796 election, the Federalists and Republicans both ran candidates at all levels from local to state and national. They had become more than mere factions, growing into strong political organizations based on firm principles. Even Madison, who had anticipated legitimate disagreement on political issues, had not expected anything other than temporary alliances built around especially controversial issues.

However, voters were inclined to take an active part in politics and were not content with simply deferring to the elite. Thus, a competitive party system sometimes marked by less than civilized debate and confrontation arose. However, the strength of this system was exposed when Washington was replaced by Adams, and later Adams by Jefferson. The peaceful exchange of power and position is a hallmark of political stability, despite Washington's insistence that parties were a grave threat to the republic.

The Federalists were supporters of centralization and a broad interpretation of the Constitution that would facilitate the use of government power to help the economy grow and develop. Those who supported Hamilton's policies promoting commerce, manufacturing, internal improvements, and national finance tended to support the Federalist Party. Merchants, creditors and the urban middle class in the Northeast and New England were prominent among these supporters.

The opposition party that emerged during Washington's presidency was called the Democratic-Republicans, now sometimes called the Jeffersonian Republicans to distinguish this party from the modern Republican Party which emerged in the 1850s. Republican supporters were a diverse bunch, led by southern planters like Jefferson, Madison, and Monroe but also including farmers throughout the country. Unlike the Federalists, who were typically of English descent, the Republicans were a more heterogeneous party with many German and Scotch-Irish voters.

James Monroe's southern plantation

In the 1796 election, Federalists portrayed themselves as the more responsible party, associated with the steady leadership of Washington. They suggested that Washington should be followed by Adams, lest dangerous radicals take over the government and bring the chaos and anarchy of the French Revolution to American soil. The Republicans, meanwhile, often portrayed the Federalists as enemies of freedom and equality, and as secretly scheming to introduce monarchy and aristocracy into the United States.

Adams thus came into power in a divided country and at a very difficult time, given the explosive international situation and continued harassment of American shipping by both sides of the European conflict. His response to the vehemence of his critics led to the serious abridgment of civil liberties through the Alien and Sedition Acts. It was a response that showed that the scope for legitimate opposition and debate was still being negotiated in the new republic.

However, Adams's heavy-handed tactics were disliked by many voters, and the election of 1800 showed that Americans' desire to participate in and influence politics was stronger than ever. The emotional appeals of the Federalists, arguing that a victory for the ungodly Jefferson would ruin the country, were not successful.

The Republican insistence on curbing the centralization of political power was more effective. They criticized the Federalist military buildup, the encroachment on freedom during the Quasi-War and the willingness of the government to borrow and spend. They argued that the government should become closer to the people by leaving more decisions to state and local governments. This message was highly popular. Jefferson and the Republicans won a decisive victory and the party remained in control of national politics for the next quarter of a century.

The expansion of slavery in the lower South and adjacent western lands, and its gradual disappearance elsewhere, began to create distinctive regional attitudes toward the institution.

Unlike the southern elite of the antebellum era, who tended to glorify slave society, most early American leaders from both the North and South saw slavery as distasteful and outdated. They envisioned that slavery would eventually die out on its own. The Virginian founders who later became Presidents (including Washington, Jefferson, Madison, and Monroe) were all slaveholders with an interest in the gradual abolition of slavery. The Northwest Ordinance also banned slavery in the vast northwestern territories of the United States without much protest from southern politicians. Southerners were content that it would be difficult to grow competing tobacco in the new territories without slave labor.

However, the introduction of new breeds of cotton and the invention of the cotton gin allowed for an explosive growth in cotton agriculture in the South. At the same time, the mechanization of textile manufacturing, the first stage of the Industrial Revolution, led to a vastly increased demand for cotton, especially in Britain. As new cotton lands opened up in the West, slaveholders in the East saw the value of their slave property increasing as the prices of slaves rapidly increased.

Eli Whitney watching the cotton gin

Meanwhile, slavery was disappearing in the North. During the Revolutionary War, blacks in New England were agitating for emancipation. During the 1780s, several states passed laws of gradual or immediate emancipation, and by 1804 all the northern states had taken such steps. In addition, Vermont had joined as a free state, and the new states carved out of the Northwestern Territory would become free states as well. However, Kentucky and Tennessee entered the Union as slave states, and the lands to the southwest were prime candidates for cotton plantations worked by large numbers of slaves.

Benjamin Franklin, a former slaveholder, became one of the most vocal opponents of slavery. In 1790, the octogenarian petitioned Congress, proposing that slavery should be abolished throughout the United States. Quakers from Pennsylvania were also agitating for the same policy. Their petitions provoked great anger and controversy in the House of Representatives. Southern representatives argued that slavery was justified by the Bible and economically necessary in the South. They also feared that any debate of this topic might inspire slave rebellions.

Some northern representatives, on the other hand, claimed that slavery was not protected by the Constitution and directly contradictory to the message

Benjamin Franklin

of the Declaration of Independence. As a response, both South Carolina and Georgia made threats to secede from the union. In order to avoid disintegration, hostilities, or possibly even civil war, Madison brokered a solution that suggested Congress had no right to abolish slavery, as it was a state matter.

Slavery continued and expanded into the new lands to the west of the original southern states. By the time of the Civil War, twice as many slaves had been taken from the Eastern Seaboard into the new states as had arrived from Africa in the whole of colonial and national history. This expansion of slavery and slave-owner power and wealth would become the most divisive political issue of 19th- century United States.

Enlightenment ideas and women's experiences in the movement for independence promoted an ideal of "republican motherhood," which called on white women to maintain and teach republican values within the family and granted women a new importance in American political culture.

The American Revolution altered women's lives as well as men's. Many women were in charge of the household and the family when the husband and other males left, and some adopted republican principles to demand greater equality for women. Abigail Adams suggested that her husband, founding father John Adams, should "remember the ladies." In general, the Revolution and the republican ideology underlying it suggested a critique of all authority, hierarchy and traditional constraint, which encouraged women to take on new roles and have opinions of their own.

However, the most important role of women in revolutionary ideology was as mothers of virtuous male citizens. Since women had the primary responsibility for rearing, nurturing and educating children, it was essential that they themselves had the proper virtue and republican outlook. Academies were built to prepare American women for this role, which some historians call "republican motherhood." While extending the rights, opportunities, and importance of women, this way of thinking also cemented the division of appropriate activities between men and women, emphasizing that the proper arena for a woman was the private sphere of the home.

PERIOD 4

1800-1848

Struggles of the new republic to define and extend democratic ideals in the face of rapid economic, territorial, and demographic changes.

Major historical events of the period:

1803 – Lewis and Clark Expedition

1804 – Underground Railroad is established

1807 – Embargo Act

1812 – War of 1812

1819 – Panic of 1819

1820 – Missouri Compromise

1823 – Monroe Doctrine is issued

1830 – Indian Removal Act

1845 – Texas joined the Union

PERIOD 4: 1800-1848

> **KEY CONCEPT 4.1:** The United States developed the world's first modern mass democracy and celebrated a new national culture, while Americans sought to define the nation's democratic ideals and to reform its institutions to match them.

The first half of 19th-century American history is characterized by the search for a national identity. The Americas were an empty slate for the Europeans who had colonized them. This, in turn, meant that the changes taking place in the newly christened United States of America were further impacted by the unstable government and lack of infrastructure. Americans had to define a national identity based on their foundational democratic ideals while rapid changes were occurring in the economy, territory, and population.

When the representatives from the colonies decided to declare independence from Great Britain, they created a unique opportunity for themselves. The government that followed would be completely new and original. There were no laws, treaties or agreements to which they must adhere. While liberating, this lack of restrictions also meant that conflicts were common, as the founders tried to create the most agreeable government for each of the very different colonies. These colonies had been founded at different times with different charters. Each one had been shaped differently by Great Britain's tyranny. This meant that one of the most difficult problems facing the newly created United States was establishing how to work together to achieve a common goal.

The nation's transformation to a more participatory democracy was accompanied by continued debates over federal power, the relationship between the federal government and the states, the authority of different branches of the federal government, and the rights and responsibilities of individual citizens.

The Declaration of Independence is an excellent example of the early influences and struggles faced by the colonies. Written by a five-person committee, though usually attributed to Thomas Jefferson, the Declaration of Independence is heavily based on the major political influences of the day, primarily the Enlightenment thinkers. The declaration of "Life, Liberty, and the pursuit of Happiness" as basic human rights in the Declaration of Independence, for instance, is an echo of John Locke's *Second Treatise,* where he explains that all men have a right to "their lives, liberties, and estates, which I call by the general name 'property.'"

Drafting the Declaration of Independence

Enlightenment concepts, such as basic human rights, spoke to the struggles that the colonies endured under King George III of England; struggles that they hoped to eradicate from their own government. Thus, the grievances listed against the King became the basis for the new government. Yet, even these were difficult to define. Jefferson originally included an entire passage denouncing slavery and blaming the entire institution on George III, despite the fact that he himself owned slaves. This passage was struck from the final document to appease Southern representatives, who knew that an end to slavery would mean crippling the economic prosperity of the South. Eventually, the document was finalized and signed. War was upon the colonies, and while their soldiers fought for their independence on the battlefield, their next challenge would be framing the new government.

The Articles of Confederation served as the first constitution of the newly created United States of America. The Articles, like the Declaration of Independence, show the effects of Britain's rule. The founders created a confederation of states which functioned almost as individual countries. These were loosely joined by a weak centralized government. This was to avoid the dictatorial control King George had exercised over the colonies. However, the Articles of Confederation had a pronounced weakness: they allowed so many rights for each individual state that they also severely crippled the power of the federal government to enhance and protect liberty.

For example, in his autobiography, Thomas Jefferson noted the issue of funding the U.S. Treasury under the Articles of Confederation. Most representatives' arguments showed an acknowledgment that the Treasury needed to be funded but lacked any intent to promise funds from their constituents. It was difficult to achieve consensus when each representative wanted to promote the interests of their own state over the interests of the new nation.

The event that best represents the country's inability to function uniformly, is Shays' Rebellion in 1786 and 1787. Upset with the tax burden placed upon them to pay for the American Revolution, protesters began speaking out in Massachusetts. They soon moved on to physical protests outside of local courthouses. While these protests did not turn violent, they did stop the county courts from meeting and disrupted the flow of business.

Anger grew as change seemed unlikely, and eventually a group of men from Massachusetts—many of them veterans of the American Revolution—marched on a federal armory under the leadership of Daniel Shays. The federal government was unable to respond, without funding for a military. Therefore, the response was weak and highlighted for many the need for change, though to what extent was another matter of contention.

Postage with an image of the founding fathers drafting the Articles of Confederation

The Constitution, despite being a short and concise document, is very well balanced. Some of the fears of the anti-Federalists were well-founded, and the framers of the Constitution took steps to address them. The primary safeguard is the system of checks and balances between the three branches. This was put in place to keep any one branch from gaining too much power.

For instance, Congress has the power to declare war, but the President does not. This would hopefully mean that all wars would have to be fully considered and debated before action was taken by the U.S. military. However, in a state of emergency, the president can deploy troops for a limited time while seeking Congress's consent for further action. This way, the president can't act alone on behalf of the nation, but still has the power to respond to unforeseen events.

Similarly, the president has the power to veto Congressional laws to protect against Congress gaining too much political sway. Congress can override a veto to protect against a president who is trying to use his power incorrectly. The Supreme Court is the final judge as to whether any law is constitutional or not. In this way, the Constitution protects against abuses of power like those seen in many of the monarchies of Europe at the time.

Once the Constitution was ratified, a list of ten amendments was added immediately. These are known as the Bill of Rights, and they outline the basic rights given to all citizens at the time of their ratification. The Bill of Rights includes the right to free speech, assembly, and religion. It grants all citizens the right to own weapons and to use them in defense of the country. It protects people against potential abuses of the military or police, like those that suffered under King George III. It's the Supreme Court's job to analyze the Constitution, its amendments and the constitutionality of laws and judicial rulings.

The Bill of Rights is a collection of the first ten amendments, but there are twenty-seven amendments in total. Many of the amendments further regulate the three branches of government. As questions about a branch's role and power have arisen, amendments have been added to ensure that there are answers. For instance, Amendment XXII defines the term limits for presidents. Other amendments are indicative of much larger social changes, like Amendment XIII, which abolished the institution of slavery in the United States. These amendments are dynamic and subject to change. Amendment XVIII, for example, prohibited the buying and selling of alcohol, ushering in the era of Prohibition. Later, Amendment XXI was used to repeal Prohibition, making the sale and consumption of alcohol legal again.

State governments are modeled on this federal ideal, with a three-branch system and a state constitution. Each state has a governor that functions as the state's executive branch. Several presidents have first served as governors of their respective states, like former president Bill Clinton, who served as the governor of Arkansas. States also have a legislative system, though these vary in title. Each state also has a state and federal court system. The state court tries violations of state laws, while the federal court tries any cases which violate federal laws.

As various constituencies and interest groups coalesced and defined their agendas, various political parties, most significantly the Federalists and Democratic-Republicans in the 1790s and the Democrats and Whigs in the 1830s, were created or transformed to reflect and/or promote those agendas.

John Jay

Two distinct political parties fought to sway public opinion on the matter of rewriting the Constitution: the Federalists and the anti-Federalists. The Federalists were led by John Jay, Alexander Hamilton, and James Madison. They believed that a stronger centralized government would better protect the fundamental human rights of the citizens and the liberties gained during the American Revolution. The Federalists were well funded and organized. They had the support of respected political figures like George Washington and Benjamin Franklin.

The anti-Federalists, however, had legitimate fears about a strong central government. They pointed out that a strong centralized government would lend itself to the types of tyranny they'd fought a war to end. The ability of the president to veto decisions made by Congress, for instance, had few legitimate restrictions. They also worried about the lack of protected rights for the citizens. Although the anti-Federalists were less organized and funded than their Federalist counterparts, they were able to force the Federalists to reevaluate their own agendas and compromise to achieve a more balanced constitution.

In the 1790s, immediately after the ratification of the Constitution, a new conflict between political parties arose. The Federalists and Democratic-Republicans had vastly different interpretations of the recently created legal system. The Federalists were focused on economic prosperity through the encouragement of wealthy investors, and therefore favored an alliance with Great Britain. They believed that Britain, as a leading European government, would promote trade and encourage exports from the United States. They also felt that too much direct influence from voters would cause confusion in the government and that after being elected, all political figures should seek to distance themselves from their constituents.

Republicans viewed Federalist tactics as a holdover from colonialism and feared the political elite taking power on a national level. Therefore, they opposed connections with Britain, favoring the French instead, as former allies from the American Revolution. They also sought to promote state and individual rights as opposed to the national rights that the Federalists focused on. This would keep the balance of power in favor of the individual states instead of allowing the federal government to have majority control.

These political parties were not stable. By the time Andrew Jackson was entering the political arena (1796), a new set of political parties were quickly replacing the Federalists and Democratic-Republicans. Democrats were in favor of reduced government spending and involvement. They found a ready constituency in those who were exposed by the market system, such as subsistence farmers. Whig politicians wanted the exact opposite: increased government spending and regulation. They were most popular with the individuals who benefitted from a market system, particularly Northerners who owned the means of production.

Supreme Court decisions sought to assert federal power over state laws and the primacy of the judiciary in determining the meaning of the Constitution.

One of the Supreme Court's most important decisions happened as a result of the Alien and Sedition Acts endorsed by Federalist President John Adams. The Alien Act allowed the government to remove (i.e., deport) citizens that were suspected of plotting against the government. This was an effort to discredit French citizens in particular, as well as those that were vocal in their criticisms of President Adams. The Sedition Act that followed allowed the punishment of those who attempted to "stir up sedition" in the United States.

Thomas Cooper

The passing of the Alien and Sedition Acts led to public outcry and widespread debate as to the constitutionality of such laws. Several of Adams' political opponents and critics were tried under the Sedition Act, including Matthew Lyon, a Republican representative from Vermont, and Thomas Cooper, who wrote publicly about the president's Alien Acts and military actions and questioned the constitutionality of both. The Sedition Act and the political split with fellow Federalist Alexander Hamilton led to a defeat for Adams in 1800 to political rival and Democratic-Republican Thomas Jefferson.

Recognizing that his power was fading after the election of his rival, Adams wanted to make sure that his party still had power in Washington. Thus, one of Adams'

last actions as President was the Judiciary Act of 1801. It was a sweeping reform and expansion of the federal judiciary. The act added sixteen judgeships for the six judicial systems and gave them jurisdiction over all cases where constitutionality was called into question.

The Republicans were worried that this might empower the federal system and weaken the state court systems. They also worried that Adams would appoint his Federalist supporters to the positions, which is exactly what he did with less than three weeks left in office. This earned Adams' appointments the title of "Midnight Judges" and meant that although Jefferson and the Republicans were taking hold of the government, they would have a difficult time passing non-federalist legislation.

Jefferson actually stopped several of the commissions for the "Midnight Judges" before they were sent out, and in doing so started proceedings on one of the most important judicial cases of the period. William Marbury petitioned the Supreme Court to force Secretary of State James Madison to send him his commission as Justice of the Peace in the District of Columbia. The court's decision for the case of *Marbury v. Madison* was not what Jefferson, or anyone else, expected.

The court decided in favor of Marbury and ruled that Madison's refusal to deliver the commission was illegal. However, they also stated that the Judiciary Act of 1789 which allowed an individual to petition the Supreme Court in this way was itself unconstitutional because it extended the Supreme Court's jurisdiction beyond that laid out in the Constitution. This decision kept Marbury from his commission but also established the practice of judicial review. Judicial review allows the Supreme Court the right to review decisions made among the lower courts. If decisions are deemed unconstitutional, the Supreme Court has the jurisdiction to readdress the case. It also allows for the review of all legislation.

After the Panic of 1819 (a financial crisis that crippled the U.S. economy until 1821) the Supreme Court, led by Chief Justice John Marshall, decided two important pro-capitalist cases. In *Dartmouth College v. Woodward*, the Supreme Court decided that private corporations could not be controlled by the state, even if the state had created them. Then in *McCulloch v. Maryland*, the Supreme Court ruled that the Bank of the United States could not be touched by the states. These were important decisions because they established the limit of government's power over private institutions and industry.

In 1830, the Indian Removal Act was passed. The act required the relocation of eastern Indians to a territory west of the Mississippi River. The act was protested by activists and tribes. The Cherokee tribe contested it in court and the Supreme Court decided in their favor in 1832. Chief Justice John Marshall ruled that the Indian tribes are "domestic dependent nations" and that the United States' function was that of a guardian. Later that same year, *Worcester v. Georgia* found that the states do not have jurisdiction over Indian nations within their borders.

The heart of these rulings was that President Andrew Jackson's removal of native people from their lands was an abuse of power, though not technically unconstitutional. The president ignored the Supreme Court's sentiment and continued the forced relocation of tribes. This laid the foundation for the United States' Native American policies. The idea of tribes as sovereign protected nations still legally holds.

With the acceleration of a national and international market economy, Americans debated the scope of the government's role in the economy, while diverging economic systems meant that regional political and economic loyalties often continued to overshadow national concerns.

As the government and the country started to grow, the United States had to deal with its place in the world as an economic market. By 1805, constant conflict between Britain and France was starting to put military, financial and social pressure on America. When British ships began targeting American vessels on the high seas and abducting American soldiers using the practice of impressment, Jefferson implemented the Embargo Act of 1807 which prohibited American goods from being exported overseas.

The intention was to withhold several of the raw materials that the British and French relied on economically, like cotton. Jefferson hoped that this would pressure both countries into leaving American vessels unmolested. Sadly, the act did more to hinder American growth than French or British aggression due to stockpiles in Europe. James Madison eventually repaired the relationship with the French, but not with Britain, setting the stage for the War of 1812.

While the Embargo Act made sense from a national standpoint, most of the states were against it because it would hurt them individually. Many of the northern states were unsuited for the agricultural specialization that flourished in the South. They were less arable and the lack of slaves in the North meant that labor was more expensive. Eventually, the northern states began to industrialize, building factories that supplied the country with materials that had been previously supplied by Europe. At the time of the War of 1812, however, Europe was supplying most farming tools and weapons to the United States. The North also protested vehemently, because the northern states were heavily involved in the shipping industry. They stood to lose a significant amount of money because of Jefferson's embargo.

In the South, agriculture was the primary profession. Products like tobacco and cotton made southern plantations very lucrative. This was, due in, part to the cheap labor provided by slavery.

Transporting cotton

Southerners primarily sold goods to Europeans, although, as the North industrialized, clothing factories began competing for southern cotton. This meant that both regions were opposed to the idea of the embargo because it gave them less of an opportunity to market and sell their goods. Disputes like this between state and federal governments persisted, as regional interests continued to differ from overarching national plans.

Many white Americans in the South asserted their regional identity through pride in the institution of slavery, insisting that the federal government should defend that institution.

Proponents of slavery ignored the pathos-driven arguments of the abolitionists and focused instead on what they considered practical reasons for slavery. They claimed that slavery was a historical constant. Slaves had existed in all major societies since ancient times as a form of fast and cheap labor. Proslavery advocates pointed out that slavery made economic sense. The Egyptians had used slaves to build the pyramids and the Americans used slaves to pick plants, which would surely whither on the vine if slavery was ended.

They also argued that not only were slaves necessary to the continued economic growth of the nation but that if all slaves were freed, there would be a huge social impact. Because slaves were not citizens and had no rights, these proslavery advocates argued that emancipation would disrupt the running of society and create widespread unemployment as slaves entered the workforce and competed for jobs.

Supporters of slavery also turned to the Bible for justification of their views. They argued that several Christians had slaves and God still supported them. King Solomon, the blessed king of the Israelites, had owned slaves. Similarly, the Ten Commandments chastised those who coveted their neighbor's possessions and supporters of slavery interpreted "possessions" to include slaves. Therefore, they argued that God both condoned slavery, and condemned attempts to take slaves away from their owners.

Furthermore, by bringing slaves to America and educating them in the Christian faith, many slave owners thought that they were saving their slaves from hell. Senator John C. Calhoun claimed in a proslavery speech to the Senate, "Never before has the black race of Central Africa, from the dawn of history to the present day, attained a condition so civilized and so improved, not only physically, but morally and intellectually." He went on to describe slavery as an institution "indispensable to the peace and happiness of both" races. Slavery, according to him, was a better condition to live in than the ignorance of their native Africa. Calhoun insisted that southerners stop apologizing for the institution of slavery, and his comments defined the proslavery arguments for the next several decades.

Concurrent with an increasing international exchange of goods and ideas, larger numbers of Americans began struggling with how to match democratic political ideals to political institutions and social realities.

Despite the fact that the Constitution had established the political future of the United States, there were still conflicts between factions and parties. The authority of the Supreme Court didn't stop people from disagreeing with the decisions it reached. With conflict occurring in the political arena, it was hard to create a stable social reality that reflected stated political goals. Many groups tried to arrange these conflicting ideas into some form of truth that supported the ideals of the country's founding documents.

The Second Great Awakening, liberal social ideas from abroad and romantic beliefs in human perfectibility fostered the rise of voluntary organizations to promote religious and secular reforms, including abolition and women's rights.

While less politically charged than many other conflicts during the time, religion was rapidly changing during the early 19th century. Before the American Revolution, most people belonged to one of three major Protestant denominations: Congregationalists, Anglicans, and Quakers. Congregationalist churches were the descendants of Puritan churches and Puritan influence on America can still be seen in many American ideals, such as hard work and community.

The Anglican Church was the American branch of the Church of England. After the Revolution, they were known as Episcopalians. The Quakers were a "peace church" like the Amish. After the American Revolution, the major denominations changed, and the three foundation denominations gave way to evangelical Methodism and Baptists, as revivals swept the nation. This period is known as the Second Great Awakening.

At the heart of the Second Great Awakening were revivals. These were large meetings, typically held in fields where a preacher, or several preachers, would stand and speak. Charles Finney, sometimes called the Father of Modern Revivalism, was one such preacher. He shared his personal faith at revivals, and his personal style impacted the movement as a whole. Finney also allowed women to pray out loud in public meetings of mixed gender, which was not done during the period due to the cult of domesticity and the national understanding of gender roles.

Charles Finney

Charles Finney created what he called the "anxious seat," which was a place for non-Christians who were considering converting. They could sit in the anxious seat to receive prayers. He also made a habit of censuring individuals by name during his services and preaching extemporaneously for an audience. Using methods like these, the energy of the crowd was masterfully controlled by these speakers. An account of a 20,000-person revival in Kentucky reads:

> *The noise was like the roar of Niagara. The vast sea of human beings seemed to be agitated as if by a storm. I counted seven ministers, all preaching at one time, some on stumps, others on wagons...Some of the people were singing, others praying, some crying for mercy. A peculiarly strange sensation came over me. My heart beat tumultuously, my knees trembled, my lips quivered, and I felt as though I must fall to the ground.*
>
> —James Finley

The ministers at these revivals reached out to their audience at the emotional level and upheld ideals that the average person could agree with. Evangelical churches generally favored ordinary people over elites. They felt that a truly pious individual was more capable of leading others to salvation than a formally trained minister, like those required by many traditional churches. These open policies meant that many flocked to the Evangelical faiths.

While these religious revivals didn't directly threaten any established order, they did encourage activism on a wide scale. The movement stressed the concept of free will and a person's choice to accept their lot in life or work to better their position. It was a very optimistic outlook, allowing the choice of religious salvation instead of the fatalistic views held by other denominations, but it was also one that encouraged conflict with the social norms.

White women, who were invited to take leadership roles for the first time, found themselves in a position to enact social change for women's rights. African Americans were also allowed to actively participate in the new religion. The stressing of individual salvation caused many to question the religion-based proslavery arguments.

While this period is characterized by conflicts over slavery, women's rights, and Native American's rights, great strides were made in other forms of activism. In 1837, Horace Mann, often called the Father of the Common School, used his position as the secretary of the newly-created Massachusetts Board of Education to enact major education reform. He started the Common School Movement to ensure that all children would have a basic education at the expense of the state.

Horace Mann

Mann believed that society could only flourish when all citizens were basically literate and had a general understanding of civics. He argued that it was only with an educated public that a democracy, dependent upon the will of that public, could reach its fullest potential. Mann was involved in creating teacher training schools, called normal schools, so that children would be educated by professionals. He also actively recruited and trained women for what was, at the time, an all-male vocation.

While Horace Mann championed the education system, Dorothea Dix was trying to bring social reform to the treatment of the mentally ill. In 1841, while teaching Sunday school at the East Cambridge Jail, a women's prison, Dix discovered that the living quarters for the prisoners were not hospitable, especially those holding the mentally ill. Many of the rooms had no heat, for instance. Outraged by the way these women were being treated, she petitioned the courts for an order to improve the standard of living in the prisons.

Concerned about the plight of others, Dix traveled around the state to research the living conditions in prisons and poorhouses. This led to her eventually writing a proposal for the Massachusetts legislature, which would expand and improve the State Mental Hospital at Worcester. Satisfied with her work at home, Dix began a national tour to improve conditions for all patients. Her continued success at the state level encouraged her to move into the federal arena. In 1848, she requested an endowment to be put aside for the treatment of the mentally ill, the deaf and the blind. Both the House and the Senate passed the bill, but it was vetoed by President Franklin Pierce. Discouraged but not defeated, Dix began to travel internationally, recommending reforms worldwide.

Scottish born Frances Wright (also known as Franny Wright) was a proponent of utopian communities and believed that they could be used to resolve the American issue of slavery (the term "utopian" comes from Sir Thomas More's *Utopia*, in which he theorized about the perfect society). These settlements tended to experiment with different models of government, marriage, labor and wealth, in an effort to find the perfect society. In 1825, Wright published *A Plan for the Gradual Abolition of Slavery in the United States without Danger of Loss to the Citizens of the South*. In the text, she urgently suggests that land is put aside for the purpose of creating a colony for freed blacks based on the utopian communities of the time.

Frances Wright

Wright was so sure that her plan would work that she invested her own money in a 640-acre tract located in present-day Tennessee. She called the land Nashoba and populated her colony with slaves that she bought and freed in exchange for being a part of her colony. Soon after the colony was founded, however, she was forced to leave. When she returned, she found it destroyed. Still insistent that her plan could work, she published a well-received newspaper article defending her idea, and in 1830 she made arrangements for the Nashoba slaves to be emancipated to Haiti.

Nathaniel Hawthorne

Several other utopian communities existed during the period. Few had any lasting impact on society, but each experimented with different social structures, an indicator that the young country was still trying to define itself. In 1841, Brook Farm was founded by Unitarian Minister George Ripley. Known as the Transcendentalist Romance, the community was the first purely secular utopian community. The foundational idea was that by living together, farming together and sharing their labors, members would have more time to spend on academic pursuits. The community disbanded relatively quickly when finances became an issue. Nathanial Hawthorne, an influential Romantic writer, was one of the community's founding members.

Author Louisa May Alcott spent seven months of her childhood at Fruitland, a utopian community founded by her father and Charles Lane. Though it claimed to be based on principles of gender equality, Alcott's scathing reflection detailed a very different story. New Harmony, in Indiana, was a more successful endeavor. Founded by social reformer Robert Owens, the community was populated by scientists and succeeded in establishing a center for scientific discovery outside of the Northeast. It disbanded after four years.

The Shakers, on the other hand, are a utopian group that still exists today. Shakers practice celibacy and communal ownership of goods. Both aspects were typical of religious utopias. However, they also believe in strict gender roles and keep the sexes separate. Their prosperity is based mainly on a source of income, namely furniture design, and manufacture.

Despite the outlawing of the international slave trade, the rise in the number of free African Americans in both the North and the South, and widespread discussion of various emancipation plans, the United States and many state governments continued to restrict African Americans' citizenship possibilities.

As the American economy began to bounce back, social issues like slavery moved to the forefront of politics. Like the economy, slavery was a complex issue that opposing sides attempted to simplify. By 1808, it was illegal to import slaves into the United States from Africa or the Caribbean. This meant that most slaves bought and sold after these times were born in the United States (although an illicit trans-Atlantic slave trade persisted after 1808). However, slaves born in America were not considered American citizens and held very few rights.

Many Southerners embraced slavery as the "peculiar institution of the South" and saw slavery as part of their regional identity. They relied on slaves as a form of cheap labor and a ready workforce. Slavery allowed for higher profits because the workforce didn't have to be paid. That is not to say, however, that all slaves were laborers. Some slaves served inside houses as domestic servants and companions. These slaves might be taught skills that were not accessible to other laborers. Domestic slaves, for instance, were the most likely to know how to read and write.

In the South, slave codes were published detailing the "rights" of slaves. These were actually manuals for slave owners and detailed how slaves could be legally treated. For instance, slave marriages were not considered legally binding, so slave families could be broken up by their owner.

In the North, most states preferred to ignore that the problem existed. Many passed laws to discourage free slaves from settling in their state, like Ohio in 1804. In 1817, the American Colonization Society was founded to try to help freed slaves return to Africa. While initially applauded as a way to assist the plight of African peoples, most people soon realized that the American Colonization Society was more worried about removing freed African Americans from northern states than improving the situation of those still in slavery.

Abolitionists, however, fought against this negligence, trying to keep slavery an issue in the minds of the public. Many slaves, unwilling to live in the horrible conditions they were subject to, attempted to escape. If successful, they would be forced to flee to Canada, where slave catchers were banned after 1819. If caught, they would be killed or returned to their owners.

In 1804, the Underground Railroad was established in Pennsylvania by abolitionists hoping to help runaway slaves. The "railroad" was actually a connected line of safe houses where slaves could hide. They would be given food and shelter and transported from one house to the next, until free. The different station houses didn't necessarily know each other, however. Runaway slaves were led by conductors, often runaway slaves themselves. Perhaps the most famous of these conductors was Harriet Tubman, who is credited with assisting over 300 slaves to freedom. She made at least nineteen trips to the South, never lost a passenger and was never caught.

Harriet Tubman,
the Moses to her people

Resistance to initiatives for democracy and inclusion included proslavery arguments, rising xenophobia, anti-black sentiments in political and popular culture, and restrictive anti-Indian policies.

While groups like the abolitionists looked at the founding documents and concluded that all humans—not just whites—had rights, many people had the opposite sentiment. Many citizens were concerned about what the inclusion-based policies of the federal government would mean if extended to all people, especially the rights afforded to citizens. Thus, a rise occurred in anti-black and anti-Indian sentiments. If these groups were made citizens, they would be able to vote, and that would change the political field. Similarly, as land opened in the West, xenophobia spread. Americans began demanding that the federal government deal with the waves of immigrants traveling to America.

While Americans celebrated their nation's progress toward a unified new national culture that blended Old World forms with New World ideas, various groups of the nation's inhabitants developed distinctive cultures of their own.

Although America tried to cultivate a cultural identity separate from the rest of the world, the creation of purely American art forms took time. Americans had not been around long enough to break away from traditional art forms, and it was very popular to mimic the highly cultured styles of Europe. This changed during the first half of the 1800s, primarily as a reaction to the opening of the western territory and the development of so many regional identities, which were then expressed and preserved.

A new national culture emerged, with various Americans creating art, architecture, and literature that combined European forms with local and regional cultural sensibilities.

As the country struggled to establish a national identity amongst the chaos of conflict, artists adapted original American styles. It became popular to document scenes of everyday life for different classes and in different regions. As territory opened in the West, landscapes became the dominant art form. Styles like the panoramic landscapes of the Hudson River School showed the country's beauty and vitality. The Tonalism and Luminism movements invoked a spiritual serenity in landscapes, reflecting the ideas of westward expansion and Americans as the chosen people. Artists were expressing the serenity of an America that was embroiled in conflicts and searching for its place in the world. They were, in a sense, capturing those fundamental ideals that founded the nation.

Painter John James Audubon established a very different style and body of work that still managed to capture the myth of America. His goal as a painter was to accurately capture the majesty of the numerous American birds. While this may sound simplistic, it made him incredibly popular in the United States and abroad. His birds managed to capture the majesty and youth of America. In addition to painting, Audubon practiced science. Audubon made the first American bird bands and used them to track and identify a group of Eastern Phoebes that returned annually to his neighbor's yard.

John James Audubon

Passenger pigeon by
John James Audubon

Romanticism, a popular literary style characterized by philosophical idealism, gave way to one of the first American literary styles, transcendentalism. Though it is sometimes mistaken for a religion, transcendentalism is about interpreting relationships. Transcendentalist authors were trying to encapsulate the same mythology as visual artists of the period; they wanted to verbally define what it meant to be an American and write about the spirit of America.

The most famous transcendentalists are Ralph Waldo Emerson and Henry David Thoreau. Emerson's essay *Self-Reliance* is still widely read and speaks to the inability of humans to obtain meaning from one another. Emerson wrote that truth had to come from the individual. Thoreau's best-known work is his essay *Civil Disobedience*. In it, he encompasses many of the same ideas that Emerson illuminated. His most well-known excerpt is his description of the night he spent in prison following his refusal to pay taxes to fund a war that he did not support. In the excerpt, Thoreau mocks the idea that a man whose conscience is clear could ever be "imprisoned." He, like other transcendentalists, valued the mental over the physical and therefore felt that his true "body" could never be touched.

Ralph Waldo Emerson (left) and Henry David Thoreau (right)

Perhaps the premier artistic style to impact the early history of America was neoclassicism, characterized by a renewed interest in classical forms and ideas. It can be seen in stunning variety in America during the early 19th century. Many of the political ideas from the Enlightenment had their roots in Greco-Roman culture. Epics, a literary form used by Greek and Roman poets, became popular and compared well with the slave narratives and westward expansionism of the day.

Even the buildings that housed the government showed an obvious homage to the Greek and Roman ruins. One of the most noteworthy members of this movement was Thomas Jefferson, who was an accomplished architect in addition to being a leading statesman. Jefferson wanted his admiration of the Roman Republic to be manifested, not only in the political institutions of the new nation but also visually in the nation's public buildings, to remind the citizens that they lived in a Republic. The White House, in particular, uses the same style of columns as the Pantheon in Rome. Neoclassicism serves as an excellent metaphor for the early American people. They were attached to the past as a way to remain connected to their ideals, yet they were prepared to change.

Various groups of American Indians, women and religious followers developed cultures reflecting their interests and experiences, as did regional groups and an emerging urban middle class.

The early 1800s saw distinct cultures emerge within numerous communities. For the Native Americans, this was a resurgence of traditional values. Through trade with the Europeans and Americans, many tribes had changed and adapted their cultural practices. They used new agricultural methods, learned to read and write in English, and adopted new technology at the expense of some of their traditional practices. Many natives encouraged a shift back to the older ways. For instance, in 1811, three Cherokee in Georgia reported that they had seen a vision denouncing European goods. The Cherokee deities were unhappy with the way Cherokees had allowed settlers to treat animals and the land, demanding that they return to the old ways.

Susan B. Anthony

Women also saw a surge in culture as they began to realize their place in the new nation. While less volatile than slavery, gender equality was another polarizing issue of the time. Women in the early 1800s didn't have a place in the public sphere and were often considered an accessory to their husband's image. This trope, often known as "the cult of domesticity," strictly defined gender roles for women and men.

As abolitionism spread, however, women began their own fight for rights. They questioned their subservience to men and felt that the abolitionist movement should be extended to include all human rights. This created a split in the abolitionist movement, particularly over whether or not women could serve as officers and speakers. When Elizabeth Cady Stanton was snubbed at the World Slavery Convention in London, she joined with Lucretia Mott and Susan B. Anthony to create a separate women's movement.

The resulting Seneca Falls Convention in New York established the women's movement in earnest. The convention encouraged speakers to share their perspective on a woman's rights in the United States, and delegates drafted a Declaration of Sentiments based on the Declaration of Independence. The declaration demanded specific rights and improvements for women, including protection in the event of divorce (especially with custody laws that tended to grant the father custody), equal property rights to men, fair wages and access to higher-level professions. The primary demand and the vehicle through which women sought to achieve these changes, was suffrage.

The right to vote would allow women to pursue the changes they wanted on a national level and would grant them equal say in other political issues, like slavery. While the women's movement was separate from the abolitionist movement, there was still significant support for abolition amongst the delegates.

Sojourner Truth demonstrated this relationship at a women's rights convention in 1851 when she gave her famous speech *Ain't I a Woman?* In the speech, she reminds her fellow women that the fight for women's rights doesn't end at suffrage for white women but is for all women. Later, this issue would divide the organization.

Enslaved and free African Americans, isolated at the bottom of the social hierarchy, created communities and strategies to protect their dignity and their family structures, even as some launched abolitionist and reform movements aimed at changing their status.

Slaves and free African-Americans were creating their own culture during this period. In 1794, Richard Allen created the first black denomination: the African Methodist Episcopal Church. Spirituals were sung in the fields as slaves worked to create a sense of community and family. They also had the dual role of acting as coded messages for runaway slaves. *Follow the Drinking Gourd*, for instance, explains how to travel north to freedom by following the Big Dipper (Ursa Major), which includes the North Star.

Frederick Douglass

Runaway and freed slaves began sharing stories that detailed their lives under former masters. Frederick Douglass wrote arguably the best known of these works: *Narrative of the Life of Frederick Douglass, An American Slave.* This text and others like it were published in the North and opened the eyes of many northerners to the evils of slavery by making slavery about a person instead of an institution.

Other African Americans served as an example of what freed slaves could be. Most notable amongst these are James Forten and David Walker. Forten apprenticed with a sailmaker in Philadelphia and took over the business when the owner passed, refusing to make rigging for any slave trading vessels. He was an inspiration to the African American community and actively fought for an end to slavery. He opposed the American Colonization Society on the basis that he was an American and belonged in the United States. Forten also financially supported William Lloyd Garrison's abolitionist paper, *The Liberator.*

Several similar publications spread across the northern states and provided a vehicle for abolitionists to band together. David Walker published his thoughts on slavery in *An Appeal to the Colored Citizens in the World* which he then smuggled into the South using sympathetic sailors as contacts. Slaves who read his works—writing that defended them against slavery in the South and discrimination in the North—were uplifted and inspired. Slaveholders soon had a bounty on his head, but he refused to flee to Canada and insisted on staying in the public eye. Another publisher, Elijah Lovejoy, was eventually killed for publishing anti-slavery messages.

Many white abolitionists encouraged the spread of African American art forms as a way to further polarize the issue and encourage more people to join the abolitionist movement. But even amongst abolitionists, there was discord. For example, with *The Liberator*, Garrison intended to bring abolitionists together and spread their ideas. Yet Garrison scorned the idea that solely political action would have any impact on ending slavery. This put him in direct opposition to the Liberty Party who tried to influence abolitionist change using the existing political system.

Others thought that by emulating and popularizing slave narratives, they could gain attention. Harriet Beecher Stowe wrote one of the most famous pieces of literature from this time period, *Uncle Tom's Cabin*. Her take on the slave narrative style was widely popular and earned her, and the abolitionist movement, a wealth of support. Some of the more extreme abolitionists took after John Brown. Brown attacked the federal arsenal at Harper's Ferry, Virginia, with the intent to lead slaves in an armed insurrection. Although Brown's actions shocked and were criticized by many, they earned him a great deal of respect from others.

Harriet Beecher Stowe

Key Concept 4.2: Developments in technology, agriculture and commerce precipitated profound changes in U.S. settlement patterns, regional identities, gender and family relations, political power and distribution of consumer goods.

The early 1800s saw some major shifts in technology and business. Suddenly, machines that could do the work of multiple men, with less strain and effort, were available. This rocked the market foundation of the country and opened the door for a number of possibilities. These changes were rapid and far-reaching, affecting everything from where new communities settled to gender roles and family relationships.

A global market and communications revolution, influencing and influenced by technological innovations, led to dramatic shifts in the nature of agriculture and manufacturing.

Samuel Morse making the telegraph

There were two major problems facing the early U.S. agricultural market: communication and transportation. With long distance communication existing only in the form of letters, it was difficult to determine markets for products and establish fair buying and selling practices. For example, a tobacco farmer in North Carolina may not have wanted to sell his tobacco in North Carolina because most of the other farmers in the state also grew tobacco, saturating the local market.

This meant that the farmer had to find a different market for his goods in order to profit. The farmer's market options were limited due to the difficulty of transportation. If the farmer could not get his items to a new market, they were essentially worthless. All of this changed as infrastructure created safer and easier transportation and with the creation of the telegraph by Samuel Morse in 1844.

Innovations, including textile machinery, steam engines, interchangeable parts, canals, railroads, and the telegraph, as well as agricultural inventions, both extended markets and brought efficiency to production for those markets.

America's development was very dependent on technological innovation. Samuel Slater, for instance, is often referred to as the father of the American factory system. After covertly memorizing the setup of a British textile mill, Slater came to the United States and put his own mill into practice. While he used methods already common in Britain, they were new to Americans and revolutionized how northerners looked at their labor force.

Slater further changed the factory system by constructing a small town for his factory. By employing families and housing them at the factory, Slater believed he could improve production. This system gave families an option outside of semi-subsistence farming—the typical lifestyle, at the time—although most factory families obtained some of their own food through farming.

Samuel Slater

Other innovators focused on agriculture. Cyrus McCormick isn't well known in the modern era, but his company became part of International Harvester, which still supplies farming equipment today. McCormick's invention, the mechanical reaper, meant that harvesting was no longer limited to the amount that could be cut by hand. Beyond that, he created an entire industry, including creditors and a service department utilizing the new concept of interchangeable parts. His business model is still relevant in a modern market, and many enterprises follow a similar plan.

Likewise, John Deere started his company with the manufacture of plows that could tackle the prairie lands where grass roots made the sod thick and difficult to penetrate. His innovative design began what is still a successful agricultural business.

Increasing numbers of Americans, especially women in factories and low-skilled male workers, no longer relied on semi-subsistence agriculture but made their livelihoods producing goods for distant markets, even as some urban entrepreneurs went into finance rather than manufacturing.

The Slater method of employment, in which entire families were housed and taken care of by the factory, was later adapted by Frances Cabot Lowell, who employed farm girls and young women instead of whole families. The girls were housed in supervised dormitories and were provided with educational and cultural opportunities. While this type of situation often raises suspicion as to working conditions and pay, the Lowell system was actually extremely beneficial to its workers.

Lowell women at the loom

Lowell drew in a ready and willing labor force by hiring young women, typically from rural communities where they wouldn't have had many opportunities to better themselves. Lowell's system had an impact on the Women's Rights Movement, helping to encourage more women to join political movements, empowering them to demand rights and education equal to their male counterparts.

With the progression of the market and the development of new factories, the discovery of anthracite coal deposits in Pennsylvania was a blessing to the nation. As industrialization continued, it became obvious that there were not enough trees to power the growing factories. Coal was a good solution; especially anthracite with its high carbon content that allows it to burn longer than most other types of coal.

Finding ways to mine and transport coal proved difficult. It took an entire generation to prepare the mountainous areas of Pennsylvania for coal mining. Canals were built to connect the coal mines with cities that needed their product. Eventually, railways replaced water transportation, which meant that more coal could reach the market at greater speed. It also meant that coal tycoons, having control of the product and the means of transportation, could sway the future of entire regions.

Regional economic specialization, especially the demands of cultivating southern cotton, shaped settlement patterns and the national and international economy.

Many scholars believe that multiple variables affected where and when settlement occurred in the United States during the 1800s. Before 1815, settlements were relatively slow to expand and branch out, particularly beyond the Appalachian Mountains, because there was very little immigration due to wars in Europe and the War of 1812 in America. Following the war, immigration to the United States increased rapidly, with the promise of new land in the Louisiana Territory.

Southern cotton furnished the raw material for manufacturing in the Northeast, while growth in cotton production and trade promoted the development of national economic ties, shaped the international economy and fueled the internal slave trade.

One of the country's most important agricultural products was cotton. While important before the Revolutionary War, cotton became one of the most influential American products in the world after Eli Whitney developed the cotton gin in 1793. Whitney's machine allowed cotton production to increase at unheard-of rates: nearly 800 percent in the first decade.

King Cotton, as it was called, was an excellent money-maker that created high competition and provided good returns on investment. It didn't spoil the way produce did, and could, therefore, be sold in domestic markets and overseas. Typically, cotton was grown in the South and sold to factories in the northern states, or to England, whose thriving textile factories couldn't be adequately fed by European wool. If sold to England—and, on average, 80 percent was—cotton was transported on northern shipping vessels. This meant that the North also prospered from the sale of cotton.

Picking cotton

The increase in production also meant an increase in labor; slavery became even more deeply ingrained into the southern economy as new labor forces were constantly needed to keep up with growing demand. Slave ships illegally transported cargo from Africa and the Caribbean to southern markets. Many slave women were encouraged or forced to produce children. Poor farmers, those who did not own slaves and couldn't afford to buy them, often stopped planting other crops to focus on cotton. Southerners were eventually forced to seek out new farmland as their one crop system quickly drained the land of its resources. This eventually raised the question of whether slavery should be allowed to spread into new territories and is why the cotton gin is often cited as a cause of the Civil War.

Despite some governmental and private efforts to create a unified national economy, most notably the American System, the shift to market production linked the North and the Midwest more closely than either was linked to the South.

Cotton wasn't the only thing tying the North and South together. John Quincy Adams, son of former President John Adams, focused on America's internal integrity using the American System. The American System was created by Secretary of State Henry Clay and consisted of three main pieces: a tariff that was designed to promote American industry, a national bank to help establish productive business and enterprise, and federal monetary support for infrastructure to help agriculture reach new, more profitable markets inside the United States.

While the American System wasn't terribly popular, especially with Adams' political opponents, it did achieve major strides in infrastructure. For example, the Cumberland Road, also known as the National Road, connected the Potomac and Ohio Rivers and allowed for westward expansion at an exponential rate. Adams also commissioned a series of canals which opened up America's waterways to encourage economic growth. This was partially due to the *Gibbons v. Ogden* Supreme Court decision in 1824, which allowed the federal government the right to regulate interstate trade. As railroads and canals made interstate commerce easier, the county's prosperity continued to grow. By the time Adams left office, the national debt had been reduced to one-third of its size.

Adams' hope was that America could be united by its continued economic growth, but many people, particularly southerners, disliked his American System because it limited the number of markets for products like cotton. This meant a limit on competition and price. The North was not as impacted because it could adapt its shipping industries inward. The North and western territories grew closer as more commerce and movement opened between the two. The South, in comparison, stayed fairly isolated by its beliefs and its economic and infrastructural differences.

Efforts to exploit the nation's natural resources led to government efforts to promote free and forced migration of various American peoples across the continent as well as to competing ideas about defining and managing labor systems, geographical boundaries, and natural resources.

Natural resources were abundant in the Americas. Virtually untouched, America had immense forests that could be turned into boats or tools. They could be shipped to Europe where lumber was more expensive and far less plentiful. Large supplies of fresh, clean water supported the creation of new towns and communities while also allowing for faster travel of people, resources and news.

America also had vast untapped mineral wealth, including coal, iron, copper, silver, and gold. As each of these resources was discovered, an industry grew to harvest it for consumption elsewhere. These jobs were dangerous but profitable, so a steady supply of labor was almost always on hand. Disease and bodily harm created concerns about job safety, and regulation became a topic of national interest.

The economic changes caused by the market revolution had significant effects on migration patterns, gender and family relations, and the distribution of political power.

Businesses tended to differ from region to region depending on the type of environment. For instance, in the agricultural areas, cities were very far apart, as settlers claimed land for farming. In areas where the growing season or land was not conducive to agriculture, people tended to band together to form larger cities for economic growth and prosperity. This meant that the societal makeup for these different areas differed greatly.

With the opening of canals and new roads into the western territories, native-born white citizens relocated westward, relying on new community systems to replace their old family and local relationships.

As with the utopian communities, new areas in the western territories created connections outside of the familial to encourage migrations. Small towns and communities were typically close-knit, as the individuals living there relied on each other for continued survival. This meant that fellowship through uniting ideals, such as religion, tended to take the place of the familial relationships, and life in town would revolve around these uniting opinions and goals.

Emigrants to the West

Migrants from Europe increased the population in the East and the Midwest, forging strong bonds of interdependence between the Northeast and the Old Northwest.

Most of the immigrants moving into the western territories were Europeans because trade with China was tentative at best and Africa was still off limits due to the legislation regarding the slave trade. These European settlers typically started in the northern states where the shipping business made it easier to travel from Europe. Then they set out west, typically among easily traveled paths like rivers or established trails. Similar groups tended to stay together, and scholars believe they may have sought locations that reminded them of their original homeland.

The South remained politically, culturally and ideologically distinct from the other sections while continuing to rely on its exports to Europe for economic growth.

While the population in the North continued to grow and change, the population in the South stayed fairly similar. This gave rise to a unique class system that further separated the North and South. While the North had industrial empires like those of the railway barons, the South had developed a landed gentry or aristocracy amongst those that could afford large plantations and the slaves to work them.

Below this class were those that could afford some slaves, but not as many as were needed to turn the massive profits of the genteel southerners. Below them were those that were too poor to afford any outside labor. Called "white trash" by their neighbors, these citizens were almost at the level of freed slaves. This social system baffled and deterred northerners and immigrants, allowing the South to further strengthen its ties with Europe.

The market revolution helped to widen a gap between rich and poor, shaped emerging middle and working classes and caused an increasing separation between home and workplace, which led to dramatic transformations in gender and in family roles and expectations.

With the rapid changes happening to industry, workers started to band together to form protective agencies called unions. Unions were focused on improving conditions for workers by creating safer working conditions and offering fair wages. In 1834, the National Trades Union made a short appearance, yet most unions functioned better on the local level than the national level.

Regional interests continued to trump national concerns as the basis for many political leaders' positions on economic issues including slavery, the national bank, tariffs, and internal improvements.

The issue of regional identity versus national identity was constant during the 1800s. Movements helping one part of the country were inevitably met by resistance from another part of the country. Slavery was seen as a necessity in the South but was abhorrent to northerners. Tariffs on imports and exports inevitably helped the North and West while hindering the potential economic development of the South, and internal improvements in the North tended to distance the South.

> **KEY CONCEPT 4.3:** U.S. interest in increasing foreign trade, expanding its national borders, and isolating itself from European conflicts shaped the nation's foreign policy and spurred government and private initiatives.

Struggling to create an independent global presence, U.S. policymakers sought to dominate the North American continent and to promote its foreign trade.

The War of 1812, sometimes referred to as the Second War for Independence, was the result of Anglo-American tension that had been brewing since the American Revolution. The tension increased with the British impressment of American sailors during the Napoleonic Wars, one of the main causes of the embargo in 1807.

War of 1812, Battle of New Orleans

As previously mentioned, Jefferson implemented the Embargo Act of 1807 in response to British ships bullying American vessels on the high seas. Jefferson intended this act to punish the British and French by withholding resources and thus convince them to leave American ships alone. This act put a strain on the relationship between America and the French and British and actually hurt American traders more than it hurt European traders.

James Madison, who succeeded Jefferson, mended the relationship with the French, but America's relationship with Britain remained tense, leading to the War of 1812. The British were also encouraging the resistance of Native Americans as settlers began to move west into the newly purchased Louisiana Territory.

In 1812, encouraged by the War Hawks in Congress, James Madison and Congress declared war on Britain. American troops were immediately dispatched to Canada (then a British colony) and were pushed back due to their under-preparedness. The British had several successes in the war, including the capture of Washington, D.C. and the burning of the White House in 1814. The Americans held control of the Northwest Territory and had several naval victories.

When Fort McHenry in Baltimore withstood more than twenty-four hours of sustained bombardment, the British Navy moved south towards New Orleans. The Treaty of Ghent was signed at this point and the war was supposed to be over. However, communication was slow, and the British did not know that the war had ended when they attacked New Orleans, where they were defeated by American troops led by Andrew Jackson. The war and its consequences highlighted the need for America to become a player in the international community.

Following the Louisiana Purchase, the drive to acquire, survey and open up new lands and markets led Americans into numerous economic, diplomatic and military initiatives in the Western Hemisphere and Asia.

Several of the foreign diplomatic initiatives during this period involved Great Britain. In 1842, Secretary of State Daniel Webster met with British Ambassador Lord Atherton to negotiate on some key points. The issue of the Canadian border was quickly resolved by establishing a fixed latitudinal border and a discussion of actions to be taken in the event of an accidental violation. The issue of the international slave trade was similarly finalized. The British agreed to stop searching American ships if the Americans agreed to police the coast of Africa to look for slave ships flying the American flag. With Anglo-American tensions relaxed, the two countries could focus on other areas, such as China.

However, tensions flared again in 1846 as the Oregon Territory became a pressing matter. In the end, England conceded its claim to some territory in exchange for uncontested control of the northern territories. With the border established from sea to sea in the North, America had almost established its present-day continental size.

In 1836, Texas successfully rebelled against Mexico and formed its own state. America, having just won a war for its own independence, offered the new territory diplomatic recognition and otherwise left it alone until 1844, when President John Tyler started negotiations for annexation. As a result, Mexico severed all economic and diplomatic ties with the U.S. Failing on the first vote, Texas was eventually added to the Union in 1845. Relations with Mexico tensed as a result, especially as the Mexico–Texas border had not been resolved before annexation.

When buying the disputed territory didn't work, President Polk gained congressional support for a declaration of war against Mexico. After American troops captured Mexico City in 1847, the treaty to buy the disputed territory was reexamined. Mexico agreed to give the United States over half of its pre-war territory, provided that the United States pay Mexico $15 million and forgive $3.3 million in debts owed by Mexican citizens.

Mexican-American War, the battle of Palo Alto

The United States sought dominance over the North American continent through a variety of means, including military actions, judicial decisions, and diplomatic efforts.

President James Monroe

In the 1820s, America began to look abroad at its influence in the international theatre. President James Monroe, in the spirit of former President Jefferson, wanted to encourage other countries to leave the Americas alone as far as colonization was concerned. To this extent, and with the support of the British, he issued the Monroe Doctrine in 1823 during a State of the Union Address to Congress.

In 1823, nearly all Latin American colonies were moving towards independence. Monroe wanted to make sure that no one would step in and fill the void as the colonies established themselves as governments. He made it very clear that any action to gain control of these colonies would be met with American intervention. In turn, he promised that America would not interfere with existing colonies. This has been referred to as the Monroe Doctrine; it has been upheld by numerous U.S. presidents and still plays an important part in American foreign affairs.

Various American groups and individuals initiated, championed and/or resisted the expansion of territory and/or government powers.

After the acquisition of the Louisiana Territory, expansion became a certainty. In 1803, Thomas Jefferson commissioned the Corps of Discovery, better known as the Lewis and Clark Expedition. Meriwether Lewis and William Clark led the Corps over 8,000 miles from 1804 to 1806, in an effort to chronicle the land, plants, animals, and people in the new territory. During the journey, Lewis recorded everything in a detailed journal, so the expedition was well preserved for posterity. They were aided by several native tribes who provided supplies and assistance, as well as their guide and interpreter Sacajawea, a native.

Meriwether Lewis (left) and William Clark (right)

Their discoveries helped to expand the knowledge of the new territory, plants, and animals that had never been seen before. The expedition was heralded as a success, and Meriwether Lewis was given a governorship upon their triumphant return. Lewis and Clark had made it all the way to the Pacific Ocean, and their example spurred others to turn west. Manifest Destiny, the belief that Americans were meant to conquer the entire continent from east to west, became a prevalent force in society. However, two issues held up the expansion of these western territories: the nation had to decide how to deal with Native Americans and the question of slavery.

Map of the general route followed by Lewis and Clark

With expanding borders came public debates about whether to expand and how to define and use the new territories.

The federal and state governments had to negotiate to create an agreement as to the role that slavery should play in the West. The government had kept a delicate balance between the number of slave and free states, splitting the twenty-two states evenly. This peace was maintained until Missouri requested to join the Union as a slave state in 1819. Fierce debate ensued, as abolitionists fought the request. The government eventually decided upon the Missouri Compromise of 1820. Missouri would be a slave state while Maine, formerly part of Massachusetts, would enter the Union as a free state.

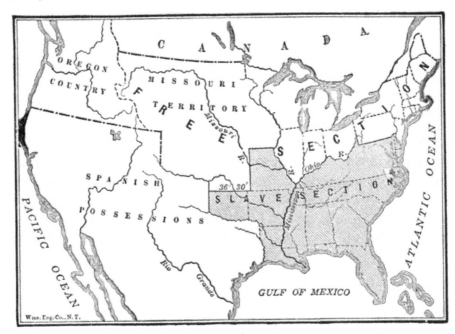

Missouri Compromise, 1820

Furthermore, the compromise drew an imaginary line across the nation to separate free and slave states. Few people were happy with the compromise. Southerners protested that the federal government was making rules related to slavery, a state issue, and northerners disagreed with the compromise on the premise that it allowed for the expansion of slavery, even if only below the compromise line. This uneasy peace existed for thirty years until it was repealed by the Kansas–Nebraska Act of 1854, which established the rule of popular sovereignty in both states. This meant that both Kansas and Nebraska could enter the Union as slave states despite the fact that they were above the compromise line.

Native American territories caused similar problems, as the tribes tried to establish their own land and rules in the face of American migration. President Andrew Jackson tried to decide this issue with his Indian Removal Act of 1830 which required the relocation of eastern Indians to a territory west of the Mississippi River. Although heavily contested, the president ignored opposition and pursued forced relocation of the American Indian tribes. While activists protested, few people were moved to do anything as the Native Americans' former territory became usable land for agriculture and settlements.

Federal government attempts to assert authority over the states brought resistance from state governments in the North and the South at different times.

While President Jackson sought to repeal parts of the American System such as the National Bank, Congress was considering another tariff, like President Adams' Tariff of 1828, which was called the Tariff of Abominations. The new tariff was very similar. It was a protectionist tariff that attempted to protect local producers from foreign competition. It did this by taxing imported goods, which would raise their price and make buying American products more appealing.

The issue was that any tariff that taxed imports was going to benefit the North over the South. The North's products, like textiles, would be cheaper than foreign products, causing northern markets to flourish. Southern markets would suffer, particularly cotton, because foreign traders would be able to buy less of these products. Southerners protested the tariff vehemently, but on July 14, 1832, Andrew Jackson signed it into law. The southern states, which were to be hardest hit, were outraged. South Carolina particularly resisted the new tariff, and in the winter of 1832, the state government declared it null and void because they considered it to be unconstitutional.

In response, President Jackson issued a proclamation disputing South Carolina's ability to ignore federal law. Congress soon passed the Force Act which would allow military force to be used against any state that refused to comply with the tariff acts. As tensions grew, a deal was brokered by Henry Clay and Vice President Calhoun. The Compromise Tariff of 1833 gradually reduced taxes back to their set levels from 1816. This conflict quickly demonstrated the tensions that still existed between the federal and state governments. It also illustrated why regionalism was inherent in American culture.

Whites living on the frontier tended to champion expansion efforts, while resistance by American Indians led to a sequence of wars and federal efforts to control American Indian populations.

President Jackson's Indian Removal Act was signed into law in 1830. From 1831 to 1839, the Five Civilized Tribes of the Southeast were relocated to the "Indian Territory" west of the Mississippi River. The conditions of their removal are often associated with the Holocaust from World War II. They were forced from their homes with few possessions and marched over land to their new territory. Disease was rampant among the natives, who had no immunity to many of the European plagues, such as smallpox. In the end, some protested the treatment of these peoples, but many were willing to ignore their plight in favor of the opportunities opened by their relocation.

Many tribes did not leave their land peaceably, however. The Seminole tribe in Florida participated in three different wars with the U.S. government to keep their land. The First Seminole War lasted from 1817 to 1818 and was a defense of tribal members. It was started when General Andrew Jackson, pre-presidency, attempted to recapture runaway slaves living with the Seminole tribe. The tribe was shaken by the encounter but defended their members.

The Second Seminole War occurred in the wake of Jackson's Indian Removal Act. The tribe had large amounts of highly coveted land that they refused to leave. This time, when soldiers approached, the tribe hid in the Florida Everglades and engaged in guerrilla warfare against the U.S. army. Their tactics were incredibly effective and might have continued that way if their leader had not been caught and ransomed back to them. After the Second Seminole War, many members of the tribe moved west. The Third Seminole War was focused on convincing the last remaining band to move west. Eventually, the federal government paid them to leave.

Seminole War: attack upon Fort King by the Indian forces under Osceola

The American acquisition of lands in the West gave rise to a contest over the extension of slavery into the western territories as well as a series of attempts at national compromise.

As northerners moved westward, balance was maintained between the free and slave states. As slavery began to move westward, however, the nation had to decide what to do about slavery and the clear division in national attitudes. The federal government tried a number of compromises before tensions became too high for them to interfere directly.

The 1820 Missouri Compromise created a truce over the issue of slavery that gradually broke down as confrontations over slavery became increasingly bitter.

While the Missouri Compromise preserved peace in the United States for thirty years, the issues with slavery grew increasingly bitter over time. As slavery spread, so did the abolitionist movement and the firsthand accounts of cruelty under slavery. Freed slaves, like Frederick Douglass, became popular orators and writers, spreading awareness to their cause and painting a picture of slavery that turned many northerners against those in the South who practiced it. This, coupled with laws that allowed hunting parties to look for runaway slaves in the North, polarized the nation and caused a breakdown between the regions.

As over-cultivation depleted arable land in the Southeast, slaveholders relocated their agricultural enterprises to the new Southwest, increasing sectional tensions over the institution of slavery and sparking a broad scale debate about how to set national goals, priorities, and strategies.

As the South finally ran out of arable land and many southerners were forced to move westward, the slavery issue sparked more public debate over how to redefine territory. The Kansas–Nebraska Act of 1854 established the rule of popular sovereignty in all new states as a way for the federal government to keep from alienating any side or faction. While a worthwhile attempt, the end result was a race to populate the state with supporters on both sides before the votes.

PERIOD 5

1844-1877

As the nation grew and expanded, regional tensions, especially over slavery, led to the Civil War, the course and consequences of which transformed America.

Major historical events of the period:

1846 – Wilmot Proviso

1846-1848 – Mexican-American War

1848 – Guadalupe Hidalgo treaty signed

1848 – California gold rush

1848 – Seneca Falls Convention

1854 – Kansas-Nebraska Act

1861-1865 – the Civil War

1862 – Homestead Act

1863 – Emancipation Proclamation

1864 – Sand Creek Massacre

1865 – the Thirteenth Amendment abolishes slavery

PERIOD 5: 1844-1877

> **KEY CONCEPT 5.1: The United States became more connected with the world as it pursued an expansionist foreign policy in the Western Hemisphere and emerged as the destination for many migrants from other countries.**

During the period from 1844 to 1877, a series of events and issues, including the expansion policy of the United States and the growing unrest among antislavery organizations, led to the Civil War. During 1844, when James K. Polk was elected president of the United States, the country attracted migrants due to its lucrative economic development policies. Polk supported expansion, as the Democrats believed in republican virtue being upheld only when more lands were opened for the yeoman farmers. Furthermore, the Texas annexation and the acquisition of Oregon County were aimed at increasing the country's influence on the continent. While organizations against slavery existed before this period, they gained political mileage only after 1840, when the Liberal Party grew discontented with abolitionist organizations and began to fight slavery via political methods.

Enthusiasm for U.S. territorial expansion—fueled by economic and national security interests and supported by claims of U.S. racial and cultural superiority—resulted in war, the opening of new markets, acquisition of new territory and increased ideological conflicts.

During the early part of the 19th century, territorial expansion became a full-fledged activity in the U.S. effort to protect its own states and to further its economic status. A key factor that influenced expansion policies, opened new markets and caused ideological conflicts was Eli Whitney's invention of the cotton gin in 1793. This machine reduced the time required to separate seeds from cotton fiber, previously a laborious process that required manual labor and primitive tools.

The cotton gin increased the profitability of the cotton industry in the South, and the increase in profits led to a rise in slavery, which many historians cite as the main reason for the Civil War. Due to the flourishing cotton industry, the American economy improved dramatically, and cotton was exported in plenty. While the South benefited from the exports, the North—particularly New England—benefited from the ample raw material supply for its textile industry.

The first Industrial Revolution (1790 to 1830) was also influenced by Whitney's production of muskets in large scale, which was one of the earliest examples of the American mass production system. The muskets were made of standardized and identical interchangeable parts, enabling faster assembly and repair. This led to the massive production of arms, which was highly profitable for the country.

Gathering cotton in the field of a plantation

The idea of Manifest Destiny, which asserted U.S. power in the Western Hemisphere and supported U.S. expansion westward, was built on a belief in the special virtues of the American people, their destiny to expand throughout the continent, and a sense of American cultural superiority; it helped to shape the era's political debates.

Manifest Destiny fueled western territorial expansion. The term Manifest Destiny was first coined in 1845 by John O'Sullivan, editor for *The United States Magazine and Democratic Review*. It was proclaimed as an effort to expand the continent, which was gifted by Providence to help the multiplying millions of Americans flourish.

Manifest Destiny encouraged the belief that the American settlers were destined to expand and move across the New World to spread their culture, traditions, and institutions, and to enlighten the primitive nations of the world. Some American settlers considered the Hispanics and Indians as inferior beings who needed to be cultivated.

John O'Sullivan

The settlers considered Manifest Destiny the best way to bring order to the country and remake the world in a way that mirrored their own image. This belief that the American people had the mission of imposing their virtuous life on others led to westward expansion, the acquisition of new territories and war with Mexico in the 1840s.

O'Sullivan's article focused on the recent Texas annexation and hinted at further annexation of the territories acquired during the Mexican-American War through negotiations with the British for Oregon and the proposed annexation of Cuba from Spain. Western expansion had some resistance from the people of the East, who worried that their dominant role in national affairs would be restricted by expansion. Regardless, in his address in 1844, President James K. Polk reiterated the commitment of the nation to the expansion of existing territories and acquisition of new ones to strengthen the bonds of the Union, provide security and economic development opportunities and grant its people more agricultural land.

The acquisition of new territory in the West and the U.S. victory in the Mexican-American War were accompanied by a heated controversy over allowing or forbidding slavery in the newly acquired territories.

The Mexican-American War (1846–1848) was the first armed conflict fought by the United States entirely on foreign land (although the U.S. had invaded Canada during the War of 1812, this was a part of a larger war which was mainly fought in what is now the United States America). Texas, which was part of northern Mexico before 1836, had rebelled from Mexico to create the Republic of Texas, which was occupied in large numbers by white American settlers from the South. The Republic of Texas further served as a haven for the African American slaves who settled there because of Mexican antislavery laws. Nearly 5,000 slaves lived in this republic, but when Texas decided to allow slavery, these people lost their rights.

David Wilmot

While at first the United States had declined to annex Texas to the Union because of the reluctance of the political powers in the North against annexing another slave state, the annexation proceeded after Polk was elected president. He wanted to re-annex Texas and reoccupy the Oregon Territory. Polk also initiated talks on purchasing New Mexico and California. Mexico refused, leading to a declaration of war.

While the war was brewing, David Wilmot drew the Wilmot Proviso in 1846 to soothe the escalating tension between the North and South. According to the proviso, southerners could acquire new territories, but slavery would be banned in the newly annexed lands. The proviso was passed in the mostly-northern House, but the Senate did not acquiesce, so the proviso was not enacted.

Mexicans led by General Antonio López de Santa Anna, who later became the president of Mexico, could not defend their territory against the advanced artillery and superior rifles of the Americans. The treaty of Guadalupe Hidalgo, signed in 1848, established the Rio Grande River as the new border between the United States and Mexico, and California and the remaining territories north of Rio Grande as part of the United States. The territories were sold for $15 million. Mexico lost New Mexico, Arizona, Nevada, Utah, and California – nearly one-third of its territories.

The Mexican-American War was controversial because it played a key role in expanding slavery. The North had been opposing the Mexican-American War, claiming that the South was trying to expand its slave power with the acquisition of new territories. The end of the war resulted in a compromise between the North and the South, but the status of slavery remained undetermined, spurring a strong debate that remained unresolved until 1863.

The desire for access to western resources led to the environmental transformation of the region, new economic activities and increased settlement in areas forcibly taken from American Indians.

During the early 19th century, the United States increased in both power and geographical size. The Louisiana Purchase more than doubled the size of the nation, and the fertility and beauty of the new lands led to more westward expansion. Additionally, the Louisiana Purchase and the Treaty of Ghent—which ended the War of 1812—removed the foreign infringements in American territory. This proved detrimental to the Native Americans, as they had received protection from these foreign powers. While some of the Indian tribes ceded all their lands, many resisted the U.S. government.

While the Native Americans—especially the Cherokee—tried to resist the takeover of their ancestral lands by founding a nation of their own, the federal government used force and trickery to expel the Indians and exert its dominance over their lands. With obvious disregard to the sentiments of the natives who had previously inhabited the lands, the government started using the land as if it rightfully owned it. The superior weapons and large number of armed troops made the settlers a dominant force, undefeatable to the Native Americans who did not have sufficient economic support or resources to fight.

The incessant westward expansion by the United States forced several Native American tribes to resettle further west by force or by reluctant submission. The Indian Removal Act of 1830, passed by the United States Congress under President Andrew Jackson, authorized the exchange of lands east of the Mississippi River for the lands on the western side. Over 100,000 Native Americans were relocated by this act. Although in theory the act was intended to be a voluntary submission of the Native Americans, immense pressure was applied to make them sign the removal treaties.

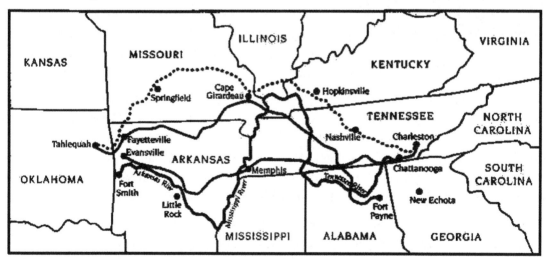

Map route of the Trail of Tears, the forced relocation march of Native Americans in the 1830s

The Indian Removal Act spurred massive destruction of the tribes, and the assimilations that followed their removal were even more devastating. The reservations to which these tribes were restricted separated them from their traditional life and forced them to embrace the European American culture. Those who acknowledged U.S. supremacy accepted the teachings of missionaries, Christianity and the inventions of white people. Some states even enacted laws forbidding settlement of non-Indians on Indian lands to prevent white missionaries from helping the Indian resistance movement.

US interest in expanding trade led to economic, diplomatic and cultural initiatives westward to Asia.

Previously, the American economy was based mainly on small-scale agriculture and local commerce. By the middle of the 19th century, America had turned into a capitalist marketplace. The Industrial Revolution changed America's economy and boosted urbanization, while agricultural development spread to the West.

As settlers moved towards the West, their conditions improved, and they flourished as hunters and farmers. The cheap land and plentiful resources attracted new settlers, and merchants and artisans followed farmers towards western occupation. Chicago, Illinois, which in 1830 had been a trading village, became the richest and largest city by the time its original settlers breathed their last. The Preemption Act of 1836 allowed people to stake claims on land, and after 1862 people could acquire their own land just by occupying it and making improvements.

The steel plow, invented by John Deere in 1837, made it easier for farmers to plow their land, while the mechanical mower and reaper invented by Cyrus McCormick in 1834 replaced manual scythes and sickles for large-scale agricultural practices. Soon mechanical seeders and threshers were introduced. The technological innovations and persistent westward movement resulted in large-scale commercial activity in the West.

The transportation revolution also helped the country economically. The pony express, steamboats, and clipper ships were some of the inventions that helped bind the nation together and connect it with other parts of the world. The clipper ships first launched in 1845 had tall masts, several sails, and could sail faster than a steamer in a good breeze. They carried highly demanded tea from China to America and transported goods to prospective merchants in California. The transportation revolution integrated the continent into a single economic and cultural entity and instilled a deeper nationalist spirit.

In addition to its westward expansion within North America, the United States also wanted to extend its base overseas, especially in Japan, for three reasons. First, the United States needed a coaling base (i.e. a fueling port) for its steamships. Since Japan was located in the same latitude as San Francisco, it served as an ideal location for a coaling base. Although Hawaii was used as a coaling base already, the U.S. Navy wanted another port in the East. Secondly, an American presence in Japan would ensure that shipwrecked sailors reaching Japan received good treatment. Lastly, the United States sought to increase its revenue by trading with other countries.

Commodore Oliver Hazard Perry

Before Commodore Perry's mission to Japan in 1854, only the Dutch were allowed to land their ships on Japanese soil, and all other countries were prohibited. After a few visits to Japan, Perry convinced the Japanese to sign the Treaty of Kanagawa in 1854, enforcing Japanese provision of food, water, coal, and other needed supplies to the American ships that docked in Nagasaki. Ultimately, Japan consented to trade with the United States, ending two hundred years of isolation.

The treaty brought in huge amounts of foreign money and greatly damaged the Japanese economy. It paved the way for Russia, France, the Netherlands, and Great Britain to also sign unequal treaties with Japan, resulting in Japan being granted fewer rights than the foreign nations. Furthermore, the treaty helped to overthrow the Shogun government in Japan, which had previously been considered an undefeatable force.

Religion, particularly evangelical Protestantism, was involved largely in the nation-building and internal expansion process in which the Americans were immersed during the entire 19th century, instigating the foreign missionary movement. The foreign missionary movement increased in intensity in the wake of the Civil War, when the critical issues of national unity and slavery were to some extent settled. This movement was in full bloom after 1900 and progressed until the 20th century, imprinting its presence in all the continents of the globe with its unique American mix of national, religious and civilizing objectives.

The early Puritan ideas of 1600, which stressed the "Errand into the Wilderness" along with the "Errand to the World" concept of the 19th century, led to the missionaries forming voluntary associations based on religion. The missionary movement evolved via internal expansion before it moved overseas. The initial challenge westward expansion presented to missionaries was providing the growing cities and towns with ministers and churches. Methodists were exceptionally skilled at missionizing and forming new congregations via their adaptable structure and circuits. The Presbyterians, Baptists, and Mormons also expanded westward. Thus, the internal religious expansion was successfully implemented except in California. Here, the Protestants did not have a big success in integrating their religion.

The internal missionary efforts focused on the Native Americans, with many missionary groups supporting the Native Americans in their fight against the federal government. The missionary movement's interaction with the Native Americans involved both cultural sensitivity and high-handedness on the part of the missionaries, and religious conversions and resistance by the Native Americans. The other area of focus for the missionaries included the African American slaves, wherein they tried to carry out their religious goals while alleviating the racist attitude of the whites and the poverty-ridden state of the blacks.

The foreign missionary movement grew based on the mission efforts and expansion policies of the Protestants within the United States. The initial step started with the formation of the American Board of Commissioners for Foreign Missions (ABCFM) in 1810 in New

England. Similar to the London Missionary Society, its British chapter formed two decades back, the organization belonged to the voluntary nondenominational category and was not managed by any ecclesiastical group. The ABCFM played a major role in all the missionary efforts of Americans overseas.

Westward expansion, migration to and within the United States, and the end of slavery reshaped North American boundaries and caused conflicts over American cultural identities, citizenship and the question of extending and protecting rights for various groups of U.S. inhabitants.

The westward expansion and migration within the country, the influx of immigrants and the end of slavery changed the social boundaries in North America. This created several conflicts due to the various cultural identities, issues of citizenship and protecting the rights of all the different groups of inhabitants—Asians, African Americans, Hispanics, and Native Americans. The unresolved slavery issue and voting and citizenship rights for immigrants and former slaves were major issues which had great economic, religious and political impacts on the nation.

Substantial numbers of new international migrants—who often lived in ethnic communities and retained their religion, language, and customs—entered the country prior to the Civil War, giving rise to a major, often violent nativist movement that was strongly anti-Catholic and aimed at limiting immigrants' cultural influence and political and economic power.

During the pre–Civil War period, many international migrants entered the United States, including more than one million Germans, over three million British and four million Irish. While prior to 1845, only Irish Protestants migrated to the United States, after 1845, Irish Catholics started migrating in huge numbers mainly due to the Great Famine. Additionally, Greeks, Italians, Hungarians, Poles and other Slavic nationals migrated to America after 1880. These immigrants served to make up the bulk of the American labor pool and were instrumental in making the country a leading economic giant worldwide.

The nativist, or Know-Nothing, movement of the 1850s had opposed the German and Irish Catholic immigration. The movement was powered by fear within the nation of the domination by Catholic immigrants who were considered opposed to American values. While the movement did not meet with much success, it was joined by many of the Protestant groups and middle-class people who

U.S. political poster for the Know-Nothing Party

---

were unresolved over the slavery issue. The Know-Nothing movement aimed at purifying American politics by ending the Irish Catholic influence. The movement wanted to uphold Republican values and curb naturalization and immigration.

The anti-Catholic sentiment that began with the influx of Irish Catholics in the 1840s resulted in the conviction that Catholic children needed to be educated in public schools to learn American values. The Irish Catholics—in spite of opposition from the Protestants—built their parochial schools on a national scale and formed the Catholic Educational Association, which was later called the National Catholic Educational Association. Piety, strict discipline and orthodoxy were prominently taught.

The Catholic schools were founded in reaction to the increasing number of schools publicly funded by Protestants. The American Bible Society in 1840 declared that the Bible would be read in each classroom. In 1875, a constitutional amendment was called for by President Grant, who favored the Know-Nothing Party, for prohibiting the use of public funds for sectarian schools and making free public schools mandatory.

The amendment was motivated by anti-Catholic views and the fear that the ambition, superstition, and greed which were believed to be fueled by the Catholic Church would go against values of intelligence and patriotism. This led to Grant's support of public schools that were free of pagan, sectarian or atheistic teachings. Although the amendment was defeated, it laid the groundwork for the Blaine Amendments, which were incorporated into the thirty-four state Constitution over the next few decades. The Blaine Amendment passed in 1880 forbade the use of tax money to fund the parochial schools or parish schools operated by the Irish to protect their Catholic religion, culture, and language.

Asian, African American, and white peoples sought new economic opportunities or religious refuge in the West, efforts that were boosted during and after the Civil War with the passage of new legislation promoting national economic development.

Smith's first vision

The white, African American and Asian populations had migrated to the West to capitalize on the plentiful economic opportunities there as well as to seek religious refuge. The Mormons' history is one stark example of a religious exodus across the continent and the successful establishment of a strong religious society. The Mormon Church originated in western New York. Joseph Smith Jr., a fourteen-year-old migrant farmer's son, claimed to have experienced supernatural revelations and spiritual visitations that led to the establishment of the Mormon Church. This Church was later named the Church of Jesus Christ of Latter-day Saints.

Mormonism attracted antebellum crowds in New York, who began to be inexplicably drawn by the promises of buried treasure, mystical visions and magical talismans that Mormonism portrayed. Smith offered hope and promise to a weak, weary and troubled group of people who were in search of divine manifestation. The antebellum people were economically backward when compared to the industrially rich northerners, and they were easily enticed by the promise of emancipation offered by the Mormons. The movement was threatened by local authorities and moved to Kirtland, Ohio, where the first temple was built, and later to Missouri and Illinois when the government ordered their extermination.

Smith was shot in 1844 by a mob while he was in prison. The anti-Mormon protests were mostly due to the struggle for political and economic power, as people believed that the Mormons with their large number of followers could upset the balance. The Mormon practice of polygamy also fueled the protests. Early 19th-century American society supported monogamy, individualism and private property. But since these principles contrasted with Mormon values, they did not accept Mormonism. The Mormons' main objective was to establish God's kingdom on earth.

Another event that influenced the economic growth of the United States was the gold rush of 1848. Prior to the peace treaty with Mexico, gold had been discovered in California in 1842 by Francisco Lopez, a Californio. The announcement of a further discovery of gold by James Marshall in 1848, in the San Francisco newspaper *The Californian,* spurred on a gold rush in which people from all over the country landed in California with shovels and picks. The gold rush also attracted people from China, Latin America, France, Germany, Australia, and Britain. The population of San Francisco spiked from 459 to 20,000 in just a few months' time and transformed it into an ethnically diverse, violent and unruly society. This sparked many murders of Native Indians, Mexicans, immigrants and white people.

Gold washing in California

The Homestead Act of 1862 was passed due to land distribution issues that had been occurring prevalently in the wake of westward migration. The land policies prior to the act made it financially impossible for prospective homesteaders to acquire land. All this changed due to the Mexican-American War in 1846. Popular pressure occurred to alter policy according to the evolving demographics, improving economy and shifting the social climate of that period.

The rise in the prices of wheat, corn, and cotton helped the southern plantations dominate the small-scale farmers. The displaced farmers moved westward to unoccupied forested land, which had more affordable conditions. Those settling in the West during this period demanded preemption, which allowed them to settle land initially and pay later. This was opposed by eastern economic forces, as they feared that the cheap labor available for their industries would be lost.

The unprecedented high number of immigrants to America also settled in the West, drawn by its economic prosperity. The advanced transportation in the form of roadways and new canals reduced the dependence of the West on the New Orleans harbor. Furthermore, England's repeal of the Corn Laws opened up new markets for American agricultural exports. Thus, the West faced a high influx of local and immigrant people in search of fertile land.

In spite of these improvements, the homesteading laws were opposed on different fronts. The North bemoaned the loss of cheap labor and the southern states were worried that the settlers would form new antislavery states. This led to homestead laws being proposed and defeated three times in 1852, 1854 and 1859. In 1860, the Homestead Bill passed by Congress was vetoed by President Buchanan.

While the early allocation methods were chaotic and arbitrary, resulting in frequent disputes over borders, the Homestead Act had great political and regional impact. When the act was signed by President Abraham Lincoln in 1862, eleven states had defected from the Union. The southern states' removal from the Union led to the act finally passing and being signed as a law. The new law established filing for application, improving land and filing for title deed as its threefold process. While initially the physical frontier conditions prevented people from making claim, the Frontier Railroad Act led to new railroads and easy access to goods, tools, weapons and other necessities for the homesteaders. Such resources allowed homesteaders to improve their facilities by building towns, schools and eventually new states.

As the territorial boundaries of the United States expanded and the migrant population increased, U.S. government interaction and conflict with Hispanics and American Indians increased, altering these groups' cultures and ways of life and raising questions about their status and legal rights.

With a marked increase in the migrant population and the expansion of territories westward, many conflicts and encounters arose with Native Americans and Hispanics, leading to questions of their legal rights and social status. Mariano Guadalupe Vallejo, born in California in 1808, was affected by the marginalization of his tribe in their own land during the territorial expansion of the Union. Born into a Californio family (i.e. a Mexican family living in Alto California) he had been groomed to lead.

When Vallejo was fifteen years old, he joined the Mexican army. He took part in many Mexican and Indian expeditions and played a primary role in quelling the Indian revolts and establishing settlements to prevent Russian settlement in California. Vallejo identified himself with Mexican Liberals in their support of an efficient government that was independent of religious authority.

Vallejo favored the governing model of the United States and in 1836 led a rebellion declaring California a free state. Although he supported the United States, he was treated badly by American rebels in 1846. He was imprisoned by General John C. Frémont, leader of the Bear Flag Revolt. Vallejo's estate was damaged, and matters improved only when the rebels were replaced by U.S. forces under the leadership of Brigadier General Stephen Kearney.

Vallejo was made Indian agent for Northern California and was elected to the Senate in 1849. In the wake of the Treaty of Guadalupe Hidalgo, Vallejo lost most of his land. His life is an example of the fate suffered by many Californians under American rule. In spite of their acceptance of the democratic U.S. government, they were treated as foreigners and were allowed to occupy only the lowest economic rung.

The Sand Creek Massacre was another effect of westward expansion on the country's Native Americans. Although the United States was engaged in conflicts with the Indian tribes due to territorial expansion, the 1851 Treaty of Fort Laramie ceded extensive territory to the Indians. However, the terms of the treaty were renegotiated in 1861 by the United States after factors like the Pikes Peak Gold Rush in 1858. In 1861, the Treaty of Fort Wise was signed by Arapaho and Southern Cheyenne chiefs. This treaty reduced Native American land to one-third the original amount. The Indian chiefs had signed mainly to safeguard their people, but certain Lakota and Cheyenne tribes who called themselves Dog Soldiers opposed the treaty.

Eyewitness' depiction of the Sand Creek Massacre

In 1864, Colonel John Chivington, under orders from Colorado governor John Evans, attacked several Cheyenne camps situated in Colorado. More attacks followed in Kansas under the command of Lt. George S. Eyre. The Cheyenne attacked in retaliation, which further increased tension between the U.S. forces and the Indians. On November 29, 1864, when most of the males were out hunting, the Colorado Territory militia, led by U.S. Army Colonel John Chivington, attacked the Indian villages of Arapaho and Cheyenne. A majority of the people slaughtered were children and women. The massacre later came to be known as the Sand Creek Massacre.

Since the gold discovery in Native American territory, tensions prevailed between the United States and the Indian tribes. When the tribes refused to move their reservations as ordered by the U.S. Army, they were attacked by Custer in the Battle of Little Bighorn. Fought in 1876 near Little Bighorn River, the federal troops under the leadership of Lieutenant Colonel George Armstrong Custer attacked Cheyenne warriors and the Lakota Sioux. The Indian tribes fighting under Sitting Bull outnumbered the armed forces and overwhelmed them in what was later termed Custer's Last Stand. Nearly 10,000 Native Americans had joined the Indian camp at Little Bighorn River, which they dubbed Greasy Grass in defiance of the war department's order to move their reservations.

In the Battle of Little Big Horn, 3,000 Native Americans defeated 600 of Custer's men within an hour. The battle was the highest victory by the Native Americans against the invading U.S. army and the worst defeat for the United States in their fight against the Indians. In the wake of the war, the government increased its efforts and confined the Cheyenne and Sioux tribes to reservations.

> **KEY CONCEPT 5.2:** Intensified by expansion and deepening regional divisions, debates over slavery and other economic, cultural and political issues led the nation into civil war.

The expansionist policies and worsening divisions regionally led to serious debates over slavery and its abolition. In addition to the raging slavery issue, the cultural, economic and political changes that occurred during the period led to civil war. These issues included the abolition of slavery, the control of governments, nullification, and sectionalism.

The institution of slavery and its attendant ideological debates, along with regional economic and demographic changes, territorial expansion in the 1840s and 1850s, and cultural differences between the North and the South, intensified sectionalism.

The main conflict that separated the North and South and increased sectionalism between them was the slavery debate. The United States was not able to bring about a balance between the northern free states and the southern slave states, although there were numerous legal documents signed in attempts to resolve the issue. The South was also feeling dominated by the North due to the increase in the northern population. This limited the chance of getting a president who supported the pro-slavery policies of the South.

The South had to face increased tariffs as it mostly relied on agriculture and plantations. The North, on the other hand, was mainly industry-based and thrived on manufacturing. The South needed more land in order to arrive at a better economic balance with the North. The economic disparity between the two sections increased tensions and led to the Civil War.

The North's expanding economy and its increasing reliance on a free-labor manufacturing economy contrasted with the South's dependence on an economic system characterized by slave-based agriculture and slow population growth.

The main economic difference between the North and South was the labor systems they employed. While industry played a key role in the North, with commerce taking priority, the South was mainly agricultural. The Southern economy was based on plantations that relied on slaves as cheap labor for their production of cotton and tobacco. The expanding economy in the North and its dependence on the free-labor manufacturing economy led to a strong divide between the North and South.

Sectionalism, a term used to describe the needs of one section of a nation being given precedence over the needs of the entire nation, was rife during the period before the Civil War. The antislavery stand of the North remained a major cause for sectionalism. Additionally, each section wanted to pass laws that benefited their land. This resulted in the free states supporting the North and the slave states supporting the South. The westward expansion further widened this divide.

Southern industry

Tariffs, which were imposed on imports, affected the South more heavily, as southerners relied on importing goods from Britain and exporting their own cotton overseas. While the North wanted the tariffs to safeguard their industries, the South opposed the tariffs, and tensions rose between the two. The South argued their right of nullification of the tariffs and antislavery laws that the North was intent on passing. Even before the Civil War, the relationship between the North and South had worsened due to taxes. While the taxes imposed on the imported goods by Congress helped the industrial development of the North, it crippled the economy of the South, because, with its agriculture-targeted economy, the South needed to import machinery from foreign countries.

During the 1850s, when recession was at its peak, Congress raised the tax on imports from 15 percent to 37 percent. In response, the South threatened to secede from the Union. The North was livid, as southern secession would greatly reduce foreign trade and strike a heavy blow to the American economy. Secession would mean that the coastwise trade, which the South dominated, would also leave the Union. Therefore, the shipping would remain idle without the involvement of the South. In view of all these economic implications, the Union decided that war was the only remaining alternative to a situation that would land them in financial ruin.

On the cultural front, the North was against slavery and the South thrived on it. Northern culture depicted the southerners as un-Christian sponges and decadent people. When the Free Labor Movement–supporting Republican Party won the elections and Abraham Lincoln was made president of the Union in 1860, southerners interpreted the move as a coup d'état by the northerners.

The war was instigated by the cultural and economic fear of the people. However, contrary to popular belief, slavery was not the only issue. Although the Republican Party was against slavery, it was not abolitionist. Abraham Lincoln's Emancipation Proclamation of 1862 supported the freeing of slaves only in the regions occupied by Confederate forces. All the other slave-holding states, which had been supporting the Union by fighting for it, were exempted.

Lincoln had addressed the issue directly, saying that he did not have the right or inclination to interfere with slavery. He said that if he could have saved the Union from division without freeing any of the slaves, he would certainly do it, but that it was not an option. According to Secretary of State William H. Steward, the Emancipation Proclamation was meant to emancipate slaves in regions where the Union could not help them and keep slaves in bondage in regions where they could easily be set free.

Abolitionists, although a minority in the North, mounted a highly visible campaign against slavery, adopting strategies of resistance ranging from fierce arguments against the institution and assistance in helping slaves escape to a willingness to use violence to achieve their goals.

The sectional conflicts and reform movements that happened during the early part of the 19th century focused on slavery and led to the abolitionist movement in the North. This movement aimed at abolishing slavery and represented the best efforts by the North to defeat the proslavery southerners. Southerners resisted this movement, and sectional conflicts grew. The abolitionist movement fought for the immediate emancipation of slaves and the ending of segregation and racial discrimination. Immediate emancipation differentiated abolitionists from the antislavery advocates whose moderate stand encouraged gradual emancipation.

The abolitionists also differed from the free soil advocates who wanted to restrict slavery to the existing areas and prevent it from spreading west. Radical abolitionism was also encouraged partly due to the Second Great Awakening fervor, which motivated people to support emancipation based on religious conviction. Abolitionist ideals became more prominent in the churches and politics in the North during the 1830s, creating more animosity between the North and South and eventually leading to the Civil War.

Of the various abolitionists, some notable personalities include:

- William Lloyd Garrison. Garrison was the publisher of the newspaper *The Liberator* and the most vocal of the abolitionists, writing in blunt and coarse language that struck at the core of the matter.

- Fredrick Douglas. Born as a slave, Fredrick Douglas became an author, orator, and reformer and devoted his entire life to the abolition of slavery and the pursuit of rights for black people.

- Harriet Tubman. This African American helped free hundreds of slaves and was the leader of the Underground Railroad that helped slaves flee to the free states or Canada.

- Sojourner Truth. Like Tubman, Truth was born a slave without any formal education. She ran away from her master and became a preacher, attacking the organized religious beliefs that favored the whites and the privileges they were given.

- Nat Turner. This preacher and black slave led one of the most famous slave revolts in the history of the United States. In 1831, he and seventy other slaves killed sixty whites in Virginia including his master, Joseph Travis. Turner was captured by Virginia militia and hanged, and this led to southern states passing stricter laws for controlling slaves, especially the slave preachers.

Nat Turner and his confederates in conference

States' rights, nullification, and racist stereotyping provided the foundation for the southern defense of slavery as a positive good.

The southern states' concern over their rights and their nullification of the laws against their economic growth led to the southern defense of portraying slavery as a good system. One of the prominent southerners in this aspect was John C. Calhoun. A noticeable representative for the antebellum South, he had helped the United States during its war with Great Britain and served as secretary of war, vice president and secretary of state.

John C. Calhoun

Calhoun opposed the Mexican-American War and the annexation of California as a free state, and he was a renowned proslavery speaker. He initially supported the 1828 Tariff of Abominations, but after receiving criticism from the South, protested against it. Calhoun was elected as a senator for South Carolina and defended the slave system against the growing antislavery protests. He dominated the American political scene from 1815 to 1850 with his gift as a debater on various political, economic, social and philosophical issues.

The proslavery sections also had support from racist minstrel shows. The shows featured blackface, a theatrical makeup where white performers used stereotyping and makeup to represent a black person. The shows were popular during the 19th century and glorified the slave stereotypes such as "dandified coon" or "happy-go-lucky darky" on the plantation. The minstrel shows started in 1830 and stayed over one hundred years, becoming a key tradition in American theater. The stereotypes embodied in the shows played a critical role in cementing as well as enhancing racist attitudes, images, and perceptions.

Repeated attempts at political compromise failed to calm tensions over slavery and often made sectional tensions worse, breaking down the trust between sectional leaders and culminating in the bitter election of 1860 followed by the secession of southern states.

Northerners attempted several measures to reduce the tensions that prevailed between the North and the South over slavery and other issues, including more power for the southern states. The various attempts to arrive at a solution over the increasing sectional tendencies over slavery worsened the situation and led to the secession of the southern states.

National leaders made a variety of proposals to resolve the issue of slavery in the territories, including the Compromise of 1850, the Kansas-Nebraska Act and the *Dred Scott* decision, but these ultimately failed to reduce sectional conflict.

The slavery conflict spurred by the annexation of territories in the wake of the Mexican-American War was resolved with the Compromise of 1850, which admitted California as a free state and allowed the territories of New Mexico and Utah to determine their slavery status by popular sovereignty. The compromise aimed at settling the border dispute between Mexico and Texas in favor of the latter and ending the slave trade in Washington, D.C., making it easier for the South to regain fugitive slaves. This compromise led to the avoidance of slavery and sectional issues for many years.

Bleeding Kansas: slavery debate in Congress

The Kansas-Nebraska Act—passed in 1854—allowed territory settlers to decide on slavery based on a popular sovereignty mandate. The bill overturned the Missouri Compromise and thus invalidated the boundary for the free and slave regions. Conflicts in the wake of this act led to what is called Bleeding Kansas, one of the various causes of the Civil War in 1861.

This act, which tried to organize the western territories, led to sectionalism and railroad development. It also split both of the major political parties, leading to the creation of a third party and a worsening of relations between the North and South. While Kansas was given statehood in 1861, southern states started to secede from the Union. The antislavery Republican Party lost the support of the Northern Whigs and independent Democrats, causing further division within the political parties.

The *Dred Scott* case was instrumental in Abraham Lincoln being elected president in 1860. Dred Scott was a slave who had gained his freedom via the American legal system. In 1857, the United States Supreme Court denied his plea for freedom, stating that a black man could not become a citizen. The abolitionists in the North were outraged by this turn of events.

The second party system ended when the issues of slavery and anti-immigrant nativism weakened loyalties to the two major parties and fostered the emergence of sectional parties, most notably the Republican Party in the North and the Midwest.

The anti-immigrant support and slavery issues that could not be resolved properly led to the disintegration of the second party system and the formation of sectional parties such as the Republican Party. While the issue of slavery was the main focus, there were economic and social changes that the country had undergone during the 19th century, leading to the reordering of the political system based on sectional lines.

During the compromise of 1850, the Democrats and Whigs were the only parties with voter loyalty. In the North, Democrats supported the compromise and Whigs opposed it. In the upper South, Whigs supported the compromise and the Democrats opposed it. This competitiveness continued with the Fugitive Slave Law, but the two merged to find a solution to the sectional conflict.

The changing economic structure made the traditional stand of the parties irrelevant and the Whig ideals became less compelling in the wake of the gold rush in California and the diversion of European investments to America. The Whigs' support of the high tariffs lost its appeal to the textile manufacturers of the North, as they wanted safety from foreign and local rivals. The issue of the railroad also caused competition between regions as opposed to political parties. The various state constitutions that were introduced from 1848 to 1852 resulted in the weakening of party machinery, as they had fewer opportunities to strengthen party loyalty. The biennial legislative system further reduced the capacity of the political system to pass laws and generated party allegiance.

In relation to nativism, the Democrats welcomed immigration and the Whigs opposed it. The Whigs were forced to get help from the Catholic immigrants in the presidential election of 1852 to get a favorable vote. The election was the death knell for the Whigs, as they won only in four states. The Democrats won with a 2–1 majority in both Houses. This was mainly due to the controversy over slavery. Furthermore, the party's decline in the South after the Compromise of 1850, its loss of support in the North and dissension within the party cadres over support of the Catholic immigrants all led to the downfall of the Whig Party. This led to the fragmentation of the second party system and realignment efforts for the formation of new parties.

Lincoln's election on a free soil platform in the election of 1860 led various southern leaders to conclude that their states must secede from the Union, precipitating civil war.

President Abraham Lincoln

Prairie lawyer Abraham Lincoln enjoyed a short span in Congress from 1847 to 1849 and later embraced his law practice fully. He joined the Republican Party in 1856 during a time when sectionalism was at its peak. The debates over the Kansas-Nebraska Act, slavery and the role of the territories in these issues made him prominent nationally, but he was unpopular in the South due to his antislavery ideals.

Lincoln was disliked by the South even prior to his taking office as president in the year 1861. He was seen as an abolitionist and a fanatic of the caliber of John Brown. The South considered him a Republican who would not fear to override the laws and constitution to arrive at a compromise of any nature. During his presidential campaign, Lincoln refrained from announcing any policies, fearing that they may be misunderstood in both the North and South.

The secession crisis emerged because of a disagreement over the validity of the election outcome (Lincoln was elected with a thin minority of the vote and less than half of the Electoral College votes) and, more importantly, a disagreement between north and south about the appropriate boundaries between state and federal governmental powers. Southerners advocated strong states' rights, while northerners favored a strong federalist system. Despite being elected by a majority of voters, Lincoln's authority was rejected by southerners. Their threats of secession were a way to pressure Lincoln and the Republicans into accepting state autonomy. The secession crisis was not new in 1860; it had already existed for over a decade. While the Compromise of 1850 had put down some of the ardor in the discord, the growing unrest among the southerners made them repeatedly resort to the threat of secession.

The secession issue caused both the slaves and southern landowners to evaluate the changing political scene. The entire social system of slave and master had been challenged after Lincoln's election. The collapse of the prevailing political system made the slaves look for new opportunities. The slaveholders, on the other hand, wanted the secession because they saw it as a positive step towards maintaining the stability of the master-slave balance. Northern intervention into their political and economic situation increased unrest among the slaves and the deteriorating relationship between the masters and slaves led to their support of secession.

In 1860, Lincoln won the election without the support of the southern states. In order to preserve the Union, Lincoln decided to fight secession rather than accept it. Lincoln believed in preserving the union of the North and South by prudent and at times forceful execution of power. His use of flexible tactics in an inflexible pursuit of reunification helped the North win the war. Lincoln's wise judgments on when to use or avoid military force (such as the strong military domination in Maryland and the moderate handling of the opposition in Kentucky) helped the North gain victory and prevent secession.

> **KEY CONCEPT 5.3:** The Union victory in the Civil War and the contested Reconstruction of the South settled the issues of slavery and secession but left unresolved many questions about the power of the federal government and citizenship rights.

While the victory of the Union upheld the antislavery stand, helped resolve slavery issues and further put a stop to any idea of secession, unresolved issues remained regarding the extent of power wielded by the federal government and the rights given to the citizens. Some of these issues included the northern states' failure to return fugitive slaves, the northern support of abolitionists and insurrectionists such as John Brown, and the religious and political beliefs of the North, which were not accepted by the southerners. The South was also against the idea of granting citizenship rights and voting rights to the slaves.

The North's greater manpower and industrial resources, its leadership and the decision for emancipation eventually led to the Union military victory over the Confederacy in the devastating Civil War.

There are many reasons the Confederacy lost the Civil War, but the main reason is that the North had more guns and men. The Union had overwhelming numbers of men, resources, and luck on its side, making it a very tough fight for the South. The large social divisions within southern society are also cited as a reason for the Confederacy's defeat. Southern society was rife with racial, class and even regional antagonisms, all of which contributed to the fall of the South. These factors, together with the lack of resources, arms and men, enabled the northern defeat of the South.

Both the Union and the Confederacy mobilized their economies and societies to wage the war even while facing considerable home front opposition.

While it is broadly believed that the Union's resources were the main reason for their defeat of the Confederate army, some historians insist that it was the Confederate's approach that led to their defeat. The Union had several advantages:

- The Union had 22 million people against 9 million in the South (of whom only 5.5 million were white).

- The firearm manufacturers in the North had greater capacity than those in the South.

- A strong naval blockade prevented the South from getting materials.

- Four slave states—Kentucky, Maryland, Missouri, and Delaware—supported the Union.

- Some people within the Confederate states were not fully supportive of its cause.

Despite their many disadvantages, southerners were confident the Confederacy would win the war. The 750,000 square miles occupied by the South were considered a huge asset, making it difficult to occupy and conquer. The South had the advantage of defending their own land instead of invading the North. Additionally, the rifles in use were best suited for defensive rather than offensive tactics.

Battle of Fort Sumter during the Civil War

Geographically, the various rivers flowing through North Virginia made it difficult for the Union armies to conquer Richmond, the capital of the Confederates. Finally, while the northerners were engaged in the war in pursuit of a reunion, the southerners had a more needy cause, that of defending their homes and lands, making their fight more psychologically immediate.

The Confederate victory in the initial major battle at Manassas confirmed Confederate supremacy, and expert opinion contends that had the Confederate forces been more proactive and brought Britain on their side, they might have been more successful. Therefore, a combination of missed opportunities and lack of luck are also cited for the downfall of the Confederates.

Lincoln's decision to issue the Emancipation Proclamation changed the purpose of the war, enabling many African Americans to fight in the Union army and helping prevent the Confederacy from gaining support from European powers.

Lincoln's Emancipation Proclamation was a key document that changed the objective of the war. It is also one of the least understood documents in U.S. history. The Emancipation Proclamation was issued twice, first in 1862 and again in 1863. It applied only to the states that rebelled and intended to restrict the Confederacy. While at first the cabinet did not support the proclamation, it later did so after witnessing the victory at Antietam and noting Lincoln's continued commitment towards executing its ideals.

While the initial aim of the Civil War was safeguarding the Union from disintegration, freedom for the slaves became the main objective after the Emancipation Proclamation was issued. Another advantage of the Emancipation Proclamation was that it prevented foreign nations from supporting the Confederates, as the European nations were against slavery. The proclamation also helped African Americans to participate in their fight for liberation. Nearly 200,000 African Americans served the Union navy and army by the end of the Civil War. The Emancipation Proclamation also encouraged the citizens to advocate and accept the abolition of slavery both in the North and South.

Although Confederate leadership showed initiative and daring early in the war, the Union ultimately succeeded due to improved military leadership, more effective strategies, key victories, greater resources and wartime destruction of the South's environment and infrastructure.

Events like Gettysburg and Sherman's March to the Sea reinforced the fact that the Union had won because of their plentiful resources, key victories, effective leadership, and efficient strategies. While the Civil War—like any other war—did not have one single moment that turned out to be the turning point, it did have many crucial moments that, in retrospect, clearly indicated the way it would end. Lee's repulse of McClellan's army in Richmond in 1862, the victory of the Union in Antietam, the Emancipation Proclamation and the successes that ensued at Gettysburg and Vicksburg in 1863 all transformed the fight significantly.

General Robert E. Lee

Lee's defeat at Gettysburg showed that victory was imminent for the Union. The clear defeat and massive damage incurred by the Confederates together with the final capture at Vicksburg demoralized them and restored control of the Mississippi River to the hands of the Union.

The March to the Sea is another landmark event that strengthened Union supremacy. Led by General William T. Sherman, the Union army destroyed most of Georgia and captured Savannah from the Confederates in 1864. While Atlanta was a Confederate stronghold, Sherman had the needed supplies and troops to defeat the Confederates and destroy Georgia.

The Civil War and Reconstruction altered power relationships between the states and the federal government and among the executive, legislative and judicial branches, ending slavery and the notion of a divisible union but leaving unresolved questions of relative power and largely unchanged social and economic patterns.

The Civil War and the period of Reconstruction that ensued changed political relationships and power dynamics in all aspects, including the legislative, executive, judicial and federal government policies. It also marked the end of slavery and the division of the Union. However, it did not resolve the questions related to the control of power and the change in the economic and social pattern. Reconstruction entailed the first step taken by the United States to develop an interracial democratic system. The war also resulted in the ratification of the Thirteenth, Fourteenth and Fifteenth Amendments of the Constitution, which declared slavery a federal crime and brought in a new dimension to citizenship and universal male suffrage. This promised new powers and an active role by the government in enforcing the amendments.

The Thirteenth Amendment abolished slavery, bringing about the war's most dramatic social and economic change, but the exploitative and soil-intensive sharecropping system endured for several generations.

The Thirteenth Amendment, passed in 1865 by the House of Representatives, abolished slavery in the United States and all places subject to its jurisdiction. During the course of the war, the purpose of the struggle changed from the restoration of the Union to freeing the slaves, which caused Lincoln to issue the Emancipation Proclamation. The Thirteenth Amendment was not accepted in 1864, as the Democrats were worried about the rights of the states. But Lincoln's election, along with Republican majority votes in both Houses, helped in passing the amendment successfully in 1865, leading to the eradication of slavery, which had left behind an indelible mark in the history of the United States.

The amendment was ratified eight months after the war ended. The Thirteenth Amendment represented the resolution of the long, drawn-out struggle for the freedom of the slaves. When the war started, some northerners were against it, as they saw it as a crusade to end slavery. While most of the Democrats and conservative Republicans in the North opposed the expansion of slavery, they were against abolishing it completely. But in the wake of the First Battle of Bull Run in Virginia, they reconsidered the role slavery played in the conflict. By 1862, Lincoln was convinced that without abolishing slavery, the war did not serve any purpose.

First Battle of Bull Run, stand of the Union troops at the Henry House

Therefore, after the big victory at the Battle of Antietam in Maryland, Lincoln issued the Emancipation Proclamation, declaring that slaves in all the rebelling territories would be declared free. The move was symbolic, as it freed only the slaves in the regions outside the control of the Union. However, it changed the main objective of the war from a reunification effort to the destruction of slavery.

Lincoln strongly believed in the need for a solid constitutional amendment to end slavery completely. While Congress debated several proposals in 1864, which included incorporating provisions that would prevent discrimination against blacks, the Judiciary Committee of the Senate was the body that provided the final language of the amendment. The conditions were actually drawn from the 1787 Northwest Ordinance, which had banned slavery from the region north of the Ohio River.

The Thirteenth Amendment was passed in 1864, and the victory of Republicans in the election guaranteed its successful implementation. The Radical Republicans wanted the complete abolition of slavery, while the Democrats wanted restoration of the states' rights. Lincoln's victory in the election ensured that the ratification of the amendment was done smoothly. When the House passed the amendment in 1865, it was sent to the states, and after Georgia ratified the amendment on December 6, 1865, slavery ceased to be an institution in the United States.

Efforts by radical and moderate Republicans to reconstruct the defeated South changed the balance of power between Congress and the presidency and yielded some short-term successes, reuniting the union, opening up political opportunities and other leadership roles to former slaves and temporarily rearranging the relationships between white and black people in the South.

With the end of the war, the fight for power emerged with renewed vigor as the moderate and Radical Republicans tried to change the power balance between the president and Congress. This led to positions of leadership and political significance among the former slaves. Notable among the Republicans were Hiram Revels, Blanche K. Bruce, and Robert Smalls.

Hiram Revels was the first African American to become a member of Congress when he was made senator of Mississippi, filling in for Jefferson Davis, the former senator and Confederate president. He was part of the committee of Labor and Education in the District of Columbia. While Revels was not predominantly for racial equality, he opposed the segregation of schools in Washington, D.C. He was also an advocate for the black people banned from working in the Navy Yard in Washington because of their racial identity.

Robert Smalls was an African American Congressman who represented South Carolina from 1882 to 1883. He was enslaved until 1862 when he piloted a Confederate ship into Union waters. He became actively involved in politics and in 1870 was a powerful leader in South Carolina. He was against segregation in railroads, eating establishments and the military, and he opposed the western emigration of African Americans in America as well as their emigration to Liberia.

Blanche K. Bruce escaped slavery during the initial phase of the Civil War. He has the distinction of being the first African American to serve as Mississippi senator full term and head a Senate session. Bruce wanted better treatment of the Native Americans and advocated army desegregation. He was part of the committee to improve navigation on the Mississippi River.

Radical Republicans' efforts to change southern racial attitudes and culture and establish a base for their party in the South ultimately failed due both to determined southern resistance and to the North's waning resolve.

Despite several arduous efforts by the Republicans, especially the Radical Republicans, resolving slavery failed to bear fruit as the South steadily resisted all the moves towards altering their racial attitude. The sectional wounds wrought by the war failed to heal during Reconstruction. While the North tried to bring the South back into the Union and give it equal footing by reviving its economy and rebuilding the southern landscape battered by war, the deep divisions in the federal government prevented the attainment of these goals. Furthermore, the assassination of Lincoln led to Andrew Johnson—a proslavery leader—becoming president.

President Andrew Johnson

Johnson started a Reconstruction plan that was against rights for the freed slaves. While the Confederates tried to enter into the power positions in the government, the Republicans who had a dominant role in Congress refused to give any leeway. While the Radical Republicans opposed the southerners, moderates and conservatives wanted the southerners to be admitted. The Radical Republicans were committed to total emancipation of slaves and equal treatment and enfranchisement of freed slaves.

During its formation in the 1850s, the Radical Republican Party—consisting of northern industrialists, altruists, practical politicians, and former Whigs—was not committed to abolitionism, yet it did attract some of the most fervent antislavery advocates. While President Abraham Lincoln insisted that restoring the Union was the main aim of the Civil War, abolitionists in Congress wanted emancipation included as well.

The Joint Committee of the Conduct of the War was formed by the Radical Republicans due to agitation over the poor performance of the Union army and the lack of attention given to emancipation. The Radicals favored including black troops and eventually broke with Lincoln over his Reconstruction policy and his reluctance to enforce the speedy abolition of slavery. The areas in the South under military control were subjected to Reconstruction under the command of Lincoln, who had planned on including only 10 percent of the southern electorate for forming the government. The Radical Republicans were not satisfied with Lincoln's Ten Percent Plan and produced the Wade Davis Bill, which required fifty percent of the white male population of a state to take an oath of loyalty and excluded an increasing number of Confederates from taking part in the restored governments.

When Lincoln vetoed the bill, the Radical Republicans were enraged and launched an effort to deny Lincoln a second-time nomination. While they welcomed Andrew Johnson when it was clear that he pursued the same lenient policies in Reconstruction, they formed the Joint Committee on Reconstruction to ensure that Reconstruction was under congressional control rather than presidential control. They passed several measures to safeguard the political involvement of blacks in the South in spite of Johnson's vetoes.

Portrait of Lincoln surrounded by Civil War scenes

Despite the Radical Republicans' efforts, white control of southern governments was gradually restored. The African Americans were frightened and prevented from participating in the polls by terrorist organizations such as the Knights of the White Camellia and the Ku Klux Klan. Furthermore, the North lost its initial zeal over the continued military occupation of the southern states, and Reconstruction efforts failed totally by the end of 1877. One reason for this failure was Northern politicians' lack of cohesiveness as a group. Their commitment to emancipation and ending racial discrimination were the only threads that held them together. They were not united over other critical issues such as labor reform, protectionism, and hard or soft money.

In the wake of the Civil War, the economic prosperity of the North—where the industrial inventions and output increased enormously—also led to a further divide between the North and the South. The subsequent depression and the northern boom served to make the Reconstruction efforts fail. Additionally, some of the white supremacy factions combined with Black Codes to dominate the freed slaves and deny them civil liberties. The Supreme Court rulings also limited the rights of the African American population. The disparity in the sharecropping system pushed the African Americans into debt which evoked their dependence during slavery. They remained an oppressed community and were afforded only second-class citizenship until the 20th century.

The constitutional changes of the Reconstruction period embodied a northern idea of American identity and national purpose and led to conflicts over new definitions of citizenship, particularly regarding the rights of African Americans, women and other minorities.

The failure of Reconstruction was due to the South interpreting its efforts as a northern concept. Furthermore, the North did not have any clear plan for properly implementing Reconstruction. This led to the failure to reintegrate the South with the Union and to various conflicts related to the rights of African Americans, minorities and women. While at the end of the war it seemed that the freed slaves were given equal rights to whites, racism prevailed. Thus, Reconstruction failed to integrate freed slaves into society.

Although citizenship, equal protection of the laws and voting rights were granted to African Americans in the Fourteenth and Fifteenth Amendments, these rights were progressively stripped away through segregation, violence, Supreme Court decisions, and local political tactics.

The Fourteenth and Fifteenth Amendments were adopted as part of the Reconstruction efforts. These were aimed at eliminating the discrimination over the right to vote based on racial identity or previous servitude conditions. Before the amendments, the states were in control of determining the qualification of voters.

Adoption of the Thirteenth Amendment

While support for the amendments was an effort to help the freed slaves, there was a deeper reason behind it. The black votes from the South would gain the majority for the supporters of the amendments. The main reason for the Fifteenth Amendment was that the Republicans wanted the support of black votes to gain a position of power in both the North and South. While the Fifteenth Amendment was temporarily and moderately successful in providing voting rights to the blacks living in northern and southern states, opposition to the amendments started in the Confederate states.

Voter intimidation, poll taxes and grandfather clauses were used to limit the voting rights of freed slaves. In the latter part of the 1870s, the southern governments nullified the Fourteenth and Fifteenth Amendments, stripped the privileges given to the African Americans and engaged in strong discriminatory practices including literacy tests, violence, and intimidation to prevent them from using their right to vote.

While the Fifteenth Amendment banned any explicit disenfranchisement based on racial factors or prior enslavement, the southerners used three overlapping alternative methods to disenfranchise blacks between 1868 and 1888. These methods included violence, illegal tactics and massive fraud, such as the cumulative poll tax by Georgia. The Supreme Court supported this disenfranchisement by gutting all the federal laws passed to protect the blacks. It undermined the executive federal powers that protected the voting rights of the blacks and refused to acknowledge racial discrimination, even if it was proven to allow constitutional violations by citing specious reasoning.

The women's rights movement was both emboldened and divided over the Fourteenth and Fifteenth Amendments to the Constitution.

While the Thirteenth Amendment abolished slavery, the complete elimination of racial discrimination was not possible due to the conflicting interests, motivations, and goals that prevailed during the Reconstruction period. The status of the freed slaves was unclear, and they did not receive proper legal protection to counter southern coercion. The Fourteenth Amendment was passed in the wake of the *Dred Scott* decision, which occurred before the war and had declared black slaves as nonpersons. The amendment sought to restore their status as citizens with natural rights, recognize their allegiance to the country and give full representation in the legislation, so that southern efforts to keep them permanently oppressed could be thwarted.

For women's rights advocates, the Fourteenth Amendment came as a big disappointment. Based on Section One of the Fourteenth Amendment, women were given the right to vote, but the Republicans, while supporting the protection of freed slaves, did not want to support women's suffrage. This was solved by the introduction of Section Two, which specified the counting criteria of the inhabitants of a state for legislative representation. The three-fifths clause of the Constitution was amended, and the specification of voting rights and citizenship to black males denied women their right to vote. This enraged the women's rights activists. Most of the Congressmen who had supported the rights of black men now opposed the women's right to vote, and the women's rights activists turned their attention to gaining women's suffrage rather than broader reforms.

The women's suffrage movement in America was founded by women who were actively involved in abolition and temperance movements. Founded in the mid-19th century, the women's rights movement met in Seneca Falls, New York, in 1848 to discuss women's rights. They passed a resolution to secure elective franchise and discussed equal rights to employment and education. Although the Seneca Falls Convention was ridiculed by the public and several supporters of the woman's rights movement refrained from supporting them, their resolution marked the beginning of the woman's suffrage movement in the country.

Lucy Stone

The first national convention on women's rights was held in 1850. It continued annually, improving the focus on the women's suffrage movement. When gender was not specified in the Fifteenth Amendment during Reconstruction, the National Women's Suffrage Association was formed. Founded by Elizabeth Cady Stanton and Susan B. Anthony, the association tried to push for women's suffrage via the U.S. Constitution. The American Woman Suffrage Association was formed by Lucy Stone and worked towards the same goal. Both these groups joined to form the National American Woman's Suffrage Association in 1890, and Wyoming became the first state in the country to grant women the right to vote.

The Civil War Amendments established judicial principles that were stalled for many decades but eventually became the basis for the court decisions upholding civil rights.

While the Reconstruction amendments—namely the Thirteenth, Fourteenth and Fifteenth Amendments—adopted in the wake of the Civil War helped to implement the Reconstruction of the South, they were also a historic step towards developing a single national identity for all Americans. The Fifth Amendment had provided a due process clause to protect the natural rights of citizens and limit the powers held by the government. The clause did not restrict the powers of the states, making it easy for them to violate the amendments, and natural rights were only partially protected.

The Fourteenth Amendment remedied the situation by extending the prohibition of natural rights violations to the states. The language of the Fourteenth Amendment clearly states that the natural rights clause should extend protection not just to citizens, but also to all persons who are part of the immunity clause or privileged beneficiaries.

Based on the equal protection clause, the government has two tasks in its function of securing rights for the people: it should not infringe upon or threaten the rights of citizens and it should take positive measures to protect the persons within its governing territory. While the former function is addressed by the due process clause, the latter is ensured by the equal protection clause. The states, however, were not duty bound to protect rights, as the original Constitution did not make it mandatory. States were thus legally free to deny rights by their own measure or by failing to prevent others from violating rights.

The amendments were required because the earlier protection clause did not have a reliable standard for providing protection to all persons. While language akin to the full protection of laws was seriously considered by Congress, these were not clear-cut standards, as they left room for violation. Equal protection provided a manageable standard, offering protection similar to that given to the most favored members of the community. By enforcing these amendments, the courts and Congress arrived at an enforceable standard.

The immunities and privileges clause does not guarantee natural rights, as it applies only to citizens, thereby lacking the universal natural right provision. Similarly, the Fifteenth Amendment is not favorable for protecting natural rights and just involves the right of a citizen to vote. This amendment denies states the right to abridge laws on a racial basis in relation to the right to vote. However, states may abridge the right-to-vote clause on any basis other than racial discrimination.

Historians have identified four different categories of rights which were debated in the nineteenth century: civil, social, political and natural. Each has different claims and statuses to protect. While natural rights are for all human beings, political rights are not universal, and eligibility is subject to the decision of the community.

The Fifteenth Amendment states that race is not a valid reason for determining the right to vote, but it leaves other ways of denying the right to vote (such as literacy) open. Thus, the actual intention of the amendment was circumvented for several years by crafty exploitation of such loopholes states used to deny minorities the right to vote. While these amendments aimed at giving freedom, rights of citizenship and voting to the slaves, they were slowly but effectively eroded by the federal court rulings and state laws – called "Jim Crow laws" after a mythical southern white racist – during the latter part of the 19th century.

Women were prohibited from voting, which led to Susan B. Anthony trying to vote in the presidential election of 1872 as an act of agitation against the rules. The Jim Crow laws passed by some states limited the rights of former slaves. Furthermore, the *Slaughterhouse* case and *Plessy v. Ferguson* case of the Supreme Court undermined the rights given by the amendments. The full effects of the rights were enjoyed by the freed slaves only after the passing of laws such as the 1964 Civil Rights Act and the 1965 Voting Rights Act.

Please, leave your Customer Review on Amazon

PERIOD 6

1865-1898

Economic, political, diplomatic, social, environmental and cultural changes as the United States was transforming from an agricultural to an increasingly industrialized and urbanized society.

Major historical events of the period:

1866 – National Labor Union is formed
1874 – Woman's Christian Temperance Union
1876-1877 – Sioux War
1876-1890 – the Gilded Age
1877 – Reconstruction ends
1881 – Booker T. Washington founds Tuskegee Institute
1890 – National American Woman Suffrage Association
1890 – Battle at Wounded Knee
1891 – Forest Reserve Act
1894 – Pullman Strike

PERIOD 6: 1865-1898

> **KEY CONCEPT 6.1: The rise of big business in the United States encouraged massive migrations and urbanization, sparked government and popular efforts to reshape the U.S. economy and environment, and renewed debates over U.S. national identity.**

The emergence of entrepreneurs, corporate conglomerations, innovators and economic and social reformers embodies the spirit of the Gilded Age and set the United States on a trajectory for the political, economic and social system existing today. Following the damage and desolation of the Civil War, it was difficult to define American spirit and national identity. This changed as Americans moved into the 20th century. Twentieth century Americans were confident, resourceful and urbanized, and they began to call into question social oppression involving gender and racial discrimination.

Mr. and Mrs. Goodhue Livingston and Mrs. Vanderbilt,
the wealthy elite of the American Gilded Age

In response to these transitions, the U.S. government set out to expand into its western lands, address workplace misgivings and lack of regulations, and embrace the newly expanding consumer and production cultures. Americans began to question the government's land use practices and for the first time were concerned with massive conservation attempts, highlighting the change in American planning from reactive policy agendas to those crafted with the future in mind.

The rise of big business in America determined the national identity associated with the United States heading into the 20th century, and without this boost in industrialization and manufacturing capacities, it is difficult to say whether the United States would have acquired and maintained its position as a global power in the 20th and 21st centuries. This exceptional rate of growth was crucial for the economic reforms in the early years of the 20th century under the Progressive movement. The major political players of the late 19th century envisioned an economic market with no restrictions, and it was because of their laissez-faire economic policies that many Americans began to question the level of control and influence these magnates held over the American political system.

Large-scale production—accompanied by massive technological change, expanding international communication networks and pro-growth government policies—fueled the development of a "Gilded Age" marked by an emphasis on consumption, marketing, and business consolidation.

As the entrepreneurial spirit swept across America, both the government and public struggled to adjust to the initial changes in urban development and technological innovations. The improvement of workplace technology, such as conveyor systems, expedited the time required to produce goods, causing an influx in goods and later services. In order to meet these demands, the American perception regarding consumerism had to change. As more Americans required more goods, the market became less saturated and more stable, propelling the economic machine of the late 19th century.

In addition to consumer trends and exponential growth in production capabilities, the American public also witnessed the beginning of monopolies with the emergence of company trusts and interlocking directorates. Such consolidation of business by buyout processes caused the wealthy elites in America to increase their fortunes while also limiting access to such ambitions. While the entrepreneurial spirit was never more evident than in this period, it is also true that the former wealthy class did not welcome newcomers and were resistant to embrace the nouveau riche of the Gilded Age.

The developments in communication technologies were unprecedented during this period; the introduction of the telephone by Alexander Graham Bell had been an impressive jump from the telegram a few decades earlier. Additional transformations in information sharing were also seen by means of mass circulation newspapers such as the *New York World,* the *New York Journal* and the *St. Louis Post-Dispatch.* National magazines and bestselling novels of the Gilded Age also transformed communication and information or idea sharing in the last years of the 19th century.

Alexander Graham Bell

In addition to technological achievements, the Gilded Age was also responsible for explosive expansion in various areas, the evolving economy, urban dwellings, and city living as well as the unparalleled growth in the West. These transitions and their initial successes caused the U.S. government to promote further growth, which would have catastrophic results for the Native American populations of the United States.

In this period, many saw the displacement and resettling of Native Americans as a necessary sacrifice for the American dream, and in many cases as an opportunity to give an uncivilized population the proper training and resources to live in the 19th century. The lasting influences of this period are all-pervasive and have had a direct impact on the economic and social systems we see today. The Gilded Age of business expansion and the American spirit of Nationalism were key in the development of today's perception of the American dream.

Following the Civil War, government subsidies for transportation and communication systems opened new markets in North America, while technological innovations and redesigned financial and management structures such as monopolies sought to maximize the exploitation of natural resources and a growing labor force.

In hopes of reunifying the United States following the disastrous Civil War, many believed growth and expansion—which would connect the Atlantic and Pacific coasts—were necessary. In order to accomplish this monumental task, the U.S. government began investing in the transcontinental railroad, which would be a source of communication, travel and much-needed work for minorities and whites.

In order to promote the success of the railroads, the government and railroad companies used land grants and other incentives to lure workers out west. Leaflets and brochures widely distributed in both the United States and parts of continental Europe proved to be a very successful advertising tactic. The draw of land and better wages following the economic and political uncertainties of the earlier 19th century caused many working-class citizens, both native-born and immigrant, to support westward expansion, thus promoting the success of the railroad and—by default—the federal government.

As the magnates of this period realized the opportunity for financial return from the new railroads, many jumped on the expansion projects, attempting to corner sectors of the market such as ownership of the only railway leading into New York City. This type of economic strategy saw the emergence of the first monopolies which were able to dictate the labor policies of the railroads while also greatly influencing the political landscape of the period.

The lasting influence of such political agendas and strategies can be seen in the monopolies created during the Gilded Age, as they were the first of their kind and extremely influential. However, the backlash these same monopolies experienced just a few years later reflected the social upheaval average Americans experienced during this period and served as a precursor to the social revolutions of the 20th century.

Businesses and foreign policymakers increasingly looked outside U.S. borders in an effort to gain greater influence and control over markets and natural resources in the Pacific, Asia and Latin America.

As the United States began its inward expansion, many influential businessmen and politicians were also looking into the global system in hopes of finding influence, resources, and alliances. In order to establish the United States as a real world power, the economic machine had to influence foreign markets in Asia and Latin America. Following this expansion-style foreign policy agenda, the United States was extremely interested in securing the natural resources required to sustain the industrial and manufacturing boom of the Gilded Age.

With the expansion of manufacturing and production, the United States and its business magnates were looking for fresh markets. Some of the most notable examples of this were the investments in Asian and Latin American countries in an attempt to gain influence within the regions. By undertaking these investment and export opportunities, the United States was setting the foundations of its 20th-century foreign policies, while at the same time creating a more pronounced rivalry between the United States and European counterparts. Such foreign policy decisions can be seen as a foreshadowing of the decisions to come in the later decades of the 20th century.

Additionally, as the U.S. government faced pushback from conservationists, some industrialists sought the natural resources of other less regulated countries. In order to maintain the massive expectations of manufacturing and production, the United States needed to secure vast amounts of natural resources including but not limited to iron ore, coal, lumber, and oil reserves.

Iron and steel company in Johnstown, Pennsylvania

The long-term implications of resource security can be seen in the World Wars and every period that follows, highlighting the incalculable value of such resources during the period of the Gilded Age, as well as the contemporary period. For the first time during this period, Americans realized the economic potential of steel and oil refining. The United States went to great lengths to cultivate the relationships and economic partnerships with countries where these commodities were not readily available, ushering in the century of American hegemony. One might also argue such policies were successful, as under President Taft a similar strategy was employed through the use of dollar diplomacy.

Business leaders consolidated corporations into trusts and holding companies and defended their resulting status and privilege through theories such as social Darwinism.

As the magnates of the Gilded Age experienced periods of criticism, many were quick to use the ideas of social Darwinism, which had transformed the social sciences also beginning in this period, to secure their new status within the political and economic systems. The most notable entrepreneurs of the Gilded Age included John D. Rockefeller and J. P. Morgan. These men initiated the economic production and markets of the late 19th century and forever transformed the notion of the American dream and the accumulation of wealth during the Gilded Age.

Some of the business practices of the Gilded Age would be considered illegal in today's markets. The use of interlocking directorates and the buying up of corporations under parent umbrellas to create monopolies were all new ideas in this period. Such tactics were wildly successful for those managing the companies. However, this was typically at the expense of shareholders and sometimes the American public. Business dealings, such as the Union Pacific interlocking directorate scandal, caused great dissatisfaction and mistrust between the working class and the ruling or business class. These sour relationships would continue until the late 20th century where, for the first time, progressive activists and presidents sided with labor instead of its big business partners.

John D. Rockefeller, born into a modest family in New York, became one of the leading magnates of this period and spent much of his time acknowledging and defending the fortune he had amassed. In 1870, Rockefeller struck liquid gold and was able to quickly thereafter establish the Standard Oil Company, which at the time was valued at one million dollars. Rockefeller perfected the use of trusts in order to weed out and eliminate his competition in the oil markets. By 1877, Rockefeller controlled close to 95 percent of the oil refineries operating in the United States, and after eliminating his competition, such as the Vanderbilt family, he was able to exercise a complete monopoly on the global petroleum market.

John D. Rockefeller

Like Rockefeller, J. P. Morgan was also a revolutionary figure of this period, however, he was able to gain his foothold in finance, drastically influencing the economic laissez-faire policies of the period. Morgan was born into a wealthy family and through his scrupulous economic dealings, he expanded his family's empire to include banking and steel. Morgan was able to perfect the use of the interlocking directorate, placing a puppet board of directors in charge of multiple companies which he oversaw. Morgan was able to buy out his competition when they were reeling from the 1890s depression. After buying out Andrew Carnegie from the steel business, Morgan formed the first billion-dollar corporation in 1901 with the creation of the United States Steel Corporation.

Andrew Carnegie

Andrew Carnegie was less than persuaded by the arguments of superiority put forth by the social Darwinists but nonetheless capitalized on the unregulated financial markets of the Gilded Age. Unlike his counterparts who bought out the competition and created monopolies, Carnegie employed a tactic known as vertical integration, where he systematically integrated all the steps in his production of steel.

Carnegie owned the coal production plants, the steamships that transported iron ore found in the Great Lakes, and railroads that transported his materials to his flagship city, Pittsburgh. By controlling all variables in the production process, Carnegie was able to improve efficiency and quality while decreasing cost.

In 1900, Carnegie sold his stock in steel to J. P. Morgan, effectively eliminating himself from further economic policies and instead focusing on philanthropic works, which he believed to be the responsibility of the wealthy elites. All of these men were instrumental in crafting the perception of the American dream to include anyone and everyone from any background. Some of these men broke through social classes and stereotypes to create some of the largest and most influential companies in American history.

As cities grew substantially in both size and in number, some segments of American society enjoyed lives of extravagant "conspicuous consumption," while many others lived in relative poverty.

The explosion of city living also brought to light the drastic and deplorable contrast between the wealthy elites and the working classes, which had never been more evident than it was during this period. As thousands of workers flooded into the city, it quickly became clear that many did not have the resources or services necessary to live in these urban metropolises. Due to a lack of space, the tenement houses were crowded and typically had communal bathrooms. The sewer and water facilities provided by the city were typically overloaded and unable to provide service to all those living in the cities, greatly straining the sanitation system. Trash piled up on the streets of New York, and Chicago health concerns mounted, partially due to the spread of communicable diseases such as tuberculosis.

The child mortality rate was extremely high in Chicago in 1900. Poverty and low standards of living caused many to despise the wealthy classes who, during this period, lived in a new sense of luxury. As a result of continued income inequality, many living below the poverty line joined neighborhood gangs, such as the Hell's Kitchen Gang or the Rock Gang, who subsided by shoplifting and other petty thefts.

In contrast to the slums many Americans inhabited in the city, the wealthy class had experienced an incredible increase in their standard of living. Leisure activities such as shopping and listening to the radio preoccupied many upper- to middle-class Americans. The introduction of vast department stores, theme parks, theaters, and operas had inspired many city dwellers to enjoy the benefits of urbanization, in contrast to the poor living conditions of those beneath their social status.

This was one of the first periods when working-class Americans were able to transition into the middle class, allowing for further consumerism. The term "millionaire" was coined earlier during the 19th century but was not actively used until this period, which should give some insight into the levels of excess and decadence experienced by the American elites. One such example of over-the-top opulence came from a formal dinner party thrown by the wife of a railroad tycoon in honor of her dog, who entered the party wearing a $15,000 (today approximately $384,000) diamond-crusted collar.

The social structure of this period, highlighted by the great income gap, had an influence on the social reforms of the period, but it is difficult to say how great of an impact it had. While many people were continuing to work towards better workplace treatment and more efficient city services, others continued to live below the poverty line. It is also interesting to note that regardless of the manufacturing and industrial accomplishments of this period, the European elites still looked down at Americans as wealthy barbarians, who had certainly achieved innovative technologies but lacked social sophistication and grace.

As leaders of big business and their allies in government aimed to create a unified industrialized nation, they were challenged in different ways by demographic issues, regional differences, and labor movements.

As industrial and manufacturing giants dominated the political landscape of the period, they were met at times with strong opposition from the immigrant classes as well as the emergence of labor unions and planned strikes. These had a drastic impact on the future of labor movements in America. As immigration labor fueled the railroad expansion, which would unify the country through transcontinental means, it was also the first to experience labor strikes as a result of the newly formed unions. One drawback of exponential labor reserves—as seen in the immigration explosions of the late 19th century—was that it made workers expendable and decreased their wages. Keeping vocational practices in this light caused increased social tensions and issues within the railroad companies, which further soured the relationship between workers and management.

These first influential labor movements allowed many Americans the right to go on strike or demand better workplace conditions in terms of health and safety. These concepts became the common workplace expectations of all Americans leading into the 20th century, forever altering the conception of union and labor movements in America. The drastic increase in labor movements and strikes highlights an American landscape in the midst of a tumultuous and challenging transition.

Strikers at the Burlington Railroad shop yards

The years between 1881 and 1900 saw close to 23,000 strikes, which involved more than six million workers. Confrontations within the railroad, steel and mining sectors all led to bloody strikes typically dispersed by the use of force by the federal government on behalf of businesses. The policies enacted by both the corporations as well as the federal government would serve to sour and detach the relationships between the working class and government.

For example, some of the Molly Maguires, who faced legal action for their role in union strikes, were convicted and hung, leading to the creation of martyr unions working against management regardless of the cost. This would continue to have a drastic impact on the labor movement of this period, as most labor activists saw little to no result of the actions taken against the railroad, coal and steel corporations.

The industrial workforce expanded through migration across national borders and internal migration, leading to a more diverse workforce, lower wages and an increase in child labor.

As the workforce continued to expand, it became increasingly clear that children and minority groups were now encompassing more and more of the workforce. Many social and labor activists detested the use of child labor, however, this was commonplace in big business leading into and during the 20th century. By 1890, close to 18 percent of the workforce was made up of children ranging in age from ten to fifteen years old. A vast expansion of women in the workforce also defined this period; between 1880 and 1890 the number of working women jumped from 2.6 million to 8.6 million, causing some men to question their quick ascension into urban work. Men in this period viewed women working for wages as a threat to the overall wage levels. This sentiment was typically shared by the majority of unions as well.

Child labor in the textile mills

As the labor movement took hold, corporations fought back against these institutions; if workers began to contest hours or working conditions, many companies would blacklist the worker and replace him or her with another worker who would be willing to work for even fewer wages and typically without the promise of any benefits. In this sense, the abundance of unskilled laborers due to immigration and migration following the Civil War was considered a negative. Workers were no longer commodities and were being treated accordingly. This influx in unskilled and skilled labor changed the economic conditions for many in the working class during this period.

However, this same workforce, which would propel the industrial and manufacturing giants to a new level of economic prosperity and influence, would also bring about the rise of the labor movement and unions, causing the business giants' eventual decline. The use of cheap labor and deplorable working conditions caused many to support the labor movement as their own means of equal representation in the industrial and manufacturing systems. The use of child labor would go mostly unchallenged until the progressive reforms. This was due in part to the financial needs of struggling families, but also because the social norm of the day was not to actively speak out against child labor.

Labor and management battled for control over wages and working conditions, with workers organizing local and national unions and/or directly confronting corporate power.

As the industrial and manufacturing giants of the period amassed wealth and influence, the working classes struggled to be protected or fairly represented. In order to combat this social and economic issue, many social activists emerged to fight for the rights of the working class. Workplace conditions in 1866 led to the first labor union, the National Labor Union, which supported implementing an eight-hour workday, the use of greenbacks, the enforcing of health and safety regulations and the repealing of laws that made importing labor easier. This latter concern embodies the sentiment of nativism, which spread during this period.

In 1869, the Knights of Labor was formed, which encompassed both skilled and unskilled laborers and worked toward equal pay amongst genders—a revolutionary concept at the time—as well as an eight-hour work day, codes for health and safety in the workplace, and the use of greenback or soft currency to expand the supply of currency being circulated while also elevating pressure on debtors. Other notable unions of this period include the American Federation of Labor (AFL), which was founded in 1886 and was an example of the emergence of craft unions. The establishment of such unions would become common in the early 20th century, as many more Americans began to embrace the idea of organized workers bargaining with management and going on strikes when an agreement couldn't be reached.

Knights of Labor pentagram

Mary Harris Jones, often referred to as "Mother Jones," was also an influential character of the labor movements of the late 19th century. She was an Irish American immigrant who worked tirelessly for the advancement and protection of industrial workers. Aside from planning and implementing vast strikes, Jones was also the co-founder of the Industrial Workers of the World in the early 20th century, which fought against child labor and the exploitation of the industrial workforce.

Some major strikes of this period included the Great Strike of 1877, where the workers of the Baltimore and Ohio railroads went on strike following a drastic pay cut of almost 10 percent. The strike was ended by the intervention of federal troops sent by President Hayes. The Homestead Strike took place in 1892 at the Carnegie Steel Company's offices in Homestead and was an industrial lockout and strike which lasted for four months and resulted in the deaths of three Pinkerton detectives and nine factory workers.

The Pullman Strike, which began in 1894, was also a result of decreased wages and increased cost of living, and resulted in violence between railway strikebreakers, sometimes called "scabs," and the rail workers. Little action was taken to address the grievances of the working class. Instead, the rail company fired all those who went on strike and blacklisted many more from working in the railroad industry. This was the typical response to strikes in the late 19th century and certainly led to the culmination of full labor reforms during the 20th century.

Pullman strikers outside Arcade Building in Pullman, Chicago

Despite the industrialization of some segments of the southern economy, a change promoted by southern leaders who called for a "New South," agrarian sharecropping and tenant farming systems continued to dominate the region.

As a result of the Confederate defeat in the Civil War, many southerners began to question the economic practices of the past, specifically the economy's sole reliance on cotton. With the emergence of the "New South," many had hoped to see a diversification of the goods and services offered there. As the southern markets and goods expanded, the South found a new market in which to invest: northern exports. Many northerners imported the tobacco grown in the South as well as industrial exports such as lumber, iron, and coal.

Though some called for the industrialization of the South, this seemed rather unlikely, as the society was agriculturally based and continued to be so after the Civil War. The introduction of secondary crops such as tobacco, rice, and sugar cane all reestablished the agrarian traditions of the past. Supported by people such as Seaman Knapp, who perfected the cultivation of crops in the South, the newly formed local and state governments were able to establish and expand agriculture education and production programs aimed at assisting those farming in the New South. This was particularly important, as much of the New South's tradition and the effects of Reconstruction still centered around the implementation of an agrarian society, rather than one dominated by the industrial and manufacturing movements seen elsewhere.

In addition to agricultural transitions, which were moving away from cotton and into tenant farming, the New South explored industry in cities such as Birmingham, Alabama. Here southerners found natural resources of iron, limestone and eventually coal, all of which were extremely important to the economic development needed in the South following the disastrous Civil War and the railroad and manufacturing booms experienced in the North, Midwest and the western territories.

Other industries which expanded during this period included lumber exports of prized southern pine trees—which were found to be in great demand around the country—and new markets for paper, clay and glass production. While the New South struggled to shed its image of outdated agrarian life, it became clear that the impact of industrialization in the Midwest and Northeast had influenced some southern politicians, but not enough to totally transform the economic landscape of the southern states. It should be noted that the reemergence of the South as a sustainable, operating entity was a vast accomplishment of the Reconstruction period and the capitalist system, and greatly influenced the future of political and social reforms, or lack thereof, in the region.

Westward migration, new systems of farming and transportation, and economic instability led to political and popular conflicts.

The expansion of westward migration opened up several new transformations in farming, mining and ranching markets. However, such expansion became possible only with the introduction of mass transportation by means of the transcontinental railroad. With the implementation of the Homestead Act in 1862, the government stopped selling land as a means of revenue and instead used it as a tool to encourage the settling of the West mainly by farming families and those moving west to find their Gilded Age niche, such as ranching, mining or working as a cowboy.

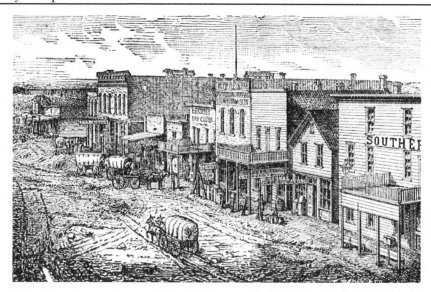

Western Expansion: street in Abilene

The main detriment of farming on the Great Plains during this period was the unpredictability of the climate, which could have disastrous effects on the crops and economic sustainability of the farm. In addition to difficulties with the weather, the political landscape of the West was barren, and a lack of law and order pervaded the West, leading many to enact forms of vigilante justice. This was especially the case in disputes between ranchers and homesteaders, who during this period still shared prairie lands on the open range.

Women experienced greater roles of independence and equality in the westward expansions than those living in the urbanized Northeast. The ratio of men to women in some frontier settlements in the West was more than 100–1. This gender differential afforded women many more privileges and the respect of their peers as they worked side by side with men in the farms and western communities.

The establishment of trading hubs on the Pacific Seaboard, such as San Francisco, embodied the West's diverse population, which was made up of nearly half immigrant populations, including but not limited to Hispanic, Asian and European backgrounds. Such diversity culminated in various sources of conflict including anti-immigration sentiment against Chinese populations in California, most notably in San Francisco, as well as Hispanic-Anglo aggression along the southern border of the United States.

Government agencies and conservationist organizations contended with corporate interests about the extension of public control over natural resources, including land and water.

As American industry exploited the natural resources of the Midwest and West, some were of the opinion that action by the federal government was necessary in order to preserve national resources including land and water. The difficult westward expansion had taught settlers the importance of protecting resources like water for future generations of farmers.

One of the first steps toward such conservation was the formation of the Office of Commission of Fish and Fisheries, also known as the Fish Commission, which was signed into law by President Ulysses S. Grant in 1871. Fisheries were one of the first renewable resources to receive the attention of the federal government, because Americans saw a drastic decline in the fisheries' production, calling into question the sustainability of fishing practices.

In addition to concerns regarding fishery practices following the industrial boom of the Gilded Age, the federal government began looking closer at its policies regarding forestry. As a result, in 1891 the Forest Reserve Act was passed, allocating lands as national forests, which later came under the control of the National Forest Service. Such policies would be expanded in the first years of the 20th century under President Theodore Roosevelt.

Others also engaged in the battle for the protection of natural resources against the machine of industrialization. One such notable example is John Muir, who in 1892 founded the Sierra Club, concerned with the protection and conservation of what was considered wild lands. Even today the Sierra Club advocates on behalf of the wildlife and for resource conservation.

The actions of conservationists during this period would have profound implications leading into the 21st century. Without these initial programs, many resources and lands might have been lost to the consumerism and manufacturing of the period. However, this was not the case, and future presidents, such as Presidents Theodore Roosevelt and Franklin D. Roosevelt, expanded these programs, bringing more water and land security to the Great Plains and the western settlements. Such advancements were crucial to maintaining the progress of the Gilded Age and migration to the West, without decimating natural resources valued by many Americans today.

Farmers adapted to the new realities of mechanized agriculture and dependence on the evolving railroad system by creating local and regional organizations that sought to resist corporate control of agricultural markets.

The transitions experienced by farmers during the late 19th century varied and sometimes met with great pushback; one notable example of this was the farmers' dependence on rail transportation of goods to East Coast markets. This new relationship was not welcomed by the majority of farmers operating in the Great Plains and eventually led to several opposition movements including, but not limited to, the Grange and Populist movements.

The Grange movement, also called the Patrons of Husbandry, was founded in 1867 and meant to facilitate the advancement of agricultural technologies, while also voicing social and economic concerns of the farmers operating in the Midwest. As the government faltered in addressing the economic, political and social concerns of farmers, the Grange movement saw a drastic increase in membership during the 1870s. Farmers were particularly upset with the rising costs of transporting goods by train, as well as the fact that the government opted for gold-backed currency instead of silver.

U.S. postage stamp honoring the Grange movement

Grangers adopted the slogan "I pay for all," which embodied their stance as the breadwinners of American society where farming was the cornerstone of American industry and progress during this period. Such policies, along with failing crops, decimated the farming populations of the 1870s, leading farmers to support Populist and later Progressive movements that were concerned with the well-being of the American farmer.

Another notable organization seeking to limit federal and state control was the Las Gorras Blancas, who took a more coercive approach to the removal of government regulations. From February 1889 until the summer of 1891, members of Las Gorras Blancas went on night rides, terrorizing the ranchers enclosing the Land Grant Common of Las Vegas, as well as railroad companies in the region. These vigilantes were taking action against what they perceived as the perpetrator of land grants in the West.

The Colored Farmers' Alliance was also influential during this period and worked against the influence of the federal and state governments, as well as racial stigma and persecution following the Civil War. The C.F.A. was formed in 1886 as a separate entity because the Southern Famers' Alliance declined the admittance of African American members. Though the Colored Farmers Alliance was a short-lived organization, it sought to advance African American farmers and citizens advocating for independence and the ownership of private property, such as homes, while also eliminating debt.

The formation of such groups shows the impact each demographic had on the political system during the late 19th century; every walk of life in America was greatly influenced by the ideals and economic strategies of the Gilded Age. This was certainly the case for those living on the western frontier, experiencing firsthand the resistance of private entities to being regulated by the federal government or corporate powers. However, this would prove to be the norm in the early decades of the 20th century, as the federal government was influenced greatly by the magnates and big businesses of the Gilded Age.

The growth of corporate power in agriculture and economic instability in the farming sector inspired activists to create the People's (Populist) Party, which called for political reform and a stronger governmental role in the American economic system.

While the farmers' call for more regulation and reforms of the influence being exercised by the railroads went unnoticed, Populism, another social movement, emerged. Like its predecessors, the Populist movement was an attempt by disenfranchised farmers to have their grievances aired and addressed. The Populist movement was especially influential in the New South, as it called upon white and African American farmers to work together toward a common cause rather than being separated on the basis of race.

By the late 1880s, farmers had experienced years of failed crops, the lack of credit institutions, insufficient marketing, a lack of regulations by the federal government to protect farmers' rights, and declining prices. These conditions, coupled with the tense relationships shared between railroad management and farmers, caused the explosion of the Populist movement in the later years of the 19th century. However, the movement dissipated by the late 1890s with the defeat of the candidates of the Populist and Democratic Parties, such as William Jennings Bryan, as the Populist Party lacked popularity among the American public. In the years following, many who supported the Populist and Grange movements would find some common ground with the Progressive movement.

Though the Populist movement was unable to maintain its popularity, it was influential because it laid the groundwork for later movements such as the Progressivism movement of the 20th century. This movement also highlights another example of division within the American population, which eventually culminated in social upheaval in later decades. This is one of the first examples of a biracial organization after the Civil War; for many in the South, this seemed an accomplishment in itself. The concept of government accountability and fair representation of all American citizens came out of such social and political movements.

Business interests battled conservationists as the latter sought to protect sections of unspoiled wilderness through the establishment of national parks and other conservationist and preservationist measures.

As industry and manufacturing giants dotted the American landscape following the Civil War, it seemed a new war on natural resources and conservation had been declared. The industrial magnates of the period exploited and sought the natural resources of continental America in hopes of continuing their dominant role within the new economy. However, many conservationists, who sought policies more in line with preserving and maintaining the natural resources and unspoiled wilderness of the United States, quickly opposed this.

The exploitation of natural resources by business interests centered mainly on iron ore, coal, oil and lumber. Iron ore was used to create steel and pig iron, which was used by the railroad companies and in the building of urban bridges and buildings. Coal was needed to propel the steam engines in the railcars, after replacing the use of wood as fuel. Other various industry machines also used coal as a fuel source, making it a necessity of the Gilded Age. Oil was used as a form of kerosene to light houses and cities during this period. It also created a new industry, petroleum refining, which would later evolve into multi-billion-dollar corporations. Lumber was also sought during this period.

Hauling coal locomotive

The creation of national parks was a great victory for conservationists and would allow for further advancements in conservation by later progressive presidents. This transition away from policies supporting big business towards those which gave a voice to workers can be seen as the transition from the Gilded Age into the Progressive Age of the early 20th century.

> **KEY CONCEPT 6.2: The emergence of an industrial culture in the United States led to both greater opportunities for, and restrictions on, immigrants, minorities and women.**

As the industrial culture emerged out of the Civil War, many African Americans, immigrant workers, and women saw their futures having more opportunities than before. This explosion of manufacturing saw the increased need for skilled labor, which had been supplied by immigration influx in the past. It seemed as though the industrial and manufacturing advancements of the Gilded Age would allow for all minority groups to expand their vocational opportunities. However, many quickly realized such ambitions would exist within the same class structure as the past and would be drastically limited in relation to the opportunities being afforded to white males.

As America entered the end of the 19th century, it was quickly becoming evident that social reform and revolution was on the horizon, and many seemed to embrace this unprecedented period of growth and transition. The impact of the Gilded Age, western expansion, urbanization, and industrialization would change the political and social landscape of America for decades to come, resulting in the global power it became by the mid-20th century.

The expansion of the western territories following the Civil War shows the greatest example of gender and racial equality of the period. In the western territories, women and minority groups such as African Americans, Chinese immigrants and other European immigrants all experienced more freedoms and vocational opportunities than were afforded to them in the urban settings of the Atlantic Seaboard. This was due to the need for skilled and unskilled laborers and the circumstances of life in the western territories.

As economic opportunities grew in the West, women who settled there were given more freedoms and responsibilities associated with running a homestead. Immigrant groups were able to settle in the West with fewer experiences of prejudice than on the East Coast while also being afforded greater financial opportunities. One notable example is the laundress and seamstress shops opened by Chinese immigrants who saw a gap in the market and capitalized on the demand for laundry services in mining communities. African Americans were also able to find greater opportunities in the West than in the New South and northern states, working as ranchers, farmers, cowboys or railroad laborers.

International and internal migrations increased both urban and rural populations, but gender, racial, ethnic, religious and socioeconomic inequalities abounded, inspiring some reformers to attempt to address these inequities.

As Americans entered an unprecedented period of economic and social development, it became clear that reform was on the horizon, and many social groups, including women, the working class and immigrants would benefit from these eventual reforms. Late 19th-century America had unregulated work environments, overzealous and sometimes corrupt politicians and a population unhappy with the influx of recent immigrants. These divisions highlighted the difficulties faced by average Americans but also showed the abundant and varying solutions and perceptions of the American public.

In hopes of addressing various forms of racial discrimination, many abolitionists and former slaves worked tirelessly to end the racial norms of the Civil War era by means of organizations and support groups whose goal was to help assimilate former slaves into post–Civil War America. Socioeconomic inequalities were addressed by attempts to reform the workplace, guaranteeing shorter workdays, protection of wages and the formation of unions.

Religious rivalries and oppression were seen during this period, which is to be expected given the transition from traditional Victorian values into more modern interpretations of religion and science. However, many immigrated during this period to experience greater freedoms of religion and escape persecution in their native lands, examples being Russian Mennonites and migrant Mormons, who made a home for themselves in Utah.

While many embraced the transitions of the period, others worked tirelessly against such changes, arguing the tradition and cultural norms of the early 19th century weren't broken and certainly didn't need fixing. However, it seems these traditionalists quickly lost the ear of the public, and many Americans were excited and eagerly awaiting the emergence of progress in the 20th century.

Increased migrations from Asia and from southern and eastern Europe, as well as African American migrations within and out of the South, accompanied the mass movement of people into the nation's cities and the rural and boomtown areas of the West.

As America began its transition westward or into urban centers, many immigrants from around the world looked to the United States as a means of accomplishing dreams unattainable in their native lands. Many immigrants moving from Europe and Asia sought better economic and vocational conditions, while others looked for expanded religious freedoms as seen with Eastern Orthodox and Jewish immigrants of the period. African Americans, who had survived slavery and the Civil War, looked for the freedoms and equality promised by the Emancipation Proclamation.

As America experienced the boom of initial urbanization, many immigrants and minority groups looked to these cities and vast economic opportunities for better wages and the amenities of city life. While many groups that had previously experienced discrimination were able to find work, social and class expectations still stifled the ambitions of many living in the city.

Westward expansion proved a little less rigid in class and social structure, allowing many African Americans and immigrant classes to hold various jobs, including those which would have previously been designated strictly for white males. Such examples included mining, ranching and homesteading. These initial opportunities would become the foundation of further calls for equal job opportunities as well as equal rights and protection within the political system.

The implications of such expansion were critical to propelling the United States into a more developed, unified country following the ravaging it had experienced during the Civil War. It also allowed many Americans to find opportunities previously unavailable, perpetuating the American dream to a new wave of citizens.

Cities dramatically reflected divided social conditions among classes, races, ethnicities, and cultures, but presented economic opportunities where new businesses proliferated.

As the manufacturing and industrialization boom continued, thousands of native-born Americans and immigrants flocked to the newly developed cities to find work. Transportation was unavailable to most working-class people during this period, so many lived within walking distance of their factories. These new cities also provided work in terms of projects and infrastructure, as housing projects and bigger buildings were necessary to accommodate the massive influx in urban populations.

Within the urban city, one could easily find mini cities divided by nationalities, such as "Little Hungary" or "Little China," where new and seasoned immigrants could enjoy some of their native traditions. These communities typically embraced their own, making the transition into American society and culture easier for each new wave of immigrants. However, the programs offered within the community were provided with the understanding that once someone had become successful, they would extend their own services to those in need, thus perpetuating the cycle.

In addition to boundaries derived from nationalities, the city grotesquely displayed the class and income inequalities of the period, with a small percentage of elites living in luxury and the working class managing through the slime of the newly minted city. This class inequality would serve as the foundations for many social movements in the later 19th and early 20th centuries.

The efficiency of the city system would prove to have drastic implications for later waves of American urbanization in the 20th century as well as establishing the expectation of urban living and production for future generations. Following the Gilded Age, Americans would never again look to agrarian means to support the economy or population. Instead, it threw all its support behind industrialization and manufacturing advancements, allowing the United States to maintain its role as a global power in the 20th century.

Immigrants sought both to "Americanize" and to maintain their unique identities; along with others, such as some African Americans and women, they were able to take advantage of new career opportunities even in the face of widespread social prejudices.

As immigrants came to America, they, like native-born citizens, sought to attain their version of the American dream, which typically meant more freedoms, better wages and an overall better day-to-day existence for the working class. During the Gilded Age, the American manufacturing sector needed skilled and unskilled labors to sustain the booming economy, and because of this demand, many industrial elites welcomed the exploding immigration patterns of the period.

These immigrants were able to maintain a sense of their homelands, as many assimilated into American culture with the help of other immigrants and lived in relatively close proximity to others who came from the same country, such as Poland, Russia or China. In the West, entire settlements consisted of Chinese immigrants who had minted the gold and silver caches of the West and supplemented agriculture during times of conflict such as the Civil War.

Toy vendor, Chinatown, San Francisco (c1900s)

Following the Civil War, women and African Americans also found new opportunities in the West and North, igniting the desire for further equality and vocational opportunities. One such example was the newly emerging cowboy, who was hired to round up and drive longhorn cattle across the Great Plains. Men from every background worked as cowboys, including Mexican settlers, former slaves and various European immigrants. Women and other minority groups could also make opportunities for themselves as homesteaders; however, like all other western ambitions, this was difficult, and many were forced to pursue other work, such as lending themselves to other farms as hands or servants.

In an urban atmosphere where access to power was unequally distributed, political machines provided social services in exchange for political support, settlement houses helped immigrants adapt to the new language and customs, and women's clubs and self-help groups targeted intellectual development and social and political reform.

As the federal government was unable to provide abundant services to the immigration and working classes seen during the explosion of urbanization, fraternal, neighborhood and social groups were able to fill the gap, garnering substantial political influence during the Gilded Age. These relationships would prove to be extremely influential in establishing the stability sought by those living in urban America during the late 19th century. Such influence caused the government to enact many social programs in the early 20th century, which placed the social dependence of the population back with the federal government, rather than privately organized ethnic or fraternal entities.

Mary Greenleaf Clement, founding member of the Woman's Christian Temperance Union

One such example of these organizations came from the Woman's Christian Temperance Union (WCTU), founded in 1874 in Cleveland, Ohio, which would move on to become one of the most influential women's groups in the 19th-century political landscape. By 1879, the leadership of the WCTU was under Frances Willard, who propelled the group to voice its opinions regarding labor laws, prison reforms, and women's suffrage. However, upon Willard's death in 1898, the group became staunch supporters of prohibition and fell away from the main stem of the women's movement.

Another notable organization that also championed social change was the National American Woman Suffrage Association, which was formed in 1890 with the combination of two former rival groups. The first president, Elizabeth Cady Stanton, sought to show the American public that women deserved the right to vote not because they were equal to men, but different, encompassing other positive traits, such as their maternal instincts and ideals equating political morality. Eventually Stanton fell away from mainstream feminism but is still attributed, along with Susan B. Anthony, with creating the foundation of the women's suffrage movement.

The implications of such organizations are paramount to understanding the social and civil movements of the 20th century. These divisions amongst the population regarding the women's suffrage movement also bring into focus, yet again, the social instability and rivalries seen during this period. Such conditions would inevitably lead to sweeping reforms and laws during the 20th century.

As transcontinental railroads were completed, bringing more settlers west, U.S. military actions, the destruction of the buffalo, the confinement of American Indians to reservations, and assimilationist policies reduced the number of American Indians and threatened native culture and identity.

In order to bring about total westward expansion, the U.S. government supported the creation of a transcontinental railroad that would provide all the resources necessary to settle the West. However, the government was also forced to address the issue of Native American settlements, which had been promised in the earlier 19th century. In order to address the issue of Native American lands, the U.S. government employed barbaric tactics, which included the extermination of the American buffalo, a life source of Native American populations. This coined the phrase "kill the buffalo and you kill the Indians."

Helen Hunt Jackson's work to bring to light the government actions against Native Americans was told in great detail in her book *A Century of Dishonor* (1881). This text perpetuated the concept of assimilation as a common good for the Native American populations, which were all but decimated by the end of the 19th century.

By 1890, all Native American tribes had lost their legal entity status and over two-thirds of their former lands, and they were now living on reservations established by the U.S. government. The implications of such policy decisions were monumental, as the U.S. government effectively eliminated an entire way of life. One so-called positive outcome of the reservation programs was the stabilization of the Native American populations following the devastation of life from ongoing military offensives, explosions of Anglican diseases brought by western settlers, and relocation programs.

Helen Hunt Jackson

However, it is difficult to make an argument for any real benefits of the reservation programs employed by the United States during this period other than the opportunity for white settlers to continue their westward expansion.

Post-Civil War migration to the American West, encouraged by economic opportunities and government policies, caused the federal government to violate treaties with American Indian nations in order to expand the amount of land available to settlers.

As the Civil War came to an end, the West was sparsely populated. There were notable settlements in Texas and lands promised to Native Americans taking up most of Oklahoma and Kansas, but other sections of the West were considered wild and unsettled. This was quickly remedied with the conception of a transcontinental railroad, which would provide the people goods and services necessary for the westward expansions called for by the government. During the 1870s and 1880s, the West grew at an alarming rate, causing many more to settle west of the Mississippi.

By means of the railroad companies and governmental policies, the United States created vast land grants that angered many settlers in the West. Examples of this can be seen throughout the Gilded Age, where disgruntled settlers attacked land grant sites, cutting off railroads and temporarily stalling the progress made by these steam giants. Such opposition did not change the policies of the U.S. government which sought to settle the wild lands of the West at any cost.

As the expansion continued, it seemed inevitable that it would be at the expense of Native American populations, who had been promised lands after being displaced from the East Coast following the initial American expansion of the Atlantic Seaboard. In hopes of bringing an end to Native American aggression, the United States sought to enact several treaties to eliminate coercive actions. These included the Medicine Lodge Treaty signed in 1867, in which the federal government recognized the Great Plains as individual tribal lands allocated by the federal government. Other notable treaties of the period included the Fort Laramie Treaty signed in 1868 which concluded warfare along the Bozeman Trail and promised vast areas of Wyoming, Montana and the Dakota territories, including the Black Hills, to the Lakota people.

Many of these treaties would eventually be violated as the U.S. government failed to secure enough land in the western regions not already promised to the Native American populations. Land grants in the West given to railroad companies greatly influenced this process and would become commonplace along the frontier and in the settled West. Additionally, the practice of land-grant colleges during this period strained the territorial resources available, while also establishing sixty-nine colleges. The Native American and Mexican populations, who believed the U.S. government would expand their territories until all other settlers were expelled and replaced with American frontier men and women, frowned upon the use of such policies, but were powerless to stop them.

The long-term implications for such policies can be seen today, especially in the western portion of the United States, where various Native American tribes maintain their traditions and culture on reservations surrounded by the unfamiliarity of the contemporary United States. Such policies also brought criticism on many Americans both during the period and in later decades; however, policies regarding Native American programs and assistance have not seen much progress.

The competition for land in the West among white settlers, Indians and Mexican Americans led to an increase in violent conflict.

As Americans began their massive westward expansion, it quickly became evident these exploits would be undertaken at the cost of great violence and instability. The Homestead Act in 1862 had given many white settlers the upper hand over Mexican or Native American settlements, which dotted the western landscape.

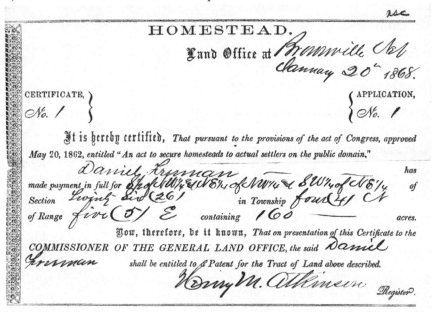

Certificate of the first homestead according to the Homestead Act

At the height of the farming and mining booms of westward expansion, the Great Plains also experienced a period of open range policies. During this period, farmers, cowboys, homesteaders and native populations struggled to maintain boundaries, which culminated in frontier justice such as vigilante courts and killings. Between the 1870s and 1880s, cowboys, ranchers, and farmers embraced the cattle industry with no feeding pattern, which would be unsuccessful and caused the end of open range farming and ranching. By the later 1880s, the Great Plains and unsettled West had been fenced up, which was made possible by Joseph Glidden's invention of barbed wire, causing further conflict as homesteaders settled in new areas already allotted to Mexican and Native American settlements.

Joseph Glidden

Geronimo

Notable acts of violence during the period include those undertaken by Geronimo, an Apache leader who waged guerrilla warfare against American and Mexican settlements in the West; Geronimo surrendered in 1886 at Skeleton Canyon, Arizona. There were also vigilante acts of terror and aggression by Mexican settlers against the railroads and the American working-class settlers. These acts would continue until the end of the 19th century and perpetuated uneasy feelings toward westward American expansion and the Mexican settlers, who had dominated the southwestern portion of the United States for decades.

Such ongoing tensions resulted in a chaotic and unlawful frontier dominated by vigilante justice and countless descriptions of terrible atrocities at the hands of whites, Mexicans and Native Americans alike. These attributes made the Southwest and the Pacific Coast seem like continuous sources of domestic conflict both welcomed and scorned by the American people following the Civil War.

The U.S. government generally responded to American Indian resistance with military force, eventually dispersing tribes onto small reservations and hoping to end American Indian tribal identities through assimilation.

As a result of westward expansion, the American government was again forced to enact domestic policies to address growing concerns over its interactions with Native American populations. In the early part of the 19th century, many Native American tribes had been allowed to remain on their native lands, with intermittent regulation attempts by the U.S. government. By the mid-19th century, the government had changed their policies in an attempt to limit Native American access to land; they enacted the concentration policy, which removed Native American populations from areas white settlers wished to inhabit.

Following the Civil War, regiments of soldiers, most notably those led by Generals William Sherman, P. T. Sheridan, and George Custer, took up military offensives against Native American tribes. The policy of forcefully dispelling resistance was commonplace in the U.S. military during this period and can be seen in the Sioux War (1876–1877) and Nez Perce conflicts, culminating in the battle at Wounded Knee in 1890.

In hopes of maintaining their livelihood and traditions, many Native Americans took up arms against the military forces and called upon their deities in hopes of evading assimilation. One notable example of the resistance movement by Native Americans comes from the Nez Perce tribe, originally located in the Northwest, mainly in Oregon. This tribe, led by Chief Joseph, fought to maintain their lands in Wallowa Valley; however, they were repeatedly engaged by American military forces and were eventually defeated in 1877.

The government initially promised relocation to ancestral lands, but instead placed the remaining tribal members in malaria-infested camps in Kansas and Oklahoma, decimating the population. In order to avoid a similar outcome, many Native Americans began practicing ghost dancing as a means of avoiding forced relocation. On the eve of each new moon, many Native American tribes would practice this ritual, which eventually caused disturbance amongst white settlers. Authorities intervened, causing deaths and further soured relations.

In addition to military confrontation, the U.S. government sought to civilize the Native American populations through assimilation and education. This was first attempted under the Dawes Act of 1887, which granted the U.S. president the authority to allot tribal lands to the heads of households and others, as well as the possibility of U.S. citizenship. While this legislation seemed beneficial to the Native American populations, it obliterated tribal customs and authority, eventually leading to the downfall of Native American culture within the United States.

> **KEY CONCEPT 6.3:** The "Gilded Age" witnessed new cultural and intellectual movements in tandem with political debates over economic and social policies.

The Gilded Age—which ranged from 1876, at the end of Reconstruction, to 1890—was a period of exponential growth and innovation in America. However, accompanying these developments was a great deal of corruption, mainly stemming from government policies and business practices. The tremendous highs of the Gilded Age experienced by the wealthy elites and the economic lows felt by the working classes and new immigrant populations highlighted the stark economic and social differences of the late 19th century.

The Gilded Age is famous for producing many of the modern amenities we appreciate today, including but not limited to the telephone, deliverable electricity and photographic and motion picture technology. Below are some of the most notable inventors of the period:

- Nikola Tesla invented the first motor that transformed alternating current (AC) electrical power into a usable mechanical force.

- Alexander Graham Bell invented the telephone in 1876, which revolutionized communication in America.

- Thomas Edison produced the first record player or phonograph in 1877 and the light bulb in 1879, culminating his lifelong achievements with the establishment of the first direct current (D.C.) electric power station in Manhattan in September of 1882, which propelled electricity throughout businesses and homes in America.

Thomas Edison

In addition to the scientific innovations of the period, America also saw the emergence of industrialized monopolies in the form of railroads and new modern factories. These transformative business practices allowed Americans to propel their economy and production capacities past those of their European rivals. However, the unchecked power and influence of monopolies within the American government also created great dissatisfaction among the working population.

The social and political rivalries prevalent between the working classes, the elites and the management in government during the Gilded Age were the precursors to the social upheavals seen during the late 19th and early 20th centuries. Such social movements and changes in perception among the American population also set the groundwork for economic reforms and the political changes of Progressivism in the 20th century.

The Gilded Age had a substantial impact on the formation of America following the devastating Civil War and leading into the two world wars. Without the industrial advances of the period, America would have lacked the resources necessary to become a world power. The manufacturing and industrial capabilities that emerged during this period laid the infrastructure of the American economy, creating railroads and the surge in factory and manufacturing production that would lead to a more efficient workforce in America.

Gilded Age politics were intimately tied to big business and focused nationally on economic issues—tariffs, currency, corporate expansion, and laissez-faire economic policy—that engendered numerous calls for reform.

The domestic politics of the United States during the Gilded Age focused primarily on economic and social transitions produced as a result of the unregulated markets and the tremendous expansion of the industrial capacities of the factories where the majority of Americans now worked. After years of struggling to subsist in their new urban surroundings, many in the working and immigrant classes began seeing the role of the government as too limited and accommodating of the members of big business.

In regards to corporate expansion, the American public had seen the rise of empire and monopoly in the United States by means of the railroad and steel companies dominated by the Vanderbilt and Rockefeller families. The banking industry of this period had been completely influenced by J. P. Morgan, who stabilized the financial markets many times before finally being defeated by the chaos of the Great Depression. These hands-off policies in the manufacturing, production, and economic sectors would end, for the most part, in the early years of the 20th century.

Tariffs were also an area of concern for many factory workers and consumers during this period, as well as factory and manufacturing owners. While the use of tariffs benefited the owners, it had the opposite effect on consumers, who typically belonged to the working class. The two types of tariffs included revenue tariffs, which fund various agencies, and protective tariffs, which allowed American companies the ability to compete with the prices and services of foreign companies at the expense of the consumer. Such policies were heavily influenced by the business elite and caused division between the management and working classes.

Currency was another topic of interest and contention during this period, causing the further division of Americans, this time into supporters and opponents of soft currency. In 1873, The Fourth Coinage Act was enacted to create the gold standard, which was opposed by those who argued silver was a more logical choice given that the mines were already producing vast silver reserves. This began a new rivalry among those who called for silver backing of currency as opposed to a gold a standard. By 1890, six new states had been acquired in the West and President Harrison was facing ever-mounting pressure to adopt some form of silver backing. In 1890, the Sherman Silver Purchase Act was enacted, requiring the government to purchase various amounts of silver every month to be converted into coins and certificates.

The influence of the currency and tariff debates allowed many Americans to have more direct say in the economic policies of the United States than ever before. With this being said, many Americans, especially the working and farming classes, were adamantly opposed to silver- and gold-backed currency, instead calling for the expansion and circulation of greenbacks, which would supply the currency markets with more money without the backing of gold or silver. Such currency would have also allowed Americans to pay their debts.

Corruption in government—especially as it related to big business—energized the public to demand increased popular control and reform of local, state and national governments, ranging from minor changes to major overhauls of the capitalist system.

Leading up to and during the Gilded Age, many Americans perceived the government's role as one that enforced law and order but stopped short of ensuring the social welfare of the American population. However, this idea began to change in the late 19th century and caused many to embrace new ideas surrounding the regulation of business and corruption by local, state and federal officials.

One notable incident that caused many to support regulation was the American transcontinental railroad scandal, where the Union Pacific and Crédit Mobilier companies had engaged in an interlocking directorate. After further investigation, it was discovered Union Pacific had paid Crédit Mobilier at highly inflated rates, making the supply company rich at the expense of the American public and Union Pacific shareholders.

East and West shaking hands at the laying of the last rail
of the Union Pacific Railroad

The Gilded Age introduced business conglomerates and trusts into a governmental system that was easily manipulated by the leading business people of their day, and this was clearly evident in the political agendas of the late 19th century. While the management and elites became wealthier, the working and immigrant classes struggled to maintain their day-to-day lives, which eventually culminated in the desire for social and political changes.

In seeking these changes, many Americans who lacked support from the government turned to neighborhood and fraternal organizations that were able to provide services to those typically neglected by state and federal institutions. However, as these organizations grew, they became substantially more powerful and were able to influence and infiltrate the political entities of the cities for which they provided services. Such influence and lack of federal or state regulations quickly led to corruption, "under the table" dealings and the establishment of the "good ol' boy" network.

As Americans saw this corruption, now fully integrated within the government system, they began to embrace ideas of socialism, which before had been completely out of the question. Reformers working against machine politics, most notably those embraced by William "Boss" Tweed at Tammany Hall in New York, were able to convince the American population of the need for reforms. These efforts culminated in the passage of the Interstate Commerce Act in 1887, which created the Interstate Commerce Commission, responsible for the federal monitoring of the economic systems.

In addition to the Interstate Commerce Commission, which was the first of its kind, Congress—under President Benjamin Harrison—passed the first of three antitrust laws, which outlawed monopolies and any limiting of trade. Some politicians believed the law was for show and difficult to enforce. The impacts of these calls for reform were monumental for the future of American economic policies, as seen in the Progressive movement and presidents such as Franklin Roosevelt. The ideas, policies, and laws enacted in regards to the economic system of this period foreshadowed the sentiment of the American people until the largest reforms of the New Deal.

Increasingly prominent racist and nativist theories, along with Supreme Court decisions such as *Plessy v. Ferguson*, were used to justify violence as well as local and national policies of discrimination and segregation.

ANOTHER JIM 'CROW CAR CASE.

Arrest of a Negro Traveler Who Persisted in Riding With the White People.

On Tuesday evening a negro named Adolph Plessy was arrested by Private Detective Cain on the East Louisiana train and locked up for violating section 2 of act 111 of 1890, relative to separate coaches.

It appears that Plessy purchased a ticket to Covington, and shortly before his arrest the conductor asked him if he was a colored man. On the latter replying that he was the conductor informed him that he would have to go into the car set aside for colored peopl This he refused to do, and Mr. Ca then stepped up and requested him go into the other coach, but he still re fused, and Mr. Cain thereupon in formed him that he would either have to go or go to jail. He replied that he would sooner go to jail than leave the coach, and was thereupon arrested.

He waived examination yesterday

Article in the Daily Picayune announcing the arrest of (Homer) Adolphe Plessy

Following the end of Reconstruction in 1877, many Americans wondered what freedoms had really been gained following the end of the Civil War. While many African Americans had found new opportunities in the northern cities, African Americans in the South faced an exponentially long road to real equality. This was the case for all minority groups, including but not limited to the Chinese as well as southern and eastern European immigrants.

As a result of Reconstruction, many southerners wondered what emancipation would look like. It was quickly realized that the South looked very similar, especially in terms of racism, as it had before the Civil War. One such example, which would have explosive implications in the future, was the *Plessy v. Ferguson* case, where the Supreme Court ruled in favor of segregation, coining the idea "separate but equal." Such examples highlight the rampant racism still evident in the 20th century.

Other sources of discrimination came in the form of religion, and as Protestants and Catholics took aggressive actions against one another, such events culminated in the creation of the American Protective Association (APA) in 1887. The founder, Henry Bowers, was a Mason and used his connections to forge great political influence. The APA quickly grew into a popular organization, while also highlighting what some would later call Protestant Paranoia. As a result of the 1893 economic crisis, the APA attracted thousands of new members and eventually, the group claimed over one million members.

During this period, many Americans embodied a sense of nativism, which was increasingly evident as immigrants continued to migrate in waves throughout the late 19th century. As these new immigrants settled into American society, many connected themselves with other nationalities who were also recent or first-generation immigrants and created transplant communities referred to as "Little Italy" or "Little Hungary." These communities fed the tensions and violence between nativists and immigrants. Such interactions would continue into the 20th century and highlight the beginnings of the anti-immigration sentiment maintained by the American public for many years.

In response to the massive influx of immigrants, the U.S. government passed the Chinese Exclusion Act in 1882, which stopped the immigration of all skilled and unskilled Chinese immigrants for ten years. This act was expanded in 1888 with the Scott Act, which banned re-entry into the United States after visiting China, regardless of legal status. Such actions greatly soured the relationship between the United States and China until 1943, when the immigration ban was lifted in hopes of garnering support for the war against Japan from Chinese nationals. However, further discrimination and oppression limited many Chinese from immigrating after the anti-immigration legislation of the 19th century.

The immigration restrictions imposed during this period highlight a change in thinking from the marginal acceptance of immigrants in the early and mid-19th century to the complete denial of further immigration during the late 19th century, coinciding with the rise in nativism and Nationalism. These movements continued to influence both domestic and foreign affairs for America leading into the 20th century, and they caused many Americans to claim racial superiority over other ethnicities. Such an attitude can be seen in the legislation passed during the Red Scare as well as the World War II internment camps used to hold thousands of Japanese Americans.

New cultural and intellectual movements both buttressed and challenged the social order of the Gilded Age.

Urbanization, which began during the Gilded Age, caused many to make social and economic transitions and inspired concern in those who worked to maintain the traditional customs with which they were comfortable. Some of the challenges faced during this period included the decline in popular religion, most notably in Protestantism, which caused many to fear the American public was becoming immoral. While many were concerned with the spiritual and social ramifications of such a trend, others saw the financial concerns associated with a declining membership base. However, the working class, particularly the factory workers, saw no need to attend church in light of their unprecedented work hours.

Some see the Gilded Age as an American Renaissance, as the American public experienced new forms of art, literature, and standards of living. In a wealthy American home of the period, one could expect to find the latest tapestries and stained-glass lighting from Louis Comfort Tiffany, a popular company of the period. Americans sought new types of literature, most notably from Mark Twain, including *Huckleberry Finn* (1885) and *Tom Sawyer* (1876). Popular poets of the period included Walt Whitman and Emily Dickinson. Painting also blossomed during the Gilded Age, and many were engrossed in the paintings of Winslow Homer, who gained fame after his publications in *Harper's Weekly*.

Mark Twain

The intellectual movements of the period highlighted a new way of thinking developed during the Gilded Age but also demonstrated the shortcomings of the period, such as racial and ethnic discrimination and gender and social inequality. The literature of the period speaks to these concerns and gives insight into the common perceptions of racism and industry following the end of the Civil War. The arts of this period also gave people hope following the Civil War, which was generally in very short supply. Culture of this period was seen as a bonus to the industrial and manufacturing initiatives of big business.

Cultural and intellectual arguments justified the success of those at the top of the socioeconomic structure as both appropriate and inevitable, even as some leaders argued that the wealthy had some obligation to help the less fortunate.

As the success of the Gilded Age continued, some argued that in light of the wealthy class' success and status within the political and social systems, they should be required to support those less fortunate. Others argued the current condition was as it was meant to be, designed with a class structure in mind and predetermined social statuses, which would inevitably lead to the right people exercising power. Such division regarding social issues highlighted the tensions and polarization of the American public leading into the 20th century.

Henry George

Leading intellectuals of the day debated the social formula necessary for creating a productive and sustainable America. One such person was Henry George, who held vocations in many areas including but not limited to writing, politics, and economics. Through his studies, George proposed the concept of a "single tax" which would be placed on all land at the undeveloped price. This tax would fund the projects required of the U.S. government without the limiting effect of other taxes levied such as income or agricultural taxes. George embodied both economic and socialistic motives, arguing that by creating land as a common property the taxes levied against it would create the funding necessary to maintain the economic models of the period.

Andrew Carnegie also shared this idea of required actions by those in economic and political positions of power regarding the protection of the lower social classes. In his famous essay, *Gospel of Wealth,* Carnegie makes the argument that successful entrepreneurs of the Gilded Age have the ability and obligation to eliminate poverty in a capitalistic society. Through philanthropy, the American society could be transformed to highlight the common and public good, rather than the opportunistic landscape seen in the cities.

Others argued against the concept of social welfare, stating that the natural order of this period was determined in the social classes, with some destined to rule and manage while others were meant to work and supply the factories. Social Darwinism, introduced in the 1870s, had influenced many to believe evolution had selected those most fit to rule. This theory was expanded upon by some American elites of the period in regards to the right to influence the political landscape.

Theories of racial superiority were also extremely influential in the early years of the 20th century and were used by Nazi Germany as support for their campaign of racial cleansing. While the theory was not employed on this level in the United States, it was applied to the Native American populations, which were viewed by many as a lesser species of human compared to the Anglo-Americans. During this period, it was common to seek the affirmation of political or social ambitions through new forms of social science, such as Darwinist and racist theories.

A number of critics challenged the dominant corporate ethic in the United States and sometimes capitalism itself, offering alternate visions of the good society through utopianism and the Social Gospel.

As intellectuals of the period struggled to conceptualize the transitions of the Gilded Age, many turned to utopian viewpoints, which were wildly popular amongst Nationalists, Populists, and Socialists. One such advocate of utopian America was Edward Bellamy, most famous for his work *Looking Backward, 2000–1887* (1888), which inspired many utopian settlements in the 1890s. Bellamy's work spurred the new concept of Nationalism, which, according to the book, can create a state with a perfectly functioning nationalized industrial sector, equal class structures and equal distribution of wealth.

In 1888, Bellamy also founded the Bellamy Nationalists Clubs, which spread his message of evolutionary-led transitions into utopian Nationalism. The works of Bellamy highlight the superbly utopian models of government and politics following the radical transition from Victorian-era policies into the more progressive ideas of the Gilded Age. While many initially supported the movement, membership waned and by the mid-1890s had all but expired. Other critics of capitalism emerged but were typically silenced, leaving many to embrace other movements such as Populism.

In addition to intellectual debates, many spiritual leaders of this period were concerned with the transition in popular religion seen in America. As factory workers adapted to their urban lives, many became less interested in religion or membership in church organizations. In response to such changes, the Social Gospel grew and tried to adapt the teachings of the Bible to contemporary issues. Many church leaders took up social causes as well; one of the most notable examples being Washington Gladden's support of the right to strike and his fight against child labor.

In hopes of addressing urban issues, churches created organizations such as the Young Men's Christian Association and the Young Women's Christian Association, which were aimed at revitalizing religion among the younger populations. Such transitions have been labeled by some as the Third Great Awakening of religion in America, which was a direct result of the urbanization of the period.

The Social Gospel and other utopian movements can be seen as a direct result of the abundant social transitions taking place during this period. As Americans struggled to find their place in an ever-evolving market and social structure, it became clear that some Americans longed for the traditional Victorian values of the early 19th century. Others looked to the future, which was full of social and economic transformation, overflowing with new opportunity and innovation.

Challenging their prescribed "place," women and African American activists articulated alternative visions of political, social and economic equality.

As many struggled with the social transitions of the Gilded Age, minority groups such as women and African Americans attempted to achieve the equality and opportunities promised to all Americans. Booker T. Washington, who was born a slave, worked tirelessly throughout his life to garner better funding for African American education, as well as overall equality for African Americans following the Civil War.

Booker T. Washington

In 1881, Washington founded the Tuskegee Institute in Alabama, which was dedicated to the education of teachers and the advancement of this vocation in an industrial economy. Washington would go on to advise the federal government on matters of education and create the National Negro Business League in 1901. During a time of great racial tension and uncertainty, Booker T. Washington advanced the rights of African Americans by means of accommodation to a place of conversation within the political system, which would lead to the civil rights movements of the 20th century.

Ida Wells-Barnett, who was also born a slave, was a critical member of the early civil rights struggles experienced during this period. Wells-Barnett worked in various capacities, such as social activism and writing, in hopes of shedding light on the white violence still experienced in this period by African Americans, specifically the practice of lynching. In 1896, with the help of her husband, Wells-Barnett organized the National Association of Colored Women, which opposed the accommodating tactics proposed by Booker T. Washington while fighting for equality in terms of race and gender.

Another notable activist concerned with the advancement of women's suffrage and civil rights in this period was Elizabeth Cady Stanton, who formed the National Woman Suffrage Association in 1870. Stanton was the front-runner of the women's suffrage movement, advocating more liberal divorce laws and the reproductive rights of women. Though Stanton was influential in the early part of the women's movement, she became more detached by the 1890s and was less in tune with mainstream perceptions and opinions. However, Stanton's work would eventually culminate in the passage of the Nineteenth Amendment, giving women the universal right to vote.

All of these activists greatly influenced the civil rights movements of their own period, as well as future periods of history, inevitably setting the foundation of future civil rights advancements. Such work was undeniable in achieving the advancements experienced by minorities and women in this period and led to further ambitions of women's suffrage and equal pay.

Please, leave your Customer Review on Amazon

PERIOD 7

1890-1945

An increasingly pluralistic United States faced profound domestic and global challenges, debated the proper degree of government activism and sought to define its international role.

Major historical events of the period:

1898 – Spanish-American War
1903-1914 – Panama Canal
1917-1918 – World War I (American involvement)
1919-1920 – Red Scare
1920 – Nineteenth Amendment
1920s – Harlem Renaissance
1920-1933 – Prohibition
1929-1939 – Great Depression
1941 – Attack on Pearl Harbor
1941-1945 – World War II (American involvement)
1945 – Atomic bombings of Hiroshima and Nagasaki

PERIOD 7: 1890-1945

> **KEY CONCEPT 7.1:** Governmental, political and social organizations struggled to address the effects of large-scale industrialization, economic uncertainty and related social changes such as urbanization and mass migration.

Following the industrial boom of the Gilded Age, which spanned from 1870 to 1900, the federal government decided to reevaluate its former laissez-faire business policies. Instead of continuing this hands-off approach, both state and national institutions began implementing more regulatory measures, falling in line with the public opinion surrounding monopolies and the desire for the government to intervene on behalf of the populace. These economic transitions, coupled with a mass explosion of urbanization, compelled many Americans to transform their day-to-day activities, which incited rivalries within the social and political classes.

In the late 19th century, the United States also saw an agricultural transition to farmers producing crops more efficiently with a smaller labor force. This smaller labor force was due to: 1) new technology (such as the steam-powered tractor) that increased efficiency; 2) increased difficulty hiring workers, due to mass urbanization and the increase of opportunities and wages created by capitalism for the average person; and 3) industrial projects that were beginning to dominate the American landscape. An explosion in industrial production and the need for unskilled workers caused a massive influx of immigrants. From 1890 to 1920, the United States admitted approximately fifteen million people. During this period, the immigration patterns were predicated on the flow of the economy; in times of prosperity immigration rose, and in times of crisis it stalled.

Hungarian immigrants celebrating the sunflower harvest in Cleveland

These years of growing immigration also spurred social unrest, as many Americans embodied a strong sense of Nationalism and were opposed to the acceptance of "new immigrants." Unlike their predecessors, these new immigrants came mainly from China or southern and eastern Europe, were typically poor and lacked any type of schooling. Furthermore, many continued to practice their old-world traditions and were less interested in assimilation, causing social tensions with some native-born Americans.

All social classes in the United States experienced the impacts of large-scale industrialization and urbanization. The elites became wealthier, maintaining a strong grip on domestic policies, while the working class was able to experience more varied vocational opportunities and an improved quality of living. However, the economic instability leading into and culminating with the Great Depression altered the spirit of the American public, causing many to question the safety and supervision being provided by the government.

In addition to economic turmoil, the American public also struggled with its own perception of massive migrations in the late 19th and early 20th centuries. While some welcomed the unskilled labor forces, particularly from Latin American countries, many others supported anti-immigration policies, again leading to escalated tensions among various social groups.

The continued growth and consolidation of large corporations transformed American society and the nation's economy, promoting urbanization and economic growth, even as business cycle fluctuations became increasingly severe.

President Harrison

The boom years of the Gilded Age brought about periods of great prosperity, research and invention; however, these same trends created monopolies and caused a transition in economic policies and schools of thought. As Americans experienced these economic changes as well as the volatility in the economy in that period, some perceived the attitudes of the bankers and industrialists to be reckless and demanded expanded government involvement and oversight.

In 1890, President Harrison took the first step with the passage of the Sherman Anti-Trust Act. Subsequent presidents added greatly to these progressive policies, such as the Hepburn Act (1906, Roosevelt) and the Clayton Anti-Trust Act (1914, Wilson). Most significant of all, though, was a campaign against both cronyism and monopolies which earned Theodore Roosevelt the name "Teddy the Trust Buster." In this period, Roosevelt used the Sherman Anti-Trust Act and the Federal courts to break up forty-five trusts, such as J. P. Morgan's Northern Securities Company, Standard Oil and U.S. Steel. President Taft confronted another seventy-five major monopolies.

These changes coupled with the rapid urbanization that followed the booming industrial periods caused many transitions in the social norms of America. As urban dwellers began earning higher wages and a middle class emerged, the new expectation of city life included department stores, banks, insurance companies, and corporate headquarters. This widespread rapid urbanization culminated in domestic economic growth and pitted traditionalists, like farmers and agrarians, against industrialists, who saw the future of America in cities and factories.

Such polarization would come to embody this period of transition, as many Americans sought new job opportunities, a change in the accepted economic class structures and a different form of government than had previously been seen. However, not all Americans embraced this sentiment of change. Many traditionalists argued for a return to the roaring prosperity and cultural expectations that had accompanied the early years of the 20th century.

Large corporations came to dominate the U.S. economy as it increasingly focused on the production of consumer goods, driven by new technologies and manufacturing techniques.

By 1894, the United States ranked first in manufacturing nations across the world, proving that a great transformation from an agrarian-based society to industrialization had certainly taken place. The key players in the later years of the Gilded Age, such as Rockefeller and J. P. Morgan, continued to influence economic and industrial affairs, though on a more restricted level, as seen in the progressive presidencies of Roosevelt, Taft, and Wilson. This influence saw continued decline leading into the World Wars and following the Great Depression. The desire of many Americans for a stronger policy against monopolies and trusts dominated the landscape leading up to this period.

The manufacturing sector was being enhanced with new technology, implementing mass production techniques that allowed companies to produce high-quality goods at a much faster rate. Given this new technology, factories could lower costs while maximizing profits. As a result of such efficient operations and an artificially high money supply, many companies produced more goods than could be sold, resulting in a saturation of the market and economic chaos. This oversupply also explains why industrialists were so interested in expanding into foreign markets in the Western Hemisphere.

President Taft

This industrial transition shed light on the widening class gap seen since the beginning of the Industrial Revolution of the 19th century. This contrast in wealth caused some to be concerned with a class war, while those that had traditionally been the elites of society were displeased with the rise in the "nouveau riche," or new rich. This created a new social rivalry characteristic of the social tensions being developed in the late 19th and early 20th centuries. Small business owners and farmers also saw the monopoly of big corporations as a negative and worked with local and federal legislators to limit the size and influence of such entities.

These corporations also held great political influence regarding foreign policy. Evidence of this is seen in the tactics used by President Taft and others who tried to infiltrate the foreign markets of the Western Hemisphere, creating an intense U.S. hegemony. Following the World Wars, this unipolarity would continue giving the United States an upper hand in many international affairs regarding both economic and political futures of the global system.

The United States continued its transition from a rural, agricultural society to an urban, industrial one, offering new economic opportunities for women, internal immigrants and international migrants who continued to flock to the United States.

As the American population began its transition from rural to urban, many new sectors of employment opened to new demographic groups, including immigrants, minorities, and women. These new opportunities, coupled with global instability, caused many to see immigration to the United States as a way to become successful and financially secure. The development of cities created new job markets. By the end of the 1890s, close to one million women had transitioned into the workforce, holding various positions as bookkeepers, telephone operators, secretaries, and seamstresses.

Most working women were unmarried and came from lower-class backgrounds, while socially acceptable vocations for upper- and middle-class women included teaching and nursing. This initial explosion in women entering the workforce set the groundwork for further vocational advances, both during the World Wars and in the following years. Once women had begun to earn better wages and hold stable jobs, they were determined to maintain these advancements and continue to fight for further recognition and equality.

This urban boom, which had created leisure time and a middle class, was driven by theological ideas, including expansion and a new American dream. Highlighted by Horatio Alger, the concept that hard work, rather than divine intervention or status, leads to success, garnered support among many in the working classes. This vision also embodied the ideals of many Americans entering into the early 20th century who wished to work for themselves and create their own versions of an urban paradise.

Horatio Alger

Immigrants and international migrants were also able to seek work in industrial and urban settings; however, many suffered workplace abuses and continued discrimination. This xenophobia caused increased tensions between native-born Americans and the massive influx of immigrants seen between 1890 and 1920. This negative perception of immigration did not lessen the number of immigrants hoping and willing to settle in America to make a more prosperous future for themselves and their families. These new vocational opportunities were the precursors for the advancement of women and minority groups seen during the war years. These transitions were instrumental in beginning the conversation of the women's and civil rights movements of the latter part of the 20th century.

Even as economic growth continued, episodes of credit and market instability, most critically the Great Depression, led to calls for the creation of a stronger financial regulatory system.

The economic uncertainties of the late 19th century and early 20th centuries can be seen as a precursor to the economic collapse of the Great Depression. Many who engaged in the markets and economic sector had experienced periods of depression and crisis leading up to the 1930s. One such example came in 1893 when the United States experienced a great period of economic depression and was only stabilized following drastic intervention by financial giant J. P. Morgan.

In 1907, J. P. Morgan was again called upon to stabilize a failed attempt at Wall Street speculation. At this point, the conservative school of thought, coupled with powerful "money trusts," dominated big eastern cities and adamantly opposed the progressive movement. However, some Americans had begun supporting progressive ideas and questioning the lack of government supervision in the stock market and banking sectors, with some calling for a central banking system.

These bouts of instability would continue, eventually leading into the Great Depression. By the 1930s, banking and industrial magnates such as J. P. Morgan were unable to buy out the American economy as they had previously done, leaving many in the public to place their support, criticism, and expectation with the federal government rather than the private businesses which had previously dominated the markets.

This was a pivotal moment for the financial and economic mindset of Americans and would be transformative in the years following the Depression. Some economic reforms had a drastic influence on banking following the Great Depression and moving into the later years of the 20th century, and they arguably molded the financial mindset of many Americans today concerning regulations and oversight. Most notable among these policies was the Regulatory Bank Act (1933), signed by President Franklin Roosevelt.

The economic instability of the early 20th century also highlighted the political polarization between progressives and conservatives; a battle that would continue into the late 1930s and beyond. This series of events also highlights how many times the United States toed the line of economic collapse before finally faltering in the Great Depression.

Progressive reformers responded to economic instability, social inequality, and political corruption by calling for government intervention in the economy, expanded democracy, greater social justice and conservation of natural resources.

Those who supported the progressive movement held the government responsible for the oversight of many sectors, most notably the economy, the environment and the workplace abuse of the early 20th century. In order to achieve the transition from a formerly conservative ruling structure to one based on progressive principles, politicians and American citizens alike championed efforts towards improved working conditions, better pay, more responsible and stable economic policies and maintenance of our national wonders and resources. This movement, supported by progressive presidents Roosevelt, Taft, and Wilson, was a transition from the conservative voices of the Gilded Age into a more progressive period.

In addition to economic and political supervision, the progressive reformers also sought to maintain, protect and enhance our natural resources and environment. This was a newer concept and an effective tool of employment in the New Deal policies by means of mandated projects such as the completion of the Hoover Dam in the 1930s and other jobs pertaining to the National Park Service. These environmental policies were instrumental in the creation and expansion of the current parks system we see today.

Hoover Dam site

In the late 1890s and the early years of the 20th century, journalists and progressive reformers—largely urban and middle class, and often female—worked to reform existing social and political institutions at the local, state and federal levels by creating new organizations aimed at addressing social problems associated with an industrial society.

As women and minority groups began expanding their roles in the economy and politics, it quickly became evident that social and political abuses were ongoing, causing many to take up their causes with local and federal organizations. The National American Woman Suffrage Association (NAWSA) was formed in 1890, which was the culmination of previously formed groups working towards the goal of women's suffrage.

Elizabeth Cady Stanton and Susan B. Anthony shared the presidency and worked tirelessly for women's rights. A few years later, Alice Paul—also working towards suffrage by different and sometimes more aggressive means, such as White House pickets and hunger strikes—founded the National Woman's Party. By 1910, most western states had granted partial suffrage rights to women, though the South and Northeast were in

Alice Paul

firm opposition to such a political transition. By August 1920, the Nineteenth Amendment had finally been signed into law by President Wilson, giving women the right to vote.

Minority groups, specifically African Americans, were also working together to be treated equally in 20th-century America. The Niagara Movement was a first attempt at national equality for African Americans. Though many whites labeled the movement as extremist, many educated African Americans saw a commonality in its theology. In 1909, four years after the Niagara Movement began, the National Association for the Advancement of Colored People (NAACP) was founded. The goal of the NAACP was the improvement of the public perception and self-image of African Americans while guaranteeing them an equal footing on the American stage.

These organizations and institutions became fundamental components of America following this period and would begin the civil rights conversation which peaked in the 1960s and 1970s. Without these grassroots efforts, many minority groups, including African Americans and women, would not have been adequately represented.

Progressives promoted federal legislation to regulate abuses of the economy and the environment, and many sought to expand democracy.

The progressive movement was in full swing by the early 20th century and climaxed with the passage of the Federal Reserve Act in December 1913. The new, hotly debated law called for compromise between the interests of the private banking sector and the popular sentiment, which was achieved through the creation of a decentralized bank. President Woodrow Wilson saw this law as a compromise between the progressive and conservative schools of thought.

The creation of the Federal Reserve Bank, as directed by the Federal Reserve Act, was instrumental in bringing stability to the economic crises of the period; however, it has also had lasting implications for the financial well-being of the United States. In 1914, President Wilson signed into law the Clayton Antitrust Act, which limited unlawful restraints and monopolies, exclusive sales contracts, local price cutting and interlocking directorates in corporations valued at $1 million or more in the same field. The progressive movement was making clear strides away from the former economic policies of the Gilded Age.

Florence Kelley

During this period, many were also concerned about the environment as well as with social exploitation in the workplace. In 1916, President Wilson created the National Park Service, which oversaw thirty-five national parks and monuments and maintained the beauty of America for future generations. Florence Kelley, born in Philadelphia in 1859, was a renowned social and political reformer who had a substantial influence on the regulation of workplace abuses. Kelley advocated for the improved treatment of women, children and factory workers, the implementation of an eight-hour workday and the protection of wages.

National, state and local reformers responded to economic upheavals, laissez-faire capitalism, and the Great Depression by transforming the United States into a limited welfare state.

The instability of markets in the late 19th and early 20th centuries, coupled with the disparity of the Great Depression, caused many American citizens to question the banking system. The lack of federal supervision embodied the former laissez-faire business policies of the 1920s leading into the economic crisis. In response to the economic instability, many progressive presidents such as Theodore Roosevelt began to transition the U.S. model away from capitalism, towards more of a welfare state that supported the needy and maintained economic norms during periods of crisis. Examples of such policies are highlighted by the New Deal, passed under later President Franklin Roosevelt. The spirit of Progressivism was championed by Presidents Roosevelt, Taft and Wilson.

The progressive school of thought argues that former laissez-faire economic policies and social Darwinist theories are intellectually incorrect; President Wilson went so far as to label these ideals as morally and intellectually unjust. Progressives also claimed that the government and the populace have the ability to right what they perceived as "wrongs" of the free market. Such ideas were perpetuated by their predecessor movements, including the populist movement, which laid the groundwork for social change.

The long-lasting implications of the progressive movement can be seen in today's social programs. It also highlights a transition in the thinking surrounding the role of the federal government in times of crisis and prosperity. Such ideals can still be seen today; notable examples were seen in the most recent economic crisis of 2008, where the federal government bailed out banks and assisted average Americans with maintaining financial health.

The liberalism of President Franklin Roosevelt's New Deal drew on earlier progressive ideas and represented a multifaceted approach to both the causes and effects of the Great Depression, using government power to provide relief to the poor, stimulate recovery and reform the American economy.

President Franklin Delano Roosevelt pursued a domestic agenda that placed the needs of the people ahead of a balanced or limited federal budget, especially during the Great Depression. In order to bring stability to the American economy, Roosevelt's first act as president was to place the banks on a four-day holiday. After the banking sector stabilized, his next task was to put people back to work in any way possible. His first request of Congress in 1933 was the passage of the Unemployment Relief Act, which created the Civilian Conservation Corps (CCC).

This Civilization Conservation Corps was responsible for employing, housing and feeding young men who were able to support their families from their earnings in the program. To support families and unemployed adults, Congress passed the Federal Emergency Relief Act (FERA), funding state works and welfare programs with an additional $3 billion. Farmers and homeowners received aid by means of the Agricultural Adjustment Act (AAA) and Home Owners' Loan Corporation (HOLC), which delayed foreclosures and repossession of farms.

Whether or not New Deal policies mitigated the Great Depression is a subject of continuing debate. The prevailing assumption among historians has always been that these interventionist policies were a success. But recently, some historians have argued the opposite. They argue that these policies actually forestalled a natural return to full employment by artificially inflating wages and prices and that World War II actually ended the depression with the immense production of war goods.

President Franklin Delano Roosevelt

To further supplement these programs, Roosevelt promoted the Tennessee Valley Authority (TVA), which became a great success and a model for future mandated projects. He also promoted the Federal Housing Administration (FHA) and National Recovery Administration (NRA), which addressed both short- and long-term concerns stemming from the economic crisis. At the same time, these policies supported the average American citizen by creating a minimum wage and maximum work hours, enhancing Roosevelt's appeal to more voters.

Roosevelt's most notable New Deal policy was the creation of the Works Progress Administration (WPA), which employed nearly 8.5 million people and created jobs through various projects including the building of bridges, public buildings, parks, roads, and airports. Additionally, subgroups of the WPA, such as the Professional Projects Division, employed women and men in federal art, theater, music and writers' projects.

The implications of the New Deal policies are vast and transformative; some argue that without these social reforms the U.S. economy may not have emerged as strongly following World War II. This, in turn, would have brought into question the dominant role it played in international affairs during the postwar and Cold War eras. New Deal programs, such as the FDIC, SEC and the Social Securities Act all set the future expectations of government assistance programs. These policies also transitioned the voting demographics of the Civil War Era; minority groups who had previously voted Republican due to President Abraham Lincoln now saw themselves more appropriately represented by the Democratic Party, a sentiment which evolved and transitioned in the years following the New Deal.

Radical, union and Populist movements pushed Roosevelt toward more extensive reforms, even as conservatives in Congress and the Supreme Court sought to limit the New Deal's scope.

The farmers and agrarian populations faced difficult times leading into and during the Great Depression; many were unable to pay the rents or mortgages maintained by East Coast financiers, leaving them hopelessly indebted to the banking sector following the collapse of the stock market. In hopes of having their concerns managed, many farmers joined the Populist movement, which originated in the 1890s as the result of a revolt led by farmers against Democrats and Republicans who had previously ignored these growing concerns.

The rural Populist movement had its roots in the Grange movement, which published a list of demands and grievances called the "Farmers' Platform" in 1857, which was directly influenced by the work of Karl Marx. Some of their grievances centered on the lending practices of East Coast banks, resentment towards the emergence of railroad monopolies, and the technological transition taking place as a result of industrial and urbanization booms.

In addition to the Populists, union movements propelled workers' rights and representation to the forefront of domestic politics. The American Federation of Labor (AFL), a notable union organization of the period, was concerned with the economic prosperity and advancement of its members. The union was spearheaded by immigrant cigar maker Samuel Gompers from 1886 until his death in 1924.

Roosevelt and his liberal politicians sought to limit the economic catastrophe of the Great Depression by means of the New Deal policies. However, conservatives met the administration with great pushback. Such resistance was seen in the judicial rulings of the Supreme Court during this period. In 1934, Congress passed the Frazier-Lemke Farm Bankruptcy Act, ordering the postponement of mortgage foreclosures for five years, but the Supreme Court struck down the law shortly thereafter.

In *Butler v. the United States* in 1935, the Supreme Court ruled that the government had collected taxes in an unconstitutional manner when trying to manage the agricultural markets. Roosevelt faced further pushback from the Supreme Court in the *Schechter* case, ruling that the government had exceeded its authority regarding the regulation of local business with no interstate connections.

The 1935 assassination of Huey Long, a radical populist and opponent of big business and Wall Street, illustrated the polarized political climate Franklin D. Roosevelt and the American population faced following the Great Depression. Many felt the government should enact policies that protected small farmers against the devastating instability of the Depression and later the disparity of the agricultural disaster of the Dust Bowl.

Huey Long on the cover of Time

Although the New Deal did not completely overcome the Depression, it left a legacy of reforms and agencies that endeavored to make society and individuals more secure, and it helped foster a long-term political realignment in which many ethnic groups, African Americans and working-class communities identified with the Democratic Party.

In addition to supporting the public through means of social programs, Franklin D. Roosevelt and his administration also sought to reform the economic sector, especially the stock market and banking industry following the chaotic periods of growth and decline in the early 20th century. Examples of this are the previously mentioned four-day bank holiday and the Emergency Banking Bill of 1933.

In hopes of limiting the continued outpouring of capital, Roosevelt gave the banks a reprieve, while at the same time using his "fireside chats" on the radio to bolster the perception of bank security and encourage Americans to keep their money in the bank instead of under the mattress. This stabilized the banking sector and eventually led to the Glass-Steagall Act and the creation of the Federal Deposit Insurance Corporation (FDIC). Such financial policies as the FDIC have been instrumental in ensuring the integrity of the bank sector for millions of Americans, both following the Depression and in the future.

In an attempt to create further reforms, Roosevelt saw to the creation of the Securities and Exchange Commission (SEC) in 1934, which oversaw and regulated all stock market trading, creating an equal footing for all investors. Leading into the Depression, many traders and anxious investors began pulling stocks to maintain their high prices. This mass exodus from the stock market manifested in a domino effect, causing further panic and market collapse in October 1929. As shareholders continued to sell their stock, the market plummeted, and between October and December 1929, the market had lost $40 billion in value. Many hoped that with the creation of federal supervision by means of the SEC, this type of trading would be limited in the future.

One of the more notable reforms of Roosevelt's New Deal is the Social Security Act of 1935. This law created a government-sponsored insurance for the disabled, dependent children, retirees and the unemployed. Again, this is an example of a policy with both short- and long-term benefits. Many conservatives opposed the passage of the Social Security Act, labeling it as an unsustainable form of socialism.

> **KEY CONCEPT 7.2:** A revolution in communications and transportation technology helped to create a new mass culture and spread "modern" values and ideas, even as cultural conflicts between groups increased under the pressure of migration, world wars and economic distress.

The evolution of communication and transportation technology drove home the appeal many Americans found in the urbanization movement during the early 20th century. Improved roads, bridges and automobiles allowed many upper- and middle-class workers to commute into big cities like New York and Philadelphia. Indoor plumbing and electricity caused many immigrants to see New York and other booming cities as utopian versions of 20th-century dwellings. The explosion of the telegraph allowed Americans to communicate much faster, all while propelling the desire for bigger and more efficient urban cities, which Americans believed would be the key to success in the transitioning international system.

This population influx caused escalated tensions between native-born Americans and immigrants; the Populist movement and monopolies; conservatives and progressives; and isolationists and interventionists. Sources of contention in this period also included the transition of women away from the traditionalist mindset of the 19th century and the vilification of alcohol by the prohibition movement. Great tensions caused many Americans to rally against others and call for the expulsion of anything that might tarnish the perception of traditional America.

1888 Prohibition poster

These advancements changed the perception of a happy life in America to one that included better wages and modern ideas and values. However, this new period was not free of conflict or tension. The lingering issues of racism, anti-immigration sentiments, and economic uncertainties caused many Americans to yearn for a more peaceful time. Examples of this change in perception can be seen most in the cultural movements of the period, including jazz, literature, flappers, and consumerism.

This would all be drastically altered following the onset of World War I when economic stresses coupled with wartime policies caused many Americans to doubt the prosperity of the early 20th century and turn to a pattern of isolationism. These concerns would only be reaffirmed with the outbreak of World War II, when Americans once again realized they would be engaged in conflict within the European theater, regardless of their isolationist mindset.

New technologies led to social transformations that improved the standard of living for many while contributing to increased political and cultural conflicts.

The new technologies of the early 20th century led to many social transitions, including the mass urbanization of the American population, which drastically changed the standard of living. The introduction of electricity, indoor plumbing, and more reliable transportation gave many urban dwellers a higher quality of life within the city establishment. Shopping became a popular pastime for both women and men. Traditionalists who favored America's past were irritated by the mass wave of urbanization and industrialization and argued for renewed investment in agriculture.

The accessibility of news also transformed the landscape of the early 20th century, allowing Americans the ability to obtain information on more topics than ever before. However, sensationalism and yellow journalism quickly emerged, using media spin and bias in hopes of forming public opinion, whether regarding the Spanish Civil War or the best car to buy. The *Saturday Evening Post* and *Ladies Home Journal* began reaching more women and rural readers, fostering a sense of American Nationalism and connectedness between the rural and urban populations.

New technologies contributed to improved standards of living, greater personal mobility, and better communication systems.

Following the industrial and manufacturing booms in the first years of the 20th century, Henry Ford revolutionized the American dream by making it possible for many to own an automobile. By 1913, Ford had perfected the assembly line and was able to pay his workers five dollars per day, causing panic amongst others in the industry, as they did not want to pay their workers that much. Such practices were certainly not the industry standard but gave many workers the desire to seek better employment.

By 1924, Ford was selling the Model T for less than $290 and, with the industrial efficiency of the assembly line, a car was being produced every ten seconds. The introduction of the car also impacted the social norms of the period, and couples and families used the car to enjoy road trips and vacations, which later became an American pastime.

Model T Ford being used for fishing, 1913

Americans also loved the mass introduction of the radio. Initially, this technology was meant for navigation and scientific discoveries rather than consumerism. However, by the early 20th century, Americans had developed a love affair with their new source of information, though it was cut short when many nations cut radio use upon entering into World War I. Americans again tuned in, following the end of the conflict, and during World War II they used the radio as a means of gathering and passing information. A notable example of the radio's popularity during this period is the "fireside chats" started by President Roosevelt during his term in office.

Americans citizens also began recognizing new heroes in American culture, such as Charles Lindbergh and Babe Ruth, reflecting an improved standard of living that allowed time for leisure activities and research into popular sciences of the time. This was also the first time Americans became overwhelmingly interested in cinema and movie stars. The motion picture industry had been relatively unknown leading up to World War I, but popularity soon engulfed the industry and allowed for the release of *The Jazz Singer* in 1927. It was the first "talkie" film, marking the end of silent movies. The motion picture industry was dominated by Paramount, MGM and Warner Brothers, which arguably created another monopoly that would greatly influence the war efforts in WWII and the consumer culture of Americans in the 20th century.

Poster for The Jazz Singer

Other notable technological advancements that improved the standard of living in America during the 20th century include the introduction of theme parks in major cities and the introduction of vaudeville productions, which traveled the country, appealing to lower-class Americans as a form of cheap entertainment. These improvements speak to the transition of the quality of life from the mid-19th century into the 20th century. Previously, families were preoccupied with the struggle of day-to-day life, with little time for leisure activities. By creating expanded job opportunities and encompassing a more diverse workforce, industrialists, using technology, enabled many Americans to pursue dreams and ambitions previously unattainable.

Technological change, modernization and changing demographics led to increased political and cultural conflict on several fronts: tradition versus innovation, urban versus rural, fundamentalist Christianity versus scientific modernism, management versus labor, native-born versus new immigrants, white versus black, and idealism versus disillusionment.

The early 20th century saw great polarization in American politics, economic policies, and immigration reforms. Evidence of this is seen in rural or agrarian prominence being replaced by urban expansion, which caused hostility, on behalf of farmers, towards the banking sector and the new wealth derived from the industrial boom. Further evidence of the tense relationships during this period came from the workers and management of industrial projects, most notably the railroad system.

Several strikes and walkouts took place during the railroad boom between 1890 and 1945. The most notable strikes included the Pullman Strike in 1894 and the United Mine Workers Strike in 1902. Management in all sectors tried to combat the rising tensions of its workers by limiting or expelling unions through yellow-dog contracts (contracts which contain a clause in which a hired worker agrees not to join a union) and lockouts.

The massive immigration influx experienced by the United States during these years also caused irritation between the native-born Americans and new groups of immigrants coming mainly from Southern and Eastern Europe and East Asia. Americans viewed these immigrants as unskilled laborers who lacked any type of education or English-speaking skills; all of which were considered undesirable in the political climate of the period. This tension was met with immigration quotas being placed on Chinese and later Jewish populations in hopes of quelling the anti-immigration sentiment expressed by Americans in this period.

Fundamentalist Christianity had also found an adversary in early twentieth-century America, as many sought to explain the world through scientific modernism. Such transitions were difficult for many Americans to embrace and received much pushback from the traditional religious groups. Again, Americans were divided on the subject. An example of this can be seen in the opposition and support for prohibition. Ratified in 1919, the Eighteenth Amendment banned the sale, manufacturing, and transportation of alcoholic beverages. Both Protestants and progressives argued that prohibition would increase production, reduce crime and limit organized crime. Many others disagreed with this position and embraced speakeasies as a means of skirting the law.

Following the World War I, many men returning from the front and some civilians, dissatisfied with current political structure, began to feel a sense of disillusionment, portrayed in some of the literature, poetry, and art of the period. However, others felt a sense of great idealism at the close of the war, creating a source of tension between those who had experienced the atrocities of the First World War and those who had not. This is another example of social tensions in America as a result of the conflicts America entered into abroad, and the domestic issues being addressed by the American government.

The division of the American public in this period made it difficult to create a unified front, regardless of the topic being discussed. However, this would change following the attack on Pearl Harbor, which incited a deep and dominant sense of Nationalism.

The rise of an urban, industrial society encouraged the development of a variety of cultural expressions for migrant, regional and African American artists (expressed most notably in the Harlem Renaissance movement); it also contributed to national culture by making shared experiences more possible through art, cinema and the mass media.

Langston Hughes

The urbanization of the 20th century saw an influx in varied cultures in America. One such example of this is the Harlem Renaissance movement, where African Americans rebuffed the norms of Jim Crow laws with art, music, and literature. Following the Great Migration, many African Americans settled in the North and found new job opportunities and other oppressed minority groups, to which they felt an association. Notable participants of the Harlem Renaissance movement include Langston Hughes, who wrote poetry and literature and worked as a social activist, and Marcus Garvey, who promoted black expressionism and racial pride.

Women during this period also experienced cultural transitions, which included continued expansion into the workforce and the introduction of a more independent woman in the flapper. These women were pushing the traditional envelope and embodied the rivalry between traditionalists and the new idea of women and feminism in the early 20th century.

Music and culture also played a substantial role in this period with F. Scott Fitzgerald calling this period the Jazz Age. Notable figures of the Jazz Age include Edward "Duke" Ellington—who was an early pioneer of jazz and began his career playing at the Cotton Club, a hub of the Harlem Renaissance—and Edward Hopper, known for his realist and watercolor paintings. Other notable cultural innovators of the period (sometimes called the "lost generation" due to the disillusioning effect of World War I), were found in American literature, where they explored new styles of writing and were interested in reaching new audiences.

Some examples include *Three Lives* (1906) by Gertrude Stein, who is credited with giving popularity to the modernist writing style of the period. F. Scott Fitzgerald, in his novels *This Side of Paradise* (1920) and *The Great Gatsby* (1925), embodied the new consumer reading culture of the 20th century. Other notable authors of the "lost generation" included William Faulkner, T. S. Eliot, and Ernest Hemingway. These newly embraced styles of writing caused many Americans to engage with literature in a way previously unknown and propelled some authors to great fame.

F. Scott Fitzgerald

The global ramifications of World War I and wartime patriotism and xenophobia, combined with social tensions created by increased international migration, resulted in legislation restricting immigration from Asia and from southern and eastern Europe.

Beginning in the late 1890s and continuing into to the 1920s, America experienced a great influx of immigrants which was met with opposition by many native-born Americans. Many Americans believed that this massive influx would change or tarnish the image of America, both internally and abroad. The sentiment was respected by the government administrations of the period through the use of immigration quotas; one notable example is the Emergency Quota Act of 1921.

This bill called for the limiting of the entrance of migrants of certain nationalities to only 3 percent of that nationality's current representation per the 1910 census. This greatly limited the number of new immigrants accepted at Ellis Island, New York. Given the census material provided, it quickly became evident that the immigration of people from Asia and eastern and southern Europe would be drastically limited in the following years.

Supplementing this bill was the Johnson-Reed Immigration Act of 1924, which extended and expanded immigration quotas leading into and following World War II. While many in government supported the anti-immigration sentiment sweeping across the United States, one notable Congressman spoke out against the bill. Robert H. Clancy, who represented various nationalities in Detroit, labeled it "un-American" and argued that Jewish, Polish and Italian immigrants were just as American as anyone. However, these policies were in place until World War II set the tone for immigration reforms moving into the 1960s.

Another situation that intensified the xenophobia seen in America, came from the Zimmerman Telegram in 1917, which caused many Americans to fear an assault by German and Mexican forces. Such concerns convinced many Americans that the country should look inward to solve problems rather than welcoming outside influences by means of immigration, again driving home the message of isolationism following the atrocities of World War I. The only exception to these anti-immigration policies was seen in Mexico, where the U.S. government encouraged thousands of Mexican Americans to migrate seasonally in order to maintain agricultural production during periods when the United States lacked an adequate workforce, most typically during World War I and World War II.

World War I created a repressive atmosphere for civil liberties, resulting in official restrictions on freedom of speech.

As with other periods of conflict, the civil liberties of Americans were sacrificed during World War I, and later during World War II, in order to maintain the national security of the country. These restrictions most notably influenced freedom of speech, causing many Americans—both native-born and immigrants—to fear the legal and judicial actions of the American government. One such example comes from the Espionage and Sedition Acts of 1917 and 1918.

The Espionage Act prohibited any negative conversation regarding the outcome of U.S. foreign policy in the war, as well as about military forces or the American flag. Those found guilty of speaking against the government during a time of war could be fined up to $10,000 or face up to twenty years in prison. The Sedition Act greatly impacted immigrants, as anyone who opposed engagement in World War I, the military draft or the newly imposed limitations on freedom of speech were susceptible to legal action taken against them, including but not limited to fines and deportation.

American Socialist Party Logo

Another implication of the Espionage and Sedition Acts was the limiting of newspaper mailing privileges of publications considered a concern by the U.S. government. These groups included German language newspapers, German American newspapers, pacifist publications and all publications owned by the Industrial Workers of the World or the American Socialist Party. Close to seventy-five newspapers lost their operating privileges as a result of the Espionage and Sedition Acts.

Though the Espionage Act initially came under fire as being considered unconstitutional, the Supreme Court inevitably supported the law as necessary during times of conflict, ruling that the government has the authority to punish anyone who would create a clear and present danger. Close to 1,000 immigrants were tried and convicted of sedition, with many being deported as a result, but none were ever convicted of spying or sabotage. The lasting implications of the Espionage and Sedition Acts are varied; the Sedition Act was removed shortly after the end of the war but was adamantly contested while in practice. The Espionage Act remained in action through the end of World War I, the Red Scare in 1919, World War II and the Cold War.

As labor strikes and racial strife disrupted society, the immediate postwar period witnessed the first "Red Scare," which legitimized attacks on radicals and immigrants.

Following World War I, America entered a period of racial and political oppression. A common practice during this period included vigilante justice by the citizenry as well as infringement of civil liberties. One such example comes from the summer of 1919, referred to as "the Red Summer" due to the vicious racial attacks on and murders of African Americans. Though the NAACP requested an investigation by President Wilson, little was accomplished at the local and federal level.

The Red Scare from 1919 to 1920 was the result of fear regarding the spread of Bolshevism in the United States following World War I. The goal of the Red Scare policies was to expose and remove radicals and socialists from the U.S. government. The Palmer Raids took place between 1918 and 1921, spearheaded by Attorney General A. Mitchell Palmer. The Red Scare raids produced little evidence of wrongdoing or malevolent intent against the United States but resulted in extensive deportations anyway.

Eventually, the public lost support for Palmer and his raids, questioning their constitutionality. Other notable events during the Red Scare include the trial and execution of Nicola Sacco and Bartolomeo Vanzetti, Italian immigrants and anarchists. Accused of murdering a guard and paymaster of a shoe factory, the trial and appeal continued for seven years and was met with great protest by many in the United States. However, in August of 1927, both men were executed, arguably because of their immigrant background.

Protest to save Sacco and Vanzetti

Several acts of Congress established highly restrictive immigration quotas, while national policies continued to permit unrestricted immigration from nations in the Western Hemisphere, especially Mexico, in order to guarantee an inexpensive supply of labor.

While the United States was against further immigration from Europe and East Asia, to meet its labor needs it found no issue with the continued influx of unskilled laborers from Latin America, specifically Mexico. This highlighted contradictions within U.S. foreign policy, causing many to wonder why the border remained virtually open to Mexico and other countries in the Western Hemisphere.

This need for unskilled laborers in agricultural production was satisfied as the Mexican Revolution intensified between 1910 and 1920, resulting in a mass exodus of refugees north into the United States, from all parts of war-torn Mexico. Close to 900,000 Mexican Americans, many of whom were sick and in poverty, immigrated to the United States between 1910 and 1920, quickly filling the void in the American workforce.

These policies also highlight the rivalry between European countries and the United States leading into and following World War I. The United States wanted to exercise hegemony within the Western Hemisphere and believed it could do so by influencing political and economic policies in Latin America and North America. By allowing the influx of Mexican American immigrants, the U.S. government believed it could hold some influence in later situations of the region. Such agreements created instability and uncertainty along the U.S.-Mexico border, as well as soured relationships between the United States and Native Americans as westward expansion continued.

Economic dislocations, social pressures and the economic growth spurred by World Wars I and II led to a greater degree of migration within the United States, as well as migration to the United States from elsewhere in the Western Hemisphere.

Following the terrible years of World War I, many around the world attempted to return their lives to some sort of normalcy, but for many in Europe, this was almost impossible. The United States, though involved in the global conflict, did not suffer extensive damages like Europe, and actually emerged from the Great War with an improved economy. This improvement, along with America's rapid industrialization, made it an appealing center of immigration from the Eastern and Western Hemispheres.

Immigration patterns can be seen as a response to economic instability caused by the two world wars, while the social pressures of immigration and rising Nationalism influenced the U.S. immigration policies in the 20th century. In hopes of quieting criticism at home, the United States instituted policies of exclusion in regards to further immigration from countries outside of the Western Hemisphere.

One such example came from California, where Japanese immigrants experienced harsh discrimination and oppression, finally resulting in segregated schooling and further cultural separation. In hopes of stopping the influx of Japanese immigrants, the United States penned the informal Gentleman's Agreement of 1907, which promised separate schooling in return for limited immigration. However, the agreement did allow Japanese women to enter the country as a way to form families with men who had already immigrated.

Although most African Americans remained in the South despite legalized segregation and racial violence, some began a "Great Migration" out of the South to pursue new economic opportunities offered by World War I.

As African Americans entered the 20th century, the conditions in the post–Civil War South were still deplorable and unjust; legalized segregation and outbursts of violence plagued many still living there. While many stayed in the South following the Civil War, others undertook the Great Migration north and west in hopes of obtaining new opportunities. Newspapers spread information regarding job recruitment, advertisements were taken out in black newspapers such as the *Chicago Defender*, and stories of successful African Americans in the northern and Midwestern workforces were printed.

As African Americans converged in northern cities, it became clear that many had similar circumstances and ambitions. All had faced segregation, oppression and lack of economic opportunity. However, as thousands made the journey north, it became clear that opportunities for work would be found in the industrialized cities. By 1919, close to one million African Americans had fled the South and were vying for jobs and housing in the crowded major cities of New York, Chicago, Philadelphia, and Detroit.

During this same period, there was a resurgence in Ku Klux Klan membership; by 1923 it peaked at five million members. In the summer of 1919, the large cities experienced a series of race riots, most notably in Chicago, which lasted thirteen days and left 537 injured and 38 dead. Such situations highlight the tense relationship between northern whites and African Americans following the initial flood of the Great Migration.

The Ku Klux Klan on parade down Pennsylvania Avenue

Many Americans migrated during the Great Depression, often driven by economic difficulties, and during World Wars I and II, as a result of the need for wartime production labor.

During the Great Depression, countless Americans traveled in search of work, consistent food, and adequate housing. Workers were displaced by more efficient methods of operation and technological advances, such as the implementation of the assembly line, and by changes in demand from industries that previously had provided steady work, such as railroads, factories, and the automobile industry. Farmers also struggled during the Depression, causing many to abandon their farms and homes to look for an income that could sustain a family.

As America prepared for World Wars I and II, the need for wartime production labor was overwhelming. As the men who had previously occupied these positions left for war, women and minority groups were expected to fill the labor gap. World War II bolstered the American economy following the Great Depression, which could not have happened so successfully if not for the domestic support of the wartime populations. Women and minority groups flocked to armament factories and industrial plants in hopes of securing higher paying jobs while also supporting the domestic war effort, which was constantly glorified by wartime propaganda. As these groups worked in various new positions, they gained a sense of importance and growth; this was an unprecedented time for women and minority groups in the workplace.

Many Mexicans, drawn to the United States by economic opportunities, faced ambivalent government policies in the 1930s and 1940s.

Following the labor shortages of the Great Depression and World Wars I and II, America solved its labor problems by continuously encouraging the influx of Mexican immigrants and seasonal workers, who maintained the agricultural production of the United States and provided an abundant source of unskilled labor. One such program was the Bracero Program, which began in 1942 and ended in 1964. This program was the result of multiple bilateral agreements between the United States and Mexico, regarding American labor shortages.

The first Braceros arriving in Los Angeles by train in 1942

During this period, some social activists fighting for Mexican labor and social causes appeared. One notable example was Luisa Moreno, who organized union workers, led labor strikes, and organized the first National Congress of Spanish-Speaking People in 1938. Moreno was a symbol of the struggle Mexican Americans felt during the social abuses of the Great Depression and world wars.

During times of inflammatory anti-immigration sentiment, most notably during the Great Depression and other periods of economic instability, thousands of Mexican American laborers and their children were deported back to Mexico. Native-born Americans harbored heightened immigration concerns during periods of economic crisis, and such deportation policies caused many in America and abroad to wonder if the United States had addressed the humanitarian concerns of Mexican immigration.

In order to deal with the chaotic deportations on the Mexican border, the U.S. Farm Security Administration (FSA) provided some families with housing, medical resources and the promise of protection from the petty crimes typically associated with migrant work camps and Mexican labor conditions. The policies enacted by the U.S. government against Mexican immigration mirrored those of other anti-immigrant sentiment, but these were particularly volatile, with great fluctuations depending on economic and social circumstances. This unpredictability in policy caused many immigrants to yearn for stability and citizenship.

KEY CONCEPT 7.3: Global conflicts over resources, territories and ideologies renewed debates over the nation's values and its role in the world while simultaneously propelling the United States into a dominant international military, political, cultural and economic position.

Under President Taft, the United States pursued a foreign policy agenda influenced by the interventionist mindset, which garnered both short-term alliances and long-term resentments. By pursuing dollar diplomacy, Taft, a staunch interventionist, was able to propel the United States into the forefront of influence in the economic, political and military sectors. However, President Wilson, an anti-imperialist, worked from a position of humanitarian diplomacy and sought to expand human rights and create a stable and lasting peace. The intent of both men to influence the international system by different means highlights the desire for American influence within the newly emerging international system.

The role of the United States in the global system had drastically changed in the years following World War I and leading into World War II. Unlike the majority of world powers, the United States had experienced minimal destruction in the Great War but was able to profit from the arms and resources sold during the war. This profit coupled with a drastic increase in economic production and manufacturing allowed the United States to directly and indirectly influence international affairs in both the Western and Eastern Hemispheres.

Many Americans began to advocate overseas expansionism in the late 19th century, leading to new territorial ambitions and acquisitions in the Western Hemisphere and the Pacific.

During the final years of the 19th century, Americans made a major push for expansion abroad. Several groups had an interest in foreign policy dealings, including industrialists who hoped to bring their goods to new markets and extract cheaper resources. Nationalism, a popular sentiment at the time, also embraced this concept of overseas expansion as a means of establishing a perception of authority and influence within the growing international system.

This type of mindset was a response to the formerly dominant European colonial models, which some Americans, such as interventionists and imperialists, now envisioned as appropriate for the U.S. Others called for the expansion of American values, democratic traditions, and religions through missionary activities. Social Darwinists argued that Americans had some sort of obligation to the less developed peoples abroad and authors like Josiah Strong perpetuated such theories.

In 1898, the last remnants of the Spanish Empire in the Americas was obliterated when America and Spain fought a short war, which America won. The spoils of victory for the U.S.A. were Cuba (where future president Theodore Roosevelt led the famous cavalry unit called the "Rough Riders"), Puerto Rico, the Philippines, and Guam. These became American territories and would each follow a different path in the twentieth century. While military means were used to subjugate these places, as well as Hawaii just before the Spanish-American War, American missionaries established schools, orphanages, leper colonies, and other philanthropic institutions in these places. These institutions were benevolent, but they played the dual role of cultural diffusion, which was actively promoted by the more cynically nationalistic Americans. Once these territories had been acquired, American natural resource industries developed in them.

From a military and political standpoint, territorial expansions and intervention abroad allowed the United States to become a global power in the time leading up to World War II. Many, including influential writer Alfred Thayer Mahan, believed the key to international influence was control of the seas, which could be accomplished in the 20th century by the expansion and maintenance of geopolitically strategic military bases. Evidence of this school of thought can be seen in the United States' acquiring naval base rights in Newfoundland and the Caribbean in return for wartime aid to the British.

Alfred Thayer Mahan

The perception in the 1890s was that the western frontier was "closed." Economic motives, competition with other European imperialist ventures of the time, and racial theories all furthered arguments that Americans were destined to expand their culture and norms to others, especially the nonwhite nations of the globe.

Following the "closure" of the western border by the Bureau of the Census in 1890, many Americans began to look abroad in hopes of influencing and maintaining America's interests in the form of newly acquired territories, such as the Philippines, Guam and Puerto Rico following the Spanish-American War. Others invested in foreign markets in order to dispel a European hegemony in the Western Hemisphere. President Taft endorsed foreign policy by constantly supporting his policies of dollar diplomacy.

By 1898, the United States had replaced many European countries as the dominant influence in international affairs, allowing for the gradual transition into a global power that surpassed European countries in consumer production and led the rebuilding effort in Europe in hopes of maintaining a stable and continuous peace.

In addition to economic interests, social Darwinism persuaded many in America to view other ethnicities and nationalities as needing guidance from a more developed people. This type of ideology, termed "survival of the fittest," caused many Americans to view themselves in a genetically dominating role. This sentiment was quickly adopted by imperialists and interventionists who were able to garner support for colonial aspirations. This mindset of a "closed" frontier was important in understanding the desire for colonialism during this period.

The American victory in the Spanish-American War led to the U.S. acquisition of island territories, an expanded economic and military presence in the Caribbean and Latin America, engagement in a protracted insurrection in the Philippines, and increased involvement in Asia.

American involvement in the Spanish-American War, the Panama Canal project and President Theodore Roosevelt's corollary policies all highlight the extensive partnership the United States was building in Latin America in the early 20th century. Military intervention coupled with dollar diplomacy was commonplace for U.S. foreign policy in the Caribbean and Latin America during this period. As Latin America and the Caribbean countries faced revolution and internal strife, the United States intervened, causing further U.S. hegemony within their territories and their neighbors.

The Panama Canal in 1915

As a result of the American victory in the Spanish-American War, the United States obtained the Philippines and the islands of Guam and Puerto Rico, furthering its influence abroad and creating rivalries with other European states for status and power. By the time the United States entered into World War I, it was a global power, maintaining various territories abroad while propelling its interests ahead of its European counterparts. These types of policies predicated the rise of U.S. influence during the two world wars, the reshaping of Europe following the collapse of Nazi Germany and the rise of the Soviet Union.

Questions about America's role in the world generated considerable debate, prompting the development of a wide variety of views and arguments between imperialists and anti-imperialists and, later, interventionists and isolationists.

As America entered into the 20th century, many questioned its role within the international system. Some supported the expansion of imperialism and argued the United States should continue to maintain its overseas colonies. The goal of many officials was to maintain U.S. international commercial interests while dispelling any European aggression. President Taft implemented dollar diplomacy, which used the economic powers of the United States as a foreign policy tool influencing markets and maximizing U.S. influence abroad.

By limiting the influence of European countries, Taft believed he would bolster the U.S. economy while also growing its international influence. This influence was intensified when the United States obtained further territories following the Spanish-American War and left many anti-imperialists calling for their release. However, interventionists believed that by influencing international affairs, the United States would maintain its interests.

As America looked toward Latin America to build further relationships, it also struggled with its neighbor Mexico and its various revolutions taking place in the early 20th century. Many fled from Mexico into the United States following the instability, causing tense border relations and ongoing conflict. Approach and response to situations like this varied greatly depending on leadership, as the United States under President Wilson, a staunch anti-imperialist, played a limited military role in the revolutions, undoing much of the foreign policy agendas of President Taft, an enthusiastic interventionist.

The implications of dollar diplomacy can be seen in the influence the United States garnered in the international system. President Taft was able to create short-term relationships that he hoped would blossom into more fruitful interactions. However, dollar diplomacy could only be so effective against the coercive policies of World Wars I and II. The lack of Mexican intervention under President Wilson is evidence of his anti-interventionist and anti-imperialist mindset; however, it contradicts his morally grounded interventions in World War I.

World War I and its aftermath intensified debates about the nation's role in the world and how best to achieve national security and pursue American interests.

Following the horrible destruction and tumultuous years of World War I, the United States questioned its role within the international system and began a direct and steady path toward isolationism, while at the same time focusing most of its energy on securing its own interests, in spite of European influence, within the Western Hemisphere. Outside of economic investments, the United States shied away from involvement on a large scale with other developed countries; many believed that after the dealings of the Great War, the only sensible foreign policy agenda was extreme isolationism. This mindset, coupled with the economic collapse of the Great Depression, which impacted American and global markets, caused many nations to look solely inward, completely ignoring their neighbors while trying to rebuild their own state system.

In order to pursue these interests, the United States continued to invest in the rebuilding of Europe and further economic engagement with Latin America, building on the previous dollar diplomacy enacted by President Taft. Such policies were designed to give American interests an upper hand in the rebuilding of the developed world, while at the same time sowing seeds of influence in the developing world. By investing in foreign markets, President Taft and those who supported dollar diplomacy hoped to buy influence within international affairs and eliminate any possible European influence within the Western Hemisphere. The United States also sought to limit arms production and negotiate peace treaties in hopes of avoiding a second global conflict.

The implications of World War I can clearly be seen in the U.S. foreign policy agenda of isolationism, which was the center of its diplomatic efforts until the mid-1930s. While America wanted to experience its role as a global power through influence, it typically did so through economic and diplomatic means, avoiding any commitment to conflict. However, soon after the end of the Second World War, it became clear that tensions and unresolved issues still remained, causing many to fear the outbreak of the next conflict. In the U.S. government, some sought to bolster aid and support of allies, the British and French, while others continued to call for complete and extensive isolation from European affairs.

After initial neutrality in World War I, the nation entered the conflict, departing from the U.S. foreign policy tradition of noninvolvement in European affairs in response to Woodrow Wilson's call for the defense of humanitarian and democratic principles.

The Presidency of Woodrow Wilson is marked by the spread of democracy, freedoms, and morality. President Wilson saw the role of the United States as one which would facilitate the spread of peace and stability throughout the international system. Following its entrance into the war in April 1917, the United States, led by President Wilson, sought to find a stable peace that would create a new period of international prosperity.

Rather than working against a German state which was already in shambles after the devastating loss, Wilson sought to move forward to create a more stable international system void of aggressive conflict and coercive policies, following World War I. (Notwithstanding this, devastating war reparations payments, demanded by the European allies, would be imposed on Germany in the Treaty of Versailles, signed by Wilson.)

In January 1918, President Wilson outlined his famous Fourteen Points speech to a joint session of Congress. These policies would become the center of the peace accords agreed to at Versailles and were respected by many leaders across the globe, notably Lenin and those in the Allied forces. Though the United States had participated in the conflict on a smaller scale than its European counterparts, President Wilson was able to drastically influence post–World War I Europe, using his political theories and models.

President Wilson (left) and French President Minister Poincaré (right)

President Wilson believed that the government's responsibilities included remedying the wrongdoing of the state and putting the needs of the people before the state. This type of foreign policy agenda is important because it influenced contemporary U.S. foreign policy regarding the expansion and maintenance of human rights and democratic institutions. As seen in the formation of the League of Nations, this type of foreign policy would dominate the international system for the next several decades. Some would argue that Wilson's policies crafted and molded the expectations for global powers, in terms of international perception and influence, in the late 20th and early 21st centuries.

Although the American Expeditionary Force played a relatively limited role in the war, Wilson was heavily involved in postwar negotiations, resulting in the Treaty of Versailles and the League of Nations, both of which generated substantial debate within the United States.

The leadership of President Wilson is apparent in the Paris Peace Conference and the Treaty of Versailles as well as the formation of the League of Nations, though America abstained from membership. Foreign policy based on morality and idealism was a key attribute of the Wilson Presidency, and this is evident when examining Wilson's reasons for entering into World War I.

The Treaty of Versailles was a culmination of the Paris Peace Conference that convened in January 1919. As a response to the end of World War I, the victorious Allied forces sought to punish the military aggression of Germany and her allies. Notable excerpts of the treaty include the limiting of German naval and armed forces, the trial of Kaiser Wilhelm II and other high-ranking German officials as war criminals, the surrender of 10 percent of Germany's prewar territories and a $5 billion immediate payment. Long-term war reparations were set at an amount which today has been estimated as the equivalent of 96,000 tons of gold or three trillion dollars U.S. The Treaty of Versailles was viewed with great animosity in Germany and contributed to the rising hostilities leading into World War II.

The League of Nations was the culmination of President Wilson's foreign policy aspirations, as well as a response to the atrocities seen during World War I. The goal of the League of Nations was the establishment of an international organization which would maintain peace, foster international cooperation and provide security for its member states. The ideas proposed by the League of Nations were popular around the world, as many countries were exhausted by the war effort and sought a return to normalcy.

However, in the United States' membership in the League of Nations was hotly debated. The opposition was led by Senate majority leader Henry Cabot Lodge, who held the opinion that membership in the League of Nations would limit the United States' ability to protect its own interests in an expensive obligatory relationship with other members. Lodge was successful in his campaign; the United States never became a member of the League of Nations.

Henry Cabot Lodge

The global implications of the Treaty of Versailles and the formation of the League of Nations were countless. President Wilson had established the international model as one free of conflict and aggression. Additionally, the agreements reached in the Treaty of Versailles left many issues unresolved in Germany and caused many Germans to hold a great sense of resentment toward the rest of Europe, which would eventually culminate in the German aggression seen at the onset of World War II.

In the years following World War I, the United States pursued a unilateral foreign policy that used international investment, peace treaties and select military intervention to promote a vision of international order, even while maintaining U.S. isolationism, which continued to the late 1930s.

Following World War I, the United States pursued a foreign policy agenda that used diplomacy by means of treaties and financial partnerships, rather than force or military commitment, in hopes of reestablishing and maintaining stability and normalcy in the international system. One of the first examples of this diplomacy was the Washington Naval Conferences in 1921 and 1922, where all the great naval powers converged to discuss disarmament and the de-escalation of conflict in East Asia.

The Stimson Doctrine that began in late 1931, following the Japanese invasion of northeast China, stated that the United States would not acknowledge any territory acquired through aggression, as it was in violation of the international system. Without committing any military action, the United States, led by President Hoover and his secretary of State Henry Stimson, was able to clearly outline its stance against aggression or coercive policies in the international system.

Continuing in its path of abstaining from European conflicts, the U.S. government passed a series of Neutrality Acts. The Neutrality Act of 1935 prohibited the trading of all implements of war, ammunition, and arms; it also stated that arms manufacturers operating within the United States must apply for an export license. It also warned American citizens traveling in conflict zones that they did so at their own risk. Americans were no longer able to extend lines of credit or loans to countries considered belligerent.

The Neutrality Act of 1937 experienced great support from the public in light of aggressive fascism in Europe and the outbreak of the Spanish Civil War. The new act forbade arms transports by U.S. merchant ships to belligerent countries, regardless of the country of origin. The act also produced the "cash and carry" policy, which allowed the transport of any materials except arms by U.S. merchant ships to belligerent countries, at the discretion of the president, in return for immediate payment. The final Neutrality Act was passed after much debate in November 1939 and lifted the arms embargo previously described, instead viewing all trade under the provisions of the "cash and carry" policy. Eventually, these policies would be scaled back as the Lend-Lease program began.

These policies would have a great impact on the outcome of World War II, as, without the U.S. aid provided to the Allied forces, Germany would have certainly overtaken British forces before the United States ever entered the war. They also greatly influenced the map of postwar Europe, which was now dominated by U.S. hegemony.

The involvement of the United States in World War II, while opposed by most Americans prior to the attack on Pearl Harbor, vaulted the United States into global political and military prominence and transformed both American society and the relationship between the United States and the rest of the world.

Following World War I and the instability of the Great Depression, most Americans had lost any appetite for conflict and, for many years leading up to World War II, they were content to maintain an isolationist mindset towards Europe. By 1940, the foreign policy of the United States had begun to transition in preparation for the inevitable conflict with Nazi Germany. Rather than entering the war, the public opinion of Americans now focused on supplying and supporting the Allies against the Axis powers.

By September 1940, the United States had agreed to give the British over fifty obsolete destroyers in return for ninety-nine-year lease agreements to territories in Newfoundland and the Caribbean. These territories would operate as joint air force bases, expanding U.S. influence throughout the Western Hemisphere. In December 1940, the British were no longer able to pay for their supplies; in response, President Roosevelt introduced the Lend-Lease Program, which required no immediate payment for the supplies being sent abroad. The Lend-Lease Program was expanded to over thirty countries and rendered close to fifty billion dollars in aid to those fighting the Axis powers.

Any resistance to entering the war was quickly dispelled when Japan attacked the United States at Pearl Harbor on December 7, 1941. The following day, President Franklin D. Roosevelt declared war on Japan. Germany quickly followed suit, declaring war on the United States and propelling America onto the global stage of the conflict. The United States now faced war on two fronts: in the Pacific against the Japanese and in continental Europe against the Axis powers.

USS California sinking at Pearl Harbor

The public perception of the war effort, molded by U.S. officials, was a fight of good against evil; protecting democracy and the human rights of those around the world. The prominence won by the United States following its military and political victories in World War II could not have been achieved without the public support of the American people.

The implications of the attack on Pearl Harbor and the U.S. entrance into World War II are almost incalculable. Some WWI historians speculate that without this attack, the United States might have waited to enter the war, allowing Germany to strengthen its grip on continental Europe and the British Isles, which could have had drastic implications for the outcome of World War II. In any event, the declaration of war against Japan by the United States caused Nazi Germany to open an additional war front, as well as involving a new player on the original fronts, which led to the decline of the Third Reich.

The mass mobilization of American society to supply troops for the war effort and a workforce on the home front ended the Great Depression and provided opportunities for women and minorities to improve their socioeconomic positions.

Rosie the Riveter

In order to be victorious in war-ravaged Europe and the Pacific, the United States and its civilian population had to fill many jobs that had been held by men now fighting in the global conflict. This allowed women and minority groups to work in positions previously unavailable to them. Close to 6.5 million women entered the workforce during the war years. The U.S. government, by means of the Office of War Information, undertook a domestic advertising campaign that encouraged women to enter the workforce and support the military effort. One notable example of this ad campaign is Rosie the Riveter. First Lady Eleanor Roosevelt convinced her husband to create women's auxiliary forces for the army (WACS), navy (WAVES), air force (WASPS) and Coast Guard (SPARS).

In addition to the actions taken by women during the war effort, African Americans also found large roles within the American war machine. Millions of African American men and women served the United States during World War II, over a million in the military and 8% of the civilian workers in the war industries. Though many served in construction or service capacities, this was a great sacrifice and opportunity for blacks in America, still reeling from racial bias and oppression.

Native Americans also engaged in the war; most notably, the Navajo Code Talkers, who assisted Allied forces by creating a code system based on the Navajo language. By the end of the war, more than 500 Navajo nation members were working for the United States Marine Corps in this capacity. Comanche fighters and over 300,000 Mexican American servicemen also engaged the Axis powers in the European theater. On the home front, Mexicans were encouraged to cross the border to assist with the harvest season in the Bracero Guest Worker Program.

The domestic war effort allowed for American and Allied troops to continue their attack on Nazi Germany and was instrumental in winning the war. It also had great economic implications, as it pulled the American markets and economy out of the Great Depression and into a period of extensive prosperity. Wartime programs gave new opportunities to women and minority groups, which would set the tone for future civil rights conversations in the 1960s and 1970s. However, even in this time of great sacrifice, the biases of racism and sexism were still present and would be seen throughout the modern history of the United States.

Wartime experiences, such as the internment of Japanese Americans, challenges to civil liberties, debates over race and segregation, and the decision to drop the atomic bomb raised questions about American values.

Some U.S. wartime policies, such as the creation of Japanese and Italian internment camps, caused debate and, at times, concern in the United States and abroad. In times of conflict or crisis, governments may limit civil liberties in order to maintain security. One such example is the Supreme Court ruling in *Korematsu v. the United States*, where the court sided with the government in preventing national security threats through detention and internment camps. Italian immigrants also faced interrogation and a policy stance similar to the Japanese. Close to 700,000 Italians were required to register as enemy aliens during World War II, and as many as 10,000 were forcibly relocated away from coastal areas.

Map showing Japanese American Internment Camps in World War II

Segregation in the armed forces caused some to question the morality of the leadership. While African Americans were eventually allowed to enter into the war, by means of two combat units and a few auxiliary forces like the Tuskegee Airmen, the racial bias remained. Other minorities serving in the military included the Navajo Code Talkers, the Comanche and several thousand Mexican Americans, who fought on the European front but were not formally segregated. Again, a racial bias remained.

The American public and leadership also questioned the brutality of the atom bombs dropped on Hiroshima and Nagasaki, ending the war in the Pacific. As a country that claimed to spread freedoms, liberties, and democracy, it is seen by many today as odd that the U.S. government ordered the use of two atomic bombs on civilian populations. This extent of U.S. military power and superiority was unprecedented, and it resulted in a drastic transition in the global system, felt most keenly during the Cold War era. However, some military strategists argued that the use of the atomic bomb was necessary and, in fact, saved thousands of American lives, as it stalled the planned invasion of Japan, codenamed Operation Downfall, which was scheduled to take place November 1, 1945.

The disregard for civil liberties in America during the two world wars caused many Americans to question the morality of their government. In the years following the internment camps, the U.S. government failed to acknowledge its mistake, and it was not until 1988 that Congress awarded surviving detainees $20,000 each in restitution.

The United States and its allies achieved victory over the Axis powers through a combination of factors, including allied political and military cooperation, industrial production, technological and scientific advances, and popular commitment to advancing democratic ideals.

The Allies were able to conquer the Axis powers through a combination of political posturing, military cooperation, and technological advancements. Such examples include the Manhattan Project, investment and research into ballistic missiles and space technology and the introduction of sonar technology.

The Atlantic Conference & Charter in 1941 was a culmination of British and American war aims, reinforcing the political alliances necessary to combat and defeat Nazi Germany and its Axis powers. Also discussed were the goals of the Allies in postwar Europe, which would determine the political landscape and U.S. hegemony leading into the Cold War era.

Advancements in sonar and radar technology allowed military leadership to plan and carry out surprise attacks against their enemies, strategies that would have severe implications for the United States and Japan; evidence of this was seen in the December 1941 Pearl Harbor attacks. This type of long-range radar navigation, also called LORAN, predated today's GPS system, clearly showing the advancement of warfare technology.

The introduction of plastics also had a great impact on the American war effort, allowing for the manufacturing of incendiary bombs, including napalm, flamethrowers and smoke screens. The factories that produced these materials had formerly been used for domestic consumer production. Following the domestic mobilization program pursued in the United States, these factories now produced materials for the war effort. Such materials were transformative in the conflict and set the stage for future conflicts as seen in the Vietnam and Korean Wars.

Medical advancements also allowed the U.S. many advantages. Service people were able to fly at higher elevations in a safer capacity, using superior technology. Penicillin and pesticides like DDT, which killed the mosquitos transmitting malaria, fought venereal and tropical diseases, were crucial for a victorious U.S. campaign in the tropical South Pacific. Scientific feats, such as the mastery of blood transfusions and supplemental oxygen, caused further innovations in the medical sector, following the end of World War II.

Various types of military cooperation were seen throughout World War II. One notable example being the North African offensive undertaken by U.S. and British forces. This offensive eventually led to the capture of General Erwin Rommel and the surrender at El Alamein. This was a decisive blow for the German forces and was seen by some as a turning point in the war.

The most notable technological advancement of World War II was certainly the atomic bomb, which was the culmination of the Manhattan Project. At the inception of the project two cities were chosen—Oak Ridge, Tennessee, and Hanford, Washington—to cultivate different processes for bomb-making: one based on uranium and the other on plutonium. The program was designed to guarantee that the United States would be the first country able to successfully create an atomic bomb. This type of efficiency and speed was necessary as Nazi Germany, Japan, and the Soviet Union were competing in the nuclear armament race.

With the help of European scientists, America was able to use both a plutonium bomb, in Nagasaki, and a uranium bomb, in Hiroshima, effectively ending World War II in the Pacific. This particular technology had unimaginable implications in the years following World War II; most notably in the Cold War and arms race undertaken by the United States and the Soviet Union.

General Leslie Groves (left), military head of the Manhattan Project, with Professor Robert Oppenheimer (right)

The dominant American role in the Allied victory and postwar peace settlements, combined with the war-ravaged condition of Asia and Europe, allowed the United States to emerge from the war as the most powerful nation on earth.

Given the military victories and political successes of the United States following World War II, including but not limited to the acquisition of new territories, the disarmament of Germany and a prestigious role in international affairs, it is no surprise that the United States maintained a dominant role within international politics in the postwar world. Even during the war itself, the United States secured its interests in postwar Europe by acquiring new allies and resources, which accompanied its rising global influence. The U.S. was able to exercise its influence at various wartime conferences. As a member of the "big three," with Great Britain and the Soviet Union, the United States enjoyed a substantial presence and position in world politics and affairs.

At the Casablanca Conference in 1943, the U.S. and British forces agreed to fight Germany until its unconditional surrender. This was crucial, as it stopped Germany from being able to eliminate the dual threat it faced on the eastern and western fronts. The Tehran Conference in 1943 promised Soviet aid to the United States against Japan, something critical to ensuring further amicable relations between the United States and the Soviet Union. However, the most critical wartime conference came in February 1945 at Yalta, where President Roosevelt and Prime Minister Churchill agreed to the eventual hegemony of the Soviet Union in Eastern Europe following the war. The big three also agreed to general occupation and war reparations for Germany, something for which Stalin desperately argued.

The Potsdam Conference in 1945 was also influential in postwar Europe, as tensions leading into the Cold War were undeniable. No agreements were reached at this conference; the United States and the Soviet Union now used these exchanges to build their arsenals against one another. The United States, under the leadership of General Douglas MacArthur, also spearheaded the occupation and reconstruction of Japan, allowing the United States to greatly influence East Asian affairs post–World War II. Such influence would be crucial in maintaining U.S. interests in the Cold War era.

Towards the end of the Second World War, it was clear that the U.S.A. was going to displace Great Britain as the unchallenged global power. Great Britain was economically drained by the war and no longer able to suppress nationalistic movements in its remaining colonies, like India and major parts of Africa and China. This was not lost on the numerous Americans who believed in America's anti-colonial origin and self-identity.

Militarily, America had the undisputed largest army and navy in the world. It was the sole occupying power of a defeated Japan, which had previously been the only modern power in all of Asia. This meant that America replaced Japan as the sole military and economic great power in the entire Pacific. America was, until 1949, the only nation with the atomic bomb. But a new threat was emerging even before the war ended: the rise of the Soviet Union. Fearing communism greatly, the U.S.A. used its military hegemony and its new image as a great liberator to gain the trust of the devastated world as the only nation that could stop the threat of Soviet expansion.

In addition, President Truman made the wise move of using economic policy to steal popularity away from communists: the Marshall Plan gave thirteen billion dollars in direct aid, as well as trade concessions, to Western European nations to enable them to rebuild their nations as capitalist democracies. Thus, the elimination of dire poverty, the U.S. government thought, would diminish support for communism there. The U.S.A. also established two other international entities immediately after the war, with the focus on stopping the spread of communism: the United Nations and the anti-Soviet North Atlantic Treaty Organization (NATO).

Please, leave your Customer Review on Amazon

PERIOD 8

1945-1980

After World War II, the United States grappled with prosperity and new international responsibilities while striving to live up to its ideals.

Major historical events of the period:

1940s-1950s – the Red Scare

1947 – the Truman Doctrine is established

1947-1991 – the Cold War

1948-1949 – Berlin Airlift Crisis

1949 – NATO is formed

1950-1953 – Korean War

1954 – *Brown v. Board of Education*

1954-1975 – Vietnam War

1958 – NASA is formed

1965 – the Civil Rights Act outlaws segregation

PERIOD 8: 1945-1980

> **KEY CONCEPT 8.1:** The United States responded to an uncertain and unstable postwar world by asserting and attempting to defend a position of global leadership, resulting in far-reaching domestic and international consequences.

As the United States emerged from World War II, it was clear that the politics and global powers of the prewar period had been forever changed, and this transition would propel the United States into a state of unipolarity within the international system. Though the United States now held more power than before, the postwar period was filled with chaos and tension that would culminate in the Cold War that spanned much of the late 20th century.

Such conditions included the rebuilding of Western Europe and establishing governments that supported the Western goals and ambitions being pursued by the United States, embodied by the Truman Doctrine. Such policies included providing countries facing authoritarian or outside aggression with economic, military and political resources. One notable example was the $400 million emergency funding of Greece on behalf of the United States.

By 1947, relations between the United States and the Soviet Union deteriorated, causing many in government and the American public to see the Soviet Union as a new adversary. As an immediate response, President Truman and his Secretaries of State George C. Marshall (1947–1949) and Dean G. Acheson (1949–1953) crafted the containment policies, which would shape the foreign policy of the United States during the Cold War.

President Truman with Secretary of Defense George C. Marshall, Secretary of State Dean Acheson, and Secretary of the Treasury John Snyder, upon the President's return from the Wake Island Conference.

Another notable event during this period that had a transformative influence on the 20th century's politics was the Chinese Revolution, which took place in October 1949 and culminated in the accession of Mao Zedong and the Communist Party in China. Such an event highlights the "sphere of influence" policies being used by the United States and the Soviet Union during this period and throughout the Cold War.

In addition to the ongoing Cold War, the United States also engaged in the Korean War (1950–1953) and the Vietnam War (1954–1975), which had significant implications for the United States internationally and domestically, seen mainly through the antiwar movements in the United States during this period. Aside from antiwar protests, the United States faced several other domestic concerns, the most notable being the civil rights movement, which dominated the 1960s.

After World War II, the United States sought to contain the growth of Communist military power and ideological influence, create a stable global economy and build an international security system.

As the Truman administration and following presidencies struggled to deal with the growing power and influence of the Soviet Union, they would enact foreign policy agendas that had one common goal: to diminish the spread and influence of Communism. Such attempts can be seen in a wide variety of policies including but not limited to containment, massive retaliation and the formation of global monetary institutions such as the International Monetary Fund (IMF) in 1944.

The United States expanded its role again in postwar Europe after it promised to rebuild and support the war-torn nations of Western Europe, while at the same time actively denouncing the rebuilding efforts of the Soviet Union. By means of the Marshall Plan, the United States was able to create a relatively stable Europe by the end of the 1950s, which greatly depended upon American financial backing as well as its military resources.

Marshall Plan aid to France: bulldozer to help rebuild French electric power system

In terms of creating a more abundant international security system, the United States quickly found itself in need of a more collective security policy. By creating the North Atlantic Treaty Organization (NATO) in April 1949, the United States and its allies formed an entity with the ability to support and maintaining peace by force and coercive policies if necessary. This enraged the Soviet Union and allowed Western Europe to feel a sense of security over the growing threat of Communism.

In addition to NATO, the United States also pursued individual peace and security agreements that set the foundation of the spheres-of-influence conflicts that would come to dominate the Cold War. In October 1949, the Mutual Defense Assistance Program was created and signed by President Harry Truman. By January 1950, bilateral agreements had been reached with eight of the NATO countries that had requested military assistance from the United States. The agreements resulted in vast military supplies and financial aid being rendered to many of the war-torn countries of Western Europe.

The long-term implications for such foreign policies are vast; some argue that without NATO and the aid of the United States, Western Europe would have staggered into the late 20th and early 21st centuries. Others argue that the presence and eventual expansion of NATO intensified and perpetuated the Cold War, leading to the ongoing rivalry of the two late 20th-century global powers, for the first time creating a true bipolarity in the international system. The alliance forged between the United States and Western Europe as a result of these foreign policies has certainly influenced the international system of the 20th and 21st centuries and arguably allowed the United States to maintain a sense of hegemony in the world.

The United States developed a foreign policy based on collective security and a multilateral economic framework that bolstered non-Communist nations.

As a result of the Soviet Union's explosive rise in Eastern Europe—and in turn, a global rise in Communism—the United States and others who opposed Communism sought to cooperate and expel such ideology from their regions and spheres of influence. Immediately following World War II, the United States pursued this expulsion via the Truman Doctrine and later the Marshall Plan. Established in 1947, the Truman Doctrine stated that the United States would come to the economic, military or political aid of any country that faced an outside threat, most notably in the form of Communism.

As former world powers, such as Britain, were preoccupied with domestic issues (including rebuilding efforts), the United States and the Soviet Union saw a power vacuum and acted accordingly. The United States, led by President Truman, argued that if aid was not given to countries where Britain had recently ceased its aid and involvement, such as Greece and Turkey, the Soviet Union would intervene and gain additional Communist satellite states. As a result, over $400 million was approved by Congress in aid to both Greece and Turkey, effectively engaging the Soviet Union in a sphere-of-influence conflict.

Following the success of the Truman Doctrine in March 1947, Congress passed the Economic Cooperation Act, more commonly known as the Marshall Plan, which funded the European Recovery Program and rendered close to $13 billion for the rebuilding projects of Western Europe. Such economic aid would allow most of Western Europe to be rebuilt by the mid-1950s and caused many European countries to become reliant upon the United States for economic cooperation and military resources.

Other examples of successful economic cooperation during this period come from the Berlin Airlift Crisis (1948–1949), in which Soviet forces exercised their power and influence within postwar Europe with frightening results. The crisis began in June 1948, when Soviet forces in East Berlin enacted a blockade of rail, road and water passages leading into West Berlin. In order to combat this threat, American, Canadian and British forces airlifted supplies into West Berlin. The blockade ended in May 1949, as Soviet forces lifted any land restrictions from West Berlin.

The United States sought to "contain" Soviet-dominated Communism through a variety of measures, including military engagements in Korea and Vietnam.

The United States tried to combat the Soviet Union and contain the threat of Communism. The policies developed by President Truman and diplomat of the Department of the State George Kennan set forth the policies of containment, which would be influential in the Cold War and later periods of the 21st century. In order to combat the Soviet threat of expansion into further satellite states and the spread of global Communism, the United States engaged in two major wars during this period: the Korean War (1950–1953) and the Vietnam War (1954–1975). Both conflicts were unpopular with the American public and seemed to only inflame the struggle between the East and West.

In addition to the conflict of the Cold War, the United States also used technological advancements to promote its status within the international system. Under the orders of President Truman, the United States actively and successfully pursued the production of the first hydrogen bomb. Edward Teller, a former Manhattan Project scientist, pursued the military and security communities during and following the end of World War II, pressing for further advancement in nuclear arms. However, not all scientists and politicians supported the project.

Edward Teller

Others in the scientific community, such as Enrico Fermi and J. Robert Oppenheimer, adamantly opposed the conception of the hydrogen bomb. Like the scientists who had produced the arms race of the 19th century and the atomic bomb of World War II, many believed the creation of such a weapon was immoral and could catapult the global system into one dominated by destruction and war.

However, production of the bomb continued, and in November 1952, the United States conducted the MIKE Test, which detonated a 10.4-megaton hydrogen device in the Marshall Islands in the Pacific. Subsequent testing included the BRAVO Test, which took place in March 1954, also on the Marshall Islands of the Pacific; this test produced the first deliverable hydrogen bomb.

Massive retaliation or response policies made famous by Secretary of State John F. Dulles under the Eisenhower Presidency in the mid-1950s were used as deterrents to the expansion of the Soviet Union. Dulles and later presidents, such as President Dwight D. Eisenhower, argued it was impractical to assert a national defense budget at the level being presented by the Soviet Union; it would, in essence, bankrupt the United States. Instead, it would deter Soviet aggression by means of nuclear weapons and the threat of full-scale American aggression.

One final military sector where the United States and the Soviet Union collided was the Space Race, made famous by Project Mercury, Warner Von Braun, and the Soviet satellite Sputnik. On October 4, 1957, the Soviet Union launched the first man-made satellite, Sputnik, causing jubilation in the Soviet Union and dread and fear in the United States. The following month, the same Soviet scientists successfully launched another satellite, this time carrying live dogs into space (along with some other species, all of which returned alive)—a monumental accomplishment for mankind.

Robert R. Gilruth, responsible for Project Mercury

Such advancements spurred the Americans to begin their own space program, and in early 1958, the United States successfully launched Explorer I, its first satellite. During this same year, President Eisenhower announced his support in the creation of the National Aeronautical and Space Administration (NASA), which also mandated that Project Mercury, newly formed, would send a man into orbit before 1959.

The Space Race was also influenced by the lack of qualified scientists and researchers being produced by the U.S. educational system during this period. In 1958, the National Defense Education Act was established to promote better teaching resources, application in math, science, and modern languages, higher education and college scholarships, all of which were intended to produce the academic minds needed to compete with the USSR in the Space Race.

The implications for the technological and military advancements during this period are far-reaching, even in today's political and international system. Without the initial advancements of the ballistic missile, the technology couldn't be transformed to create the intercontinental ballistic missiles of today. Additionally, the development of the hydrogen bomb set a new precedent, even above that of the nuclear annihilation seen in Japan following World War II, which troubled many scientists and American families alike.

The investment in academics and research as a result of the creation of NASA has been monumental in maintaining the perception of the United States as a global power, and the results have transcended the physical boundaries previously in place for humankind. Additionally, the space technology that had once been such a source of rivalry between the United States and the Soviet Union eventually became a bridge to further cooperative interactions between the two countries.

The Cold War fluctuated between periods of direct and indirect military confrontation and periods of mutual coexistence (or détente).

As the bipolarity of the Cold War system emerged, it became clear that neither side would be able to actively or sustainably wage war on its rival. Thus, periods of great conflict followed by nonaggression and coexistence were seen during much of the Cold War. The most notable examples of direct conflict between the United States and the Soviet Union are the Vietnam and Korean Wars.

Both wars created intense polarization amongst the American public and the international community in regards to the spread of Communism and the anti-Communist campaigns of the West. These wars were also instrumental in the spreading or expulsion of Communism during this period. Other examples of indirect conflict in the sphere-of-influence battles between the Soviet Union and the United States were illustrated by Communist satellite states and the establishment of NATO.

While both global powers maneuvered to secure their position within the international system, they found themselves in periods of détente—a French word meaning a release of tensions—which eased the nuclear ambitions of both sides. One such example came from President Nixon, who in 1972 made historic trips to China and the Soviet Union to meet with foreign leaders, trips that allowed him to highlight his foreign policy successes rather than his domestic blunders.

President Richard Nixon and Premier Alexei Kosygin sign the Cooperation in the Fields of Science and Technology Agreement between the United States and the Soviet Union

The détente period ended with the signing of the Strategic Arms Limitation Talks (SALT) and was revisited with subsequent trips in June 1973 and 1974. These later talks produced little to no agreement as was seen in the original talks but did perpetuate a sense of common peace between the two powers. Such foreign policy ambitions were aimed towards the increase of trade between the countries, as well as nuclear de-escalation, which both parties hoped for.

These periods of fluctuating tensions would be important to setting the groundwork for future Russian and American relations following the end of the Cold War and the collapse of the Soviet Union. These periods of relaxed relations also allowed the American public to see the Soviet Union as less of a threat, which was crucial to lowering the anti-Communistic rhetoric seen in the United States following World Wars I and II.

As the United States focused on containing Communism, it faced increasingly complex foreign policy issues, including decolonization, shifting international alignments and regional conflicts, and global economic and environmental changes.

A period of decolonization began following the end of World War II, and the United States struggled to find an even tone of authority and security while maintaining its stance as a champion of democracy and self-representation in the international system. From 1945 to 1960, over three dozen new states were formed in Asia and Africa, bringing into context the global transition away from colonization.

However, not all governments were pleased with this new policy agenda; many in America feared that the relinquished colonies would quickly be influenced or intimidated by the Soviet Union, in turn causing further expansion of Communism. It seemed that decolonization could cause further security concerns for the United States and its allies. Examples include the Indonesian War of Independence (1945–1950) against its colonial rulers in the Netherlands and the conflict between the Vietnamese and French (1945–1954).

Political revolts and rebellions in Eastern Europe also plagued the Cold War period. Notable examples include the Hungarian Revolution, which ended in November 1956, and the revolt of the Czech population, ending in August 1968 at the hands of Soviet forces. Such transition and instability caused the United States to pursue a foreign policy agenda that included financial aid and support, military intervention when it was deemed necessary, expansion of alliances to include the new influx of states created following World War II and an end to popular colonialism.

Postwar decolonization and the emergence of powerful nationalist movements in Asia, Africa, and the Middle East led both sides in the Cold War to seek allies among new nations, many of which remained nonaligned.

As the Cold War heated up and the United States and the Soviet Union continued to pursue aggressive policy agendas, it was clear to the newly emerging countries of the 20th century that each must support or oppose Communism. However, many states wanted to be excluded from the sphere-of-influence conflict and decided to form the Non-Aligned Movement, which focused on internal development rather than foreign policy agendas. The Non-Aligned Movement was cultivated in 1955 at the Bandung Conference; it quickly gained momentum among newly nationalized or formed states.

These newly created independent states became even more of an interest in the 1950s and 1960s when the international community saw the influence such states could have on the United Nations council. These particular states were typically wary of European-style government and management due to their colonial past and spent time trying to distance themselves from the former ruling models they had seen used in Europe and North America.

Cold War competition extended to Latin America, where the United States supported non-Communist regimes with varying levels of commitment to democracy.

In hopes of limiting the influence of the Soviet Union and Communism within the Western Hemisphere, the United States took drastic and sometimes concerning actions to welcome non-Communist based governments into its fold. The first formal attempt at welcoming these alliances following World War II came from the Inter-American Treaty of Reciprocal Assistance, also known as the Rio Treaty enacted in 1948, which stated that aggression against one country in the Americas would be seen as an attack on all the countries.

Such foreign policy decisions would have significant impacts on the relationships between American states, as well as Soviet relations with these same states, causing some to turn towards Communism and others to turn towards other forms of government, in most cases not true democracies. Before the two world wars, the United States had consistently pursued a path of isolation from global affairs; however, following the wars—and certainly during the Cold War era—this was neither practical nor possible.

As the United States worked to install and support governments opposed to Communism, it also found itself orchestrating the demise of the governments it perceived as pro-Communist. Such examples can be found throughout the Cold War era and include the US-sponsored coup in Iran in August 1953, Guatemala in June 1954 and Chile in September 1973, all of which resulted in the overthrow of acting governments.

The United States attempted to stay the tide of negative perception in Latin America due to its extensive involvement in the early 20th century. Notable examples include the Organization of American States (OAS), which was formed in 1948 shortly after the Rio Treaty and called for the cooperation of American states against the spread or infiltration of Communism into the Western Hemisphere.

The global ramifications for such policies can be seen in the immediate Latin American response as well as future relationships between the American countries. Mistrust and concerns grew from the relationship between Latin America and the United States during this period. The United States failed to see substantial results from OAS, which never experienced the surge of anti-Communism they hoped to see in the Latin American countries. Additionally, the continued unilateral use of force by the United States in Latin America caused many to question whether the United States had genuinely embraced a new path of foreign policy towards its American continental neighbors or just insisted upon being perceived in this way.

Ideological, military and economic concerns shaped U.S. involvement in the Middle East, with several oil crises in the region eventually sparking attempts at creating a national energy policy.

During World War II, the Soviet Union deployed and maintained military resources to Iran, an oil-rich nation, in order to protect its resources from Axis aggression. However, its continued military presence in the country following the war caused many Americans to be concerned about the future of the Middle East following the end of the two world wars. After the Soviet Union backed an armed rebellion in 1946, it became clear that Soviet "satellite states" in the Middle East were a real concern, and U.S. involvement in the region escalated as a result of the Tehran Conference violations. In hopes of eliminating threats to the global oil markets, the United States and other global and regional powers established institutions that could better control the markets.

One such institution is the Organization of the Petroleum Exploring Countries (OPEC), which was created in September 1960 at the Baghdad Conference. Original members included Iraq, Saudi Arabia, Iran, Kuwait, and Venezuela. Its main goal was to regulate and unify member state policies regarding oil production in order to produce fair and stable petroleum markets for producers. Following several oil crises, the formation of OPEC was seen as a safeguard against future mishandlings.

OPEC ministers

However, this was not necessarily the case, and OPEC took actions against what it perceived to be its threats and adversaries. In 1973, oil diplomacy was enacted by OPEC; it called for an embargo on oil against states that supported Israel's Yom Kippur War against Egypt, Syria, and Jordan. This included the United States and other western allies who had relied upon the oil of the Middle East to feed their energy needs.

The Suez Crisis also highlighted the energy concerns of the postwar period. On October 29, 1956, Israeli military forces invaded Egypt and progressed toward the Suez Canal. This military offensive came after the canal was nationalized by Egyptian President Gamal Abdel Nasser in July 1956. The conflict escalated when British and French forces joined with Israel, almost enticing the Soviet Union, which supplied Nasser with arms, into the conflict. Forces were eventually withdrawn in late 1956 and early 1957.

As the Eisenhower Presidency worked to deter its allies from inciting a Soviet conflict, it also had to be careful of policies that seemed soft or too accommodating of Soviet expansion. The long-term implications of the formation of OPEC would cause the United States to pursue national policies toward the oil markets and its producers, namely OPEC states. Later administrations would attempt to influence Middle Eastern states, most notably Saudi Arabia, Iran, and Iraq, in order to stabilize the global oil markets while at the same time exercising American influence in the hopes of accomplishing a greater hegemony in the region. This is also ascribed to the sphere of influence during the Cold War, which positioned states against other states in the Soviet-American game.

Cold War policies led to continued public debates over the power of the federal government, acceptable means for pursuing international and domestic goals, and the proper balance between liberty and order.

As American presidents exerted unprecedented executive power, the American people began to question certain policies and legislation, causing an influx of both criticism and support for the executive branch and its newly acquired authority. One of the earliest examples of executive authority during this period comes from President Truman, who was able to craft the rebuilding of Western Europe and the financing of various states threatened by Communism through unprecedented legislation. Such actions would mold the international system in postwar Europe, and by the actions of one man allowed the United States to ascend into its position of hegemony.

President Dwight D. Eisenhower

Another example of early executive authority came in the form of infrastructure development by means of the Federal Highway Act of 1956, which granted President Eisenhower the ability to build and develop a vast federal highway system, a crucial component for war in continental America. In order to finance the project, Congress approved a rise in gas taxes and instituted highway and toll taxes for some roads; the federal government would end up financing close to 90 percent of the project. Some argue this legislation is the largest domestic success of the Eisenhower administration while others insist the excessive force used to produce these highways decimated farming lands and isolated parts of the country.

The most notable and far-reaching example of executive authority during this period comes from the Gulf of Tonkin Resolution, which effectively gave the executive branch the authority and means to pursue total war against the Northern Vietnamese. Many argued that the escalation of the Vietnam War was due to the reactive policies of the Johnson administration that allowed the conflict to be perpetuated into a chaotic state of total war. Later presidents such as Nixon would also cite the resolution when defending military offensives, most notably against Cambodia in 1970.

The American sentiment surrounding expanded executive powers was hot and cold; at certain times the public called upon the federal government to protect their interests and promote social programs, however, during times of conflict or dissatisfaction, the public turned away from these expansive powers. Long-term implications for such political events and contexts would be seen in contemporary times as the United States entered the 2003 Iraq War, where the American public again called into question the absolute authority of the executive branch.

Americans debated policies and methods designed to root out Communists within the United States, even as both parties tended to support the broader Cold War strategy of containing Communism.

During this period, the greatest concern of many Americans was the rapid spread of the Soviet Union and its Communist ideology. In order to prevent an infiltration of Communism in America, many argued that staunch regulations, legislation, and policies should be in place to prevent such a political and social crisis, as Communism stood against everything valued by Americans.

A second Red Scare dominated the American public during the late 1940s and early 1950s, and in response, President Truman enacted some of the first anti-Communist policies in the United States during this period. Executive Order 9835, issued in 1947, allowed the attorney general to list membership in Fascist, Communist and subversive organizations as grounds for dismissal from work. Many academic institutions, such as Harvard and Columbia, were targeted by the government for supporting Communist sympathizers or discussing the political and social attributes of Communist society. Between 1947 and 1953, close to 13 million workers were questioned and investigated by the federal government by means of the Federal Loyalty Program, resulting in the termination of approximately 3,000 workers and the resignation of nearly 11,000 more.

Such policies would eventually bring about the installation of the House Un-American Activities Committee (HUAC) and the Internal Security Act, all of which actively sought to label and expel those working against America on American soil. By 1954, the American public—as well as those in the Senate and the Eisenhower administration—had grown tired of right-wing Joseph McCarthy and his exaggerated claims of Communist infiltration within the U.S. government. Though McCarthy himself lost the support of the American public, the sentiment of anti-Communism and anti-subversive policies continued for many years and is arguably perceived as his legacy following his death in 1957.

The implications for such domestic policies were far-reaching and left the American public weary of federal investigations. Many Americans were wrongfully accused of supporting subversive movements or Communism itself, which brought into question the use of the federal government's power against its own population.

Although the Korean conflict produced some minor domestic opposition, the Vietnam War saw the rise of sizable, passionate and sometimes violent antiwar protests that became more numerous as the war escalated.

The Vietnam War was a source of bitter contention in the United States during this period, as many of the older generations saw the need for stability in Southeast Asia without the influence of the Soviet Union, while the younger generations saw the conflict as unnecessary and sometimes even criminal. This sentiment was widely expressed in the counterculture and would come to dominate domestic politics during this period. As affluent young Americans were afforded the opportunity for higher education, a division between the counterculture and its parent generation emerged and continued into the later years of the 20th century. Events like the Berkley free speech fight in 1964 caused many young Americans to view the college setting as one in which rebellion and revolution could be fostered, cultivating the historical "teach-ins" of the Vietnam era.

As the war continued, the young American demographic waged protests against the use of napalm and other chemical weapons, massive aerial bombings—now commonplace in the war—and the killing of Vietnamese civilians at the hands of American military personnel. By 1968 and 1969, hundreds of antiwar protests had taken place and were continuing to be organized throughout the country. One such

Vietnam War: Thunderchief pilots bomb military target in Vietnam

notable example took place on November 15, 1969, when as many as 250,000 protestors descended on Washington, D.C., and peacefully called for the withdrawal of American troops from the Vietnam War.

Many Americans, especially those who had fought in the two world wars, saw the protests as disrespectful, unpatriotic and even treasonous. Other younger Americans who took part in the protests saw the actions of the American government in Vietnam as exercising unbridled authority, which many came to see as inappropriate in democratic states such as the United States.

Forms of protest against the war were also seen in the military, where many who did not support the war or were tired of the endless campaign began speaking out against the policies of the Vietnam War. As American troops finally began to withdraw, many others waiting to leave the war actively spoke out against military leadership and the overall morale of the American forces. Thousands of servicemen were dishonorably discharged for desertion, while close to 500,000 men dodged the draft between 1965 and 1973, many fleeing to Canada. All of this exemplified domestic reaction to the occupation of Vietnam, the war itself, and the presidential administrations in the United States that continued to perpetuate America's role in the conflict.

The role of the United States in the Vietnam War and the domestic challenges it presented certainly had lasting implications for the United States and the international system. In the future, Americans would be less certain of their military superiority, something they had clearly embraced following the two world wars. The conflict also brought financial strain to a nation experiencing a period of great economic growth, eventually culminating in massive inflation and the oil crisis of 1973.

Additionally, the American public harbored great division among each other and military servicemen following the conflict. Some saw the returning soldiers as murderers, and others saw them as the vanquished; neither was a comfortable perception for the American population. Medical issues later arose from the use of chemical weapons, such as Agent Orange, used against the Vietnamese and affecting many U.S. service people who were exposed to them. These types of policies would cause frustration and resentment on behalf of the military forces involved in the conflict toward the federal government, perpetuating the perception of a failed military offensive in Vietnam.

US Army spraying Agent Orange in Vietnam

Americans debated the merits of a large nuclear arsenal, the "military-industrial complex," and the appropriate power of the executive branch in conducting foreign and military policy.

As Americans attempted to assimilate into the Cold War period, it became clear that the use of nuclear weapons was a concern for almost all Americans and caused many to question the use and maintenance of a vast nuclear arsenal. Some Americans saw this arsenal as protection against the threat of the Soviet Union and its nuclear arsenal, others believed that nuclear war was imminent and built bomb shelters in their backyards.

The "military-industrial complex" was a term used before the Cold War era by those in World War I and II to describe war profiteering. The term gained particular prominence during the farewell speech given by President Dwight D. Eisenhower in 1961. This particular sentiment was a culmination of the arms races and struggles seen during the Cold War by those living in the United States and the Soviet Union. While President Eisenhower believed a degree of military-industrial complex was necessary to deter the use of nuclear weapons by the Soviet Union, the increased military spending during his presidency also concerned him because it limited his ability to adjust the tax levels below those of Presidents Roosevelt and Truman.

President Eisenhower saw the expansion of ideas such as the military-industrial complex as an expansion of federal power which he did not necessarily support. President Eisenhower, like other conservatives, sought to limit the authority of the federal government in most matters and believed that state and local representation had the best ability to address the majority of American issues. While many supported this concept, others sought to illustrate the negatives of the military-industrial complex, arguing it would greatly alter the source of power within the United States by placing it in the hands of a few elites. Others argued it was a wasteful policy that allowed the overspending of the national security budget while hampering the arms-reduction efforts that were fiercely pursued in light of the period and nuclear threats.

As Americans tried to adjust to the Cold War's nuclear scares and their own nuclear past in Hiroshima and Nagasaki, many began to look to the federal government to limit the threat to national security. Some demanded a more aggressive foreign policy against the Soviet Union, and others sought to question the role of the president in foreign and military affairs. Such concerns were highlighted in the 1960s.

For example, President Lyndon B. Johnson was given rights by Congress via the Gulf of Tonkin Resolution to take whatever actions he deemed appropriate against North Vietnamese attacks in order to maintain the peace and security of Southeast Asia. These types of decisions by the federal government would perpetuate the conversation regarding the president's role in contemporary conflicts and politics. This particular legislation had a far-reaching influence, as it was the legal foundation from which Presidents Lyndon B. Johnson and Richard Nixon would launch their campaigns in the Vietnam War.

> **KEY CONCEPT 8.2:** Liberalism, based on anti-Communism abroad and a firm belief in the efficacy of governmental and especially federal power to achieve social goals at home, reached its apex in the mid-1960s and generated a variety of political and cultural responses.

Americans moved into the 1960s with a new sense of stability and prestige, and the successes of the previous decade seemed to spur on new social movements, most notably the civil rights movement and counterculture movement, which dominated domestic politics during the 1960s. During this period, the United States continued to expand its influence within the international system as a constant adversary to Communism, which was in line with how many Americans believed the foreign policy of the period should be handled.

In order to address the failed system of segregation, the United States finally began to adopt legislation and policies that would eventually bring equality to African Americans. In order to address the social concerns of the counterculture, the federal government attempted to expand rights in the workplace, ending segregated hiring practices and limiting gender discrimination practices. However, many struggles were yet to come, and many would march, protest and sit in before any real action was taken.

Americans looked to the federal government for economic assurances and protection of their freedoms. In 1965, President Lyndon B. Johnson issued an executive order requiring that all federal contractors use affirmative action in its hiring process, eliminating workplace discrimination for minorities and women. Many large companies that held government contracts were now required to hire more minorities and women.

President Johnson, who supported the civil rights movement, also attempted to recognize the concerns of the African American population by appointing Thurgood Marshall to the Supreme Court; Marshall was the first African American to hold this position.

U.S. Supreme Court Justice, Thurgood Marshall

The actions of the 1960s set in motion the future social expectations of the 20th and 21st centuries. After this decade, many Americans concluded that everyone should have an equal voice in the democratic principles of the United States, minorities and women included. Social demonstrations became an avenue many Americans accessed in order to have their grievances heard and addressed, perpetuating the idea that the United States is a land of freedom and opportunity for all.

Seeking to fulfill Reconstruction-era promises, civil rights activists and political leaders achieved some legal and political successes in ending segregation, although progress toward equality was slow and halting.

During the late 1940s and 1950s, civil rights activists continued to fight the social and racial inequalities being experienced by many African Americans in the United States. While progress was sometimes slow or even stagnant, the movement persevered and eventually culminated in the end of racial segregation.

Rosa Parks and
Dr. Martin Luther King Jr.

Initial victories were seen in *Brown v. Board of Education* (described further in this chapter) and the Montgomery Bus Boycott after the arrest of Rosa Parks in December 1955. The Bus Boycott also sparked further progress within the civil rights movement, this time across the country, as news reports regarding the boycott garnered civil rights support from the American public. Eventually, it was determined by lower courts that the segregation of the public bus system was unconstitutional.

The emergence and leadership of Dr. Martin Luther King Jr. also sparked renewed interest and support of the civil rights movement, continuing the momentum that culminated in the Civil Rights Act of 1965.

Following World War II, civil rights activists utilized a variety of strategies—legal challenges, direct action, and nonviolent protest tactics—to combat racial discrimination.

In order to stem the tide of segregation and racism in America, many social activists worked tirelessly with the help of the federal government to create equality for all in the late 20th century. Many notable social activists came from this period, including Fannie Lou Hamer, Thurgood Marshall, and John Lewis; all worked by different means to bring social equality to the United States.

Fannie Lou Hamer was a civil rights activist who worked for the Student Nonviolent Coordinating Committee and co-founded the Mississippi Freedom Democratic Party in 1964. Hamer worked endlessly against racial discrimination in politics, promoting democratic voting rights and systems to inadequately represented African Americans. In 1962, Hamer, along with seventeen other African American activists, registered to vote in spite of local and state obstruction by police forces and white Americans in the South, who met such actions during this period with fierce resistance and interference. As a result, Hamer was fired from her job at a plantation where she had lived and worked for two decades. However, Hamer saw this action as a blessing and began pursuing civil rights on a more intensified scale.

John Lewis was a U.S. Congressman and avid activist of the civil rights movement who championed the rights and freedoms of all Americans. Lewis maintained roles of leadership in various organizations, and he was the Chairman of the Student Nonviolent Coordination Committee and the director of the Voter Education Project (VEP). Lewis was also instrumental in the 1963 March on Washington, where he was the keynote speaker and the Selma march that took place on March 7, 1965. Lewis was arrested more than forty times during the civil rights era and was able to put in place a monumental framework for racial and social equality.

Thurgood Marshall was another influential civil rights activist who maintained membership with the NAACP and championed the early court cases of *Brown v. Board of Education*. He was appointed associate justice of the United States Supreme Court by President Johnson in October 1967 and served through October 1991. Marshall was the 96th justice and first African American on the Supreme Court.

Such events had a vast impact on the civil rights movement. The use of sit-ins, boycotts, freedom rides, peaceful marches and the protection offered by the Supreme Court facilitated slow but constant progress in the fight for racial equality.

Decision-makers in each of the three branches of the federal government used measures including desegregation of the armed services, *Brown v. Board of Education* and the Civil Rights Act of 1964 to promote greater racial justice.

In attempts to create real racial equality, the U.S. government—by means of the judicial, legislative and executive branches—facilitated great progress in the civil rights movement of the 1950s, 1960s, and 1970s. Notable examples included the entire desegregation of the armed services following the historic Supreme Court ruling in May 1954 in *Brown v. Board of Education*. The Supreme Court ruled that the "separate but equal" segregation laws in public schools were unconstitutional, transforming the civil rights movement. This ruling would be used over and over to delegalize federal and state segregation.

The Civil Rights Act of 1957 established the Civil Rights Division of the Department of Justice, which empowered the federal government and prosecutors to obtain court injunctions against interference with the right to vote. This was monumental in accomplishing fair democratic representation of the African American population. Adding to this success was the Twenty-Fourth Amendment, which eliminated the poll tax that required payment to participate in federal elections and limited voting. The Civil Rights Act of 1964 outlawed discrimination based on race, color, religion, sex or national origin, enforced equal employment and ended segregation in public places.

These acts of legislation and rulings by the Supreme Court forever altered the political and judicial landscape of the United States, finally affirming to the nation and others that true equality is obtainable through the cooperative efforts and hard work of social activists and the American public.

Continuing white resistance slowed efforts at desegregation, sparking a series of social and political crises across the nation, while tensions among civil rights activists over tactical and philosophical issues increased after 1965.

As civil rights activists made progress in their pursuits, some Americans—most notably in the South—adamantly rejected desegregation and equal rights for African Americans. This sentiment was embodied in several crises of the period including the Montgomery Bus Boycott, the Little Rock desegregation and the Watts riots. Following the call for public desegregation, many in local and state governments in the South attempted to pursue their own policies by raising funds to create white-only private schools or defunding public school programs, as exemplified in 1956 by Virginia legislatures.

Black students turned away in Little Rock, Arkansas

During this period, southern state legislatures passed close to 500 laws attempting to block the Supreme Court decision of *Brown v. Board of Education*. Unfortunately, the measures taken by state governments opposed to desegregation were quite efficient and the federal government typically lacked the ability or desire to intervene. However, by 1957, the federal government was forced to intervene in Little Rock, Arkansas, as the school system refused to integrate African American students. With the help of the National Guard, nine students were escorted to school and protected by federal troops. As a result, the Virginia legislature ordered that all public high schools close rather than be fully desegregated, which was enforced until April 1959 following the Supreme Court ruling that the school system reopen.

The racial tensions of this period created serious sources of conflict and aggression; most times these actions were taken against African Americans. However, in August 1965, African Americans protested in Watts, California, leading to massive riots that lasted upwards of a week and left thirty-four dead and countless injured. These initial riots would foreshadow further unrest in the summer of 1966 and embodied the sentiment of frustration among young African Americans. These racial riots spread across the country and impacted cities such as Cleveland, Chicago, and Detroit, which had to request federal troops and National Guardsmen to quell the riots. Such racial tensions between young African Americans and the police forces in urban areas would continue into the 21st century.

Stirred by a growing awareness of inequalities in American society and by the African American civil rights movement, activists also addressed issues of identity and social justice, such as gender, sexuality, and ethnicity.

During this period, all demographics of the American population experienced publication and social activist recognition, this was also the case regarding the emergence of sexuality following the counterculture. Many women activists such as Gloria Steinem sought to shed light on the gender inequalities and discrimination of the period. One notable example of such activism came in 1963 when Steinem went undercover at the notorious New York City Playboy Club, where she detailed the degrading experience women faced in the workplace. Such publications were read everywhere and received by many women as a gratifying criticism of the sexism faced in America.

Activists began to question society's assumptions about gender and to call for social and economic equality for women and for gays and lesbians.

During this period, the feminist movement took a strong position within the American public and caused the equality conversation to not only encompass women but gays and lesbians as well. This conversation would begin during the 1960s but continued to evolve in the 21st century. Notable figures of the feminist movement during this period included Betty Friedan and Gloria Steinem.

Betty Friedan's *The Feminine Mystique* (1963) criticized domestication and challenged the perception of women as housewives, which was widely circulated in the 1950s. This book sought to educate women on vocational opportunities outside of the home and encouraged women to be more than housewives. Gloria Steinem was also a social activist and writer of the period who worked to promote women's rights and equality by means of political and vocational opportunities. Steinem worked to create *New York* magazine in the 1960s, and during the 1970s founded the National Women's Political Caucus and *Ms. Magazine*, a feminist publication. The feminist movement of this period would eventually catapult into a full gender movement encompassing the rights and freedoms of gays and lesbians within the American community.

Latinos, American Indians, and Asian Americans began to demand social and economic equality and a redress of past injustices.

Cesar Chavez

As African Americans and women began seeing the progress of the civil rights and women's movements, other minorities who had faced similar oppression and prejudice worked to promote their own equalities and bring to light injustices. One such example comes from Cesar Chavez, who was the leader of the United Farm Workers, a nonviolent labor movement, from 1963 until 1970. This movement would lead to the unionization of Mexican American farm workers, and for the first time gave appropriate credence to the difficulties faced by immigrant and nonimmigrant workers in the American Southwest.

Other organizations who pursued equality for Mexican Americans was La Raza Unida, or the National United Peoples Party, which successfully elected many Mexican Americans to local and state government positions. The goal of La Raza Unida was the procurement of better-paying jobs, better educational opportunities, and more adequate housing.

Native Americans were also pursuing better recognition and rights on behalf of the U.S. government during this period. The American Indian Movement (AIM) was an Indian activist organization created to monitor police activities, promote cultural renewal and coordinate vocational opportunities among both urban and rural Native American populations. The AIM was a source of concern for the federal government in the early 1970s, as it occupied the Bureau of Indian Affairs headquarters in 1972 and the Pine Ridge Indian Reservation at Wounded Knee, South Dakota, in 1973.

Despite the perception of overall affluence in postwar America, advocates raised awareness of the prevalence and persistence of poverty as a national problem, sparking efforts to address this issue.

As many Americans experienced unprecedented growth and leisure, many others still struggled to maintain a reasonable standard of living, typically falling below the poverty line, which during this period constituted making less than $3,000 annually.In order to combat these issues, President Kennedy and President Johnson enacted great legislative measures by means of social programs in order to address poverty in America. Under President Kennedy, Congress appropriated close to $5 million in urban renewal efforts aimed at easing poverty in cities across America. The passage of the Area Redevelopment Act in 1961 also worked to provide economic aid to impoverished rural and urban populations, while attempting to address unemployment in these demographics. President Johnson continued these efforts through his version of the New Deal, which provided additional aid and support to the lower income demographics.

President John F. Kennedy

As many liberal principles came to dominate postwar politics and court decisions, liberalism came under attack from the left as well as from resurgent conservative movements.

During the postwar years, many liberal presidents, most notably Presidents Kennedy and Johnson, were able to use this school of thought to bolster domestic affairs, while struggling to maintain foreign affairs. Due to this shortfall in global politics, many in the government, most notably conservatives, began to question the soft policies toward Communism and domestic spending on social programs, which led to a revitalization of conservative movements in the American public and government.

Liberalism reached its zenith with Lyndon Johnson's Great Society efforts to use federal power to end racial discrimination, eliminate poverty and address other social issues while attacking Communism abroad.

Under President Lyndon B. Johnson, the United States experienced the largest expansion of domestic social programs since those of President Franklin D. Roosevelt. Many Americans viewed the "Great Society" advanced by President Johnson as a means to combat poverty and political and social inequalities determined by race and gender. President Johnson's firm stance against Communism caused many Americans to view the presidency of Johnson as a continuation of the ideals put forth by President John F. Kennedy.

President Lyndon B. Johnson

In March 1964, President Johnson wrote to Congress calling for the end of poverty in America, which he hoped to accomplish through social programs comparable to the reforms of the New Deal. In order to deal with poverty in rural America, President Johnson initially proposed a $962 million aid package; however, by 1966, this package had grown close to $3 billion. President Johnson also sought to create jobs by means of social programs that would bolster aid and federal support to educational services, the civil rights movement and the poor, following in the footsteps of President Kennedy, who founded the Volunteer in Service to America (VISTA) program, which provided volunteer services to rural and underprivileged areas across the United States.

President Johnson also embraced the civil rights movement and continued to show presidential support for the equality of African Americans across the country. By asking Congress to continue President Kennedy's legacy by means of civil rights legislation, President Johnson was able to form and enact the greatest civil rights reforms since the Reconstruction era, and in 1965 he heralded the Voting Rights Act as monumental legislation.

Continued expansion of social programs and oversight by President Johnson resulted in forming the Department of Housing and Urban Development, initiating Medicare and Medicaid. Additionally, implementing a Head Start program allowed preschool students to be better prepared in the educational system. Other notable policies of the Great Society included conservation efforts emerging throughout the country, the creation of the food stamps system and the protection of the American public as consumers.

President Johnson differed from his predecessor on foreign affairs such as involvement in the Vietnam War and the expulsion of Communism at any price. During this period, Johnson cautiously expanded the United States' role in the conflict by signing secret negotiations and policies that allowed American military forces to take covert actions against the North Vietnamese. These policies expanded to limited bombing raids on Northern Vietnam, and following the passage of the Gulf of Tonkin Resolution, President Johnson led the United States into a full-scale war against the North Vietnamese and Communism.

Liberal ideas were realized in Supreme Court decisions that expanded democracy and individual freedoms, Great Society social programs and policies and the power of the federal government, yet these unintentionally helped energize a new conservative movement that mobilized to defend traditional visions of morality and the proper role of state authority.

The United States Supreme Court ruling in the case of *Miranda v. Arizona* in 1966 resulted in the decision that police officers are required to make detainees aware of their constitutional rights to an attorney and self-incrimination upon arrest. The case highlighted the judicial struggles of Americans against a system they did not always understand.

Ernesto Miranda, a Phoenix resident, was arrested on charges of rape, kidnapping, and robbery, and after a police interrogation confessed to the crimes. However, Miranda held less than a high school education, had a history of mental illness and had no legal counsel present at the time of interrogation. Given the circumstances, Miranda appealed to the Supreme Court, arguing that his confession had been acquired through unconstitutional means. This ruling resulted in the "Miranda rights," which are read to all those arrested by the police.

Another important Supreme Court ruling during this period comes from the *Griswold v. Connecticut* case of 1965, which ruled that a federal ban on contraceptives violated the privacy of marriage. Estelle Griswold was the executive director of the Planned Parenthood League of Connecticut and provided many women with contraception; she was eventually convicted by a Connecticut court for violating a law passed in 1879, which prohibited the facilitation of contraceptives. The Supreme Court ruled that this was unconstitutional and eliminated the ban on contraceptive use.

Estelle Griswold

As these cases were influencing the American population of the time, conservative opponents of such legislation worked adamantly to restore the traditional values of the American family and pastime. Many argued against contraception and abortions, citing moral and religious concerns.

However, these cases would have a drastic influence on the future rights of the American public. Future legal battles would cite cases such as *Miranda v. Arizona*, *Griswold v. Connecticut* and *Roe v. Wade* as examples of the expansion of judicial protection, freedoms, and controversial American rights.

Groups on the left also assailed liberals, claiming they did too little to transform the racial and economic status quo at home and pursued immoral policies abroad.

As the civil rights movement lagged, some activists began to seek a different way to achieve racial equality. Prominent black separatist Malcolm X had been advocating a drastic departure from King's methods for a number of years, but still did not garner the public support necessary to propel his social revolution. Malcolm X embodied a different perception of the civil rights movement, as he was willing to resort to violence in order to right the wrongs of American society.

The Black Panther Party for Self-Defense—also known as the Black Panther movement—founded in Oakland in 1966 by Huey Newton and Bobby Seale, employed similar tactics. The movement, which attempted to police minority communities against the threats of the federal government, also wished to enact a type of revolutionary socialism for the minority and working classes. The Black Panther movement highlighted the frustration of many African Americans who argued that the federal government had done too little to grant equality to all races.

Groups like the Black Panthers argued that no real action had come from the accommodating policies of Dr. Martin Luther King Jr., and acts of violence would more effectively force the hands of the federal government into action. The Student Nonviolent Coordination Committee (SNCC) also followed the path of Malcolm X and the Black Panthers. The SNCC had previously been part of the MLK camp of nonaggression towards racial injustice. Stokely Carmichael from Brooklyn led the organization and called for active participation in Freedom Rides aimed at desegregating the bus systems.

While the federal government faced criticism at home regarding its stalled interaction with the civil rights movement, other organizations began to criticize the United States for its foreign policies. The Students for a Democratic Society, who initially voiced concern over income inequality, racial justice, and participatory democracy, quickly gained traction in the antiwar protests of the period. This particular group was a more radical entity of the counterculture and worked against the U.S. military actions domestically and abroad.

Such social movements were influential in creating the perception of free speech among university campuses across the country while giving a voice to urban impoverished minorities who had been ignored for decades. These organizations were critical of the federal government and allowed many students to march against inequalities and injustices, a freedom that is greatly prized by many Americans today.

KEY CONCEPT 8.3: Postwar economic, demographic and technological changes had a far-reaching impact on American society, politics and the environment.

During the postwar years, many Americans changed their perception of the American dream to one that included living in a Sun Belt state, such as California, Texas, or Florida, with many consumer amenities like radios and refrigerators. This ideal American life had changed from those eager to work in industrial or manufacturing jobs while living in big northern cities to those interested in new sectors of work like the military installations or factories of the Sun Belt. For the first time, Americans were less interested in the East Coast and focused their attention west into the southwestern states, propelling massive immigration into these regions and cementing the American transition out of the two world wars and into the Cold War era.

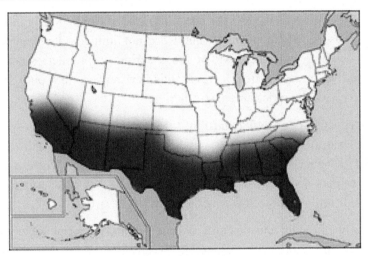

Sun Belt states

In addition to the formation and federal stimulation of the Sun Belt, the American population experienced an unprecedented surge that produced baby boomer generation, which quickly outnumbered any other demographic in the United States. Such numbers alone would allow this generation to greatly influence American culture and the future of American society, for example, the emergence of rock and roll music, suburbanites and the explosion of the middle class.

In this period, Americans were concerned with the state of American lands and natural resources and for the first time were able to enact federal regulatory standards and institutions aimed at preserving and maintaining the splendor of the United States. Examples of this are seen in the formation of the Environmental Protection Agency in 1970 and the first regulatory law of pollutants, the Clean Air Act, also passed by Congress in 1970.

The long-term implications for this period can be seen in the transition of the American population away from staunch traditionalism to one supported by various groups of revolution and social movements, such as the counterculture. The emergence of Sun Belt states also paved the way for millions of Americans to live their version of the American dream in new and various ways.

Rapid economic and social changes in American society fostered a sense of optimism in the postwar years as well as underlying concerns about how these changes were affecting American values.

As the U.S. economy exploded out of the postwar years, many Americans began experiencing a quality of life previously unknown to the middle and lower classes, and traditionalists were concerned with the social implications of this economic development. During the 1950s, most Americans experienced a prolonged period of economic achievement, growth, and stability. Many Americans were now earning more, causing an explosion of the middle class, which by this time included close to 60 percent of the population. Middle-class earners in this period were those who earned between $3,000 and $10,000 annually.

There was also rapid expansion into suburban living by the baby boomers, which also caused a new market of housing and financing to develop, further propelling the American economy. Enhancing this new life were the consumer amenities previously out of range for the middle or lower classes, which included but were not limited to refrigerators, secondary automobiles, and washing machines. All of these consumer products were meant to show Americans how to live an easier life. However, this new movement would spark a consumer culture that caused various rivalries amongst Americans.

As the new generations took control of the economic and political spheres during this period, it became clear that a transition was underfoot from the traditionalist mindsets of their parents to a modern concept of the American dream and family. These new ideas greatly concerned many parents and conservatives, as they instead saw a deterioration of the social system they had so heartily embraced during the early 1950s.

These newly emerging tensions and rivalries within American society caused many to be concerned about the implications economic expansion had on the public. The lives of teenagers during this period were drastically different from those of their parents, inciting the counterculture movements of the late 20th century.

A burgeoning private sector, continued federal spending, the baby boom and technological developments helped spur economic growth, middle-class suburbanization, social mobility, a rapid expansion of higher education and the rise of the "Sun Belt" as a political and economic force.

As Americans began to settle into the prosperous times of the 1950s and 1960s, the United States experienced an unprecedented explosion in the population, leading many to call this generation the baby boomers. The period that saw the most growth was from 1946 to 1964, with the greatest rise in population taking place in 1957. This movement was unexpected, but greatly influenced the culture and political landscape we see today, as this generation sparked the counterculture movement and expanded U.S. hegemony around the globe leading into the 21st century.

This population explosion, which saw the addition of nearly 50 million babies by the end of 1950, also catapulted the emergence of the Sun Belt as a political force. Following the postwar years, Americans began to settle in Sun Belt states such as California, Arizona, Texas and Florida at a much more rapid rate than the northeastern industrial communities. This transition was due in part to the influx of investment and political influence stemming from these states, but also the draw of living in states with better wealth distribution and climates more forgiving than the Midwest or Northeast.

In addition to an improved community and climate, the federal government encouraged many thousands of people to move to Sun Belt states by providing an abundance of jobs by means of federal defense spending on weapons systems and the completion of military installations. Furthermore, larger portions of the federal budget were being sent to Sun Belt states and were financing infrastructure development in the region.

While the population's attention shifted its focus to the Sun Belt states, former industrial sectors in the Midwest and Northeast, most notably in the Ohio Valley, were impacted very negatively by the boom and the expansion of other states. Former industrial giants and other manufacturing states eventually became known as the Frostbelt or Rustbelt and were becoming increasingly dissatisfied with the domestic policies of the United States, which now transitioned away from its industrial and manufacturing roots and instead intensified its focus on a service-based economy.

Small family farms also felt the pinch of the explosion of Sun Belt states, as larger agribusiness models were limiting and replacing small family-run farms. Such transitions between big and small businesses, East and West Coast perceptions and influences and service versus industry all set the stage for social tensions that would divide the country in the following years.

These economic and social changes, in addition to the anxiety engendered by the Cold War, led to an increasingly homogeneous mass culture as well as challenges to conformity by artists, intellectuals and rebellious youth.

As the baby boomers grew into young adulthood and responded to the Cold War pressures, new social movements emerged that were often centered on nonconformity and individualism. The emergence of music as a social revolution was first introduced in the early 1950s, as many teenagers sought to find a music genre that embodied their interests and ambitions. This was a transition from early periods where music choice was typically decided by race, as Caucasians typically embraced country and gospel genres, and African Americans preferred rhythm and blues tracks. In 1951, a Cleveland disc jockey named Alan Freed coined the term "rock and roll" as a way of characterizing the young white population's interest in blues music. From this point on, the movement exploded and would carry itself into contemporary periods.

Trading card photo of Alan Freed

In 1956, Elvis Presley released his first radio sensation, "Heartbreak Hotel," which horrified many traditionalists and excited the younger populations. Examples of this can be seen in the appearances Elvis made on the *Ed Sullivan Show* during the 1950s and 1960s, known across the country as a traditional family program. Initial rock and roll music had a connotation of rebellion and sexuality, which would later be seen to a greater extent in the counterculture. Easy access to radios, Dick Clark's television program *American Bandstand* and 45-rpm records all propelled the music revolution to be a mainstay of this generation.

Elvis Presley

The Beat movement of the 1950s can also be seen as a precursor to the counterculture movement, as many popular writers glorified wanderlust and free love in their novels. One such example comes from Jack Kerouac, who in 1957 published *On the Road,* which detailed two men's journeys across the United States, highlighted by drug experiences, free love and what would later be described as the counterculture. Other notable figures of the Beat movement included Allen Ginsberg and William Burroughs. Another important literary work from this period is *The Affluent Society* by economist John Kenneth Galbraith, which detailed the rise of the middle class and economic growth following the war years, specifically World War II.

Conservatives, fearing juvenile delinquency, urban unrest and challenges to the traditional family, increasingly promoted their own values and ideology.

As the American political and military landscape changed during the Cold War, the American family also experienced a great transformation during this period. As the "greatest" generation returned from war and settled back into American society, it was clear that an age of American prosperity was on the horizon that included domestic economic stability and growth, as well as the newly championed position as a global power. However, not all saw the United States in this light during the 1960s and 1970s. The conservative school of thought saw these transitions as attacks against the traditional family structure, as well as the American perception of the formal social structure.

In order to promote what they believed to be the best path for America, many conservatives spoke out against rock and roll music and the later counterculture movement, and reminded the American public of its traditional values, including stay-at-home mothers and obedient children. However, many of these conservatives experienced great backlash and were marginalized by the 1970s movements.

As federal programs expanded and economic growth reshaped American society, many sought greater access to prosperity, even as critics began to question the burgeoning use of natural resources.

As the Sun Belt gained prominence among Americans and politicians, many saw the draws of California and the Southwest as very desirable, causing massive population influxes to the regions. It became evident that the federal government planned to extract and use natural resources in an almost reckless manner in order to feed the machine of postwar expansion.

The federal funding of the Sun Belt states caused many formerly prestigious industrial and manufacturing cities, such as Cleveland and other Rust Belt cities, to lose their draw, and instead encouraged many Americans to embrace the military installations and job opportunities being presented in the Sun Belt states. However, these states were less easily tamed by the American population, with extreme weather conditions, including the hot deserts of the Southwest, and the lack of water necessary to sustain the population influx. As a result, many Americans began questioning the expansion of Sun Belt states at the expense of American natural resources, which were beginning to become more respected and protected. The depletion of resources and the declining Rust Belt states caused many Americans to view the expansion as risky and at times unnecessary.

Internal migrants, as well as migrants from around the world, sought access to the economic boom and other benefits of the United States, especially after the passage of new immigration laws in 1965.

As Americans experienced vast economic progress, their concerns regarding immigration quotas became less and less evident, pointing to the fact that America has been open to immigration during times of prosperity, but opposed it during periods of economic crises or uncertainty. Many immigrants continued to view the United States as the land of opportunity and worked tirelessly to obtain passage to America and citizenship in the country.

In October 1965, Congress, under the Presidency of Lyndon B. Johnson, passed the Immigration and Nationality Act, also known as the Hart-Celler Act, which ended the immigration quotas of the early 20th century. Rather than enacting across-the-board quotas, immigration into the United States would now focus on skill sets and the relationships to relatives who were already citizens or living in the country.

Restrictions were placed on visas, capping them at 170,000 per year with various exceptions including people born in "independent" nations in the Western Hemisphere— highlighting the age of the Cold War—and former citizens, ministers, and employees of the U.S. government. These laws reflected a change in the perception of Americans; formerly many saw the influx of immigrants as troublesome and unproductive, now Americans were vastly more concerned with the spread of Communism and the Soviet Union.

Responding to the abuse of natural resources and the alarming environmental problems, activists and legislators began to call for conservation measures and a fight against pollution.

Following the period of wartime industrial production, the U.S. government began to evaluate the environmental concerns being raised by conservationists and the American public. Previously, the federal government had taken small steps towards maintaining the natural resources of the country, but it was not until the 1960s and 1970s that the American public truly became concerned with pollutants and the status of the environment.

One of the early advocates of conservation and environmentalism was Rachel Carson, who was a writer, social activist, and ecologist. Carson studied many subject areas relating to the environment and the sciences; she received a Master of Arts in Marine Biology from Woods Hole and undertook graduate studies in zoology at Johns Hopkins University. In 1962, Carson released *The Silent Spring*, which raised concerns among the American public regarding the use of pesticides (particularly DDT) in the American agricultural system. In June 1963, Carson testified about the misuse of pesticides before the U.S. Senate Subcommittee on Government Operations.

Rachel Carson and Robert Hines

Rachel Carson was one of the first conservators to speak out against the mistreatment of America's lands and natural resources during this period and greatly influenced others to continue this same cause. Other notable activists of this period include Wisconsin Senator Gaylord Nelson, who championed the creation of Earth Day in 1969, mimicking the teach-in activists seen during the Vietnam War. Senator Nelson was like many other Americans who were influenced by the environmental concerns of the period and sought to use the federal government to regulate and protect the environment.

Public perception during this period led to various government responses including The Wilderness Protection Act. Signed into law in 1964, this act designated wilderness areas as defined by the law as the most protected forms of federal land. The establishment of the EPA in 1970 and the passage of the Clean Air Act in the same year demonstrate the federal government's active attempts to regulate and protect the American public against the harms of pollution.

The Clean Air Act gave the federal government the ability to control and regulate air pollutants considered hazardous to human health. Such legislative initiatives and social movements would set the stage for future generations to pursue conservation efforts.

New demographic and social issues led to significant political and moral debates that sharply divided the nation.

As the middle class emerged following the boom of the 1950s, many Americans struggled to gain an identity in the new country. Some insisted upon maintaining the traditional values of the American family through hard work and faith, others argued this was a period of revolution and worked towards the civil rights and feminist movements.

During this period, the American public was divided on a great many things including but not limited to the civil rights movement, desegregation and the distinction and tensions experienced between conservatism and liberalism in this period. Some Americans embraced the counterculture while others saw it as an attack on the traditionalist views of the American public. Americans began to question the authority and leadership of the presidency as a result of expanded executive powers and the Watergate scandal which engulfed President Richard Nixon. Additionally, many Americans wanted the federal government to regulate and conserve the natural resources and lands of the country, while others felt this was unnecessary.

Marine Corps scaling wall during the Korean War

The Korean and Vietnam Wars are two of the largest sources of contention among the American public, as many saw these conflicts as murderous and unwanted and others believed the threat of Communism was so great that any action was necessary to impede Soviet expansion. Debates regarding the sexual and reproductive rights of women during this period also caused great controversy and left the American public with the task of deciding the morality of others, making many feel uncomfortable. All of these divisions show the transition America experienced in the postwar years, and while it was prosperous and exciting to many of the baby boomer generation, others saw these polarizations as the context for future tensions in America.

Although the image of the traditional nuclear family dominated popular perceptions in the postwar era, the family structure of Americans was undergoing profound changes as the number of working women increased and many social attitudes changed.

Following the booming 1950s, most Americans viewed the family structure in a traditional sense, with a domesticated stay-at-home mother and a father who worked outside of the home. Such perceptions were amplified following the baby boom, which projected women as subservient maintainers of the traditional values of family. However, other women, mainly those who had occupied various vocational posts during the war years, wanted to experience a new American dream of working outside of the home while also maintaining their families and personal lives. This change in public opinion resulted in the popularity of feminist movements during the period, but also highlighted a counter movement that viewed women's rightful place in the home and worked to promote the social norms maintained during the 1950s.

As the American population adjusted to the postwar political climate, it became clear that women would continue to maintain many roles acquired during the war years, especially in the workforce. Following the domestic war boom, former munitions factories and manufacturing plants, which had been used for arms production and military rearmament, were transformed to meet the demands of the newly emerged consumer culture, providing new avenues of work for women.

During World War II, many women joined the workforce in factories and cities, filling the void left behind by the predominantly male workforce that had gone to war. During this period, close to 25 percent of the workforce was made up of women. However, during the later years of the 20th century, women continued to expand their roles within the workforce, and between 1945 and 1960, they made up nearly 50 percent of the total American working population.

This transition in social perceptions would be monumental for continued women's movements of the late 20th and early 21st centuries. It also highlights the social divisions of the period and shows the United States as a country striving to provide equal rights and opportunities for all. Women and other minorities would continue to experience setbacks—such as the failure to ratify the Equal Rights Amendment in 1972—but would continue to work towards equality.

Young people who participated in the counterculture of the 1960s rejected many of the social, economic and political values of their parents' generation, initiated a sexual revolution and introduced greater informality into U.S. culture.

The young Americans who began the counterculture movement had an unknown ally amongst them—the sheer volume of participants following the years of the baby boom. The counterculture generation held the largest sector of the American population and due to size alone had transformative influence over the American culture of the late 20th and early 21st centuries.

The counterculture embraced nonconformity and a transition away from traditional or parental values; many were labeled as hippies who worked against everything their traditional parents had established during the prosperous years of the 1950s. As young Americans sought to find themselves away from suburban neighborhoods and the confines of traditional American family values, their parents worked to discredit the counterculture movement and bring back their conservative values. Instead, the counterculture movement embraced many social taboos, such as public nudity, free love and the open use of recreational drugs (e.g. LSD, marijuana).

The counterculture also embraced communal existence and saw the rise of many couples living together outside of wedlock, something unheard of during the 1950s. In addition to testing social norms, the counterculture also provided Americans with access to healthier foods such as granola, yogurt, and wheat germ, all of which were completely alien to the American diet before this period. As young men and women sought to find their individuality, the explosion of tie-dyed shirts, afros and long hair tied with wildflowers all embodied the transformative idea of the counterculture, frightening many traditionalists who thought the American family and core values had been tarnished.

The emergence of a sexual revolution was also seen during this period, which promoted free love and the use of birth control. While many initially saw this as the most expressive form of the counterculture movement, downsides of such openness were quickly seen in terms of venereal diseases. The counterculture also embraced drug use, most notably LSD and marijuana, and notable academics such as Harvard professor Dr. Timothy Leary argued in support of the open use of LSD. However, drawbacks to such attitudes were quickly seen in drug addictions and "bad trips." The ramifications of the counterculture can still be seen today in dietary changes by the American public (towards both healthier and less healthy choices), acceptance of recreational drugs—notably marijuana use in recent years—and the continued perception of individuality as a key attribute.

Timothy Leary arrested by the DEA in 1972

Conservatives and liberals clashed over many new social issues, the power of the presidency and the federal government, and movements for greater individual rights.

As Americans moved into the later years of the 21st century, many began seeing an intense polarization and divide among the American public and government officials. New social issues arose out of this period, and many saw the need for reforms distinct from previous movements. Instead, Americans sought to embrace a new identity that would mold the international perception of the United States in the coming years.

An example of the monumental conditions of the period comes from Watergate, which rattled the faith of the American people in the office of the president and the federal government as a whole. Several burglars were apprehended inside the Democratic National Committee, a federal building in Washington, D.C. while attempting to place wiretaps and illegally retrieve federal documents. While it was unclear if President Nixon ordered or had knowledge of such acts, it was immediately clear that he had actively attempted to cover up the wiretap scandals.

Watergate complex

President Nixon offered hush money to those initially questioned by law enforcement in regards to the burglary and attempted to obstruct investigation by the Federal Bureau of Investigation. Nixon fired staff unwilling to support his position in the scandal and physically destroyed evidence of his administration's wrongdoing. In August 1974, President Richard Nixon resigned as the full extent of his involvement reached the American public. President Gerald Ford quickly and assertively pardoned President Nixon, removing any possibility of legal action. Such events greatly divided the American public, causing some to side with President Nixon and others to vehemently despise him and his presidency.

Other examples of public divide during this period came from the legal proceedings of *Bakke v. University of California*, where the United States Supreme Court ruled it unconstitutional to use the basis of race for college admittance above merit, or as the only determining factor. The court ruled against meeting racial quotas, but argued affirmative action was acceptable if it was used to promote greater diversity and used on a case-by-case basis. Some argued that such events highlighted a new problem of reverse discrimination and showed that while the attempt at creating an equal America was underway, it was far from over.

Women also struggled for equality during the 1950s, 1960s, and 1970s, and such divisions were colorfully demonstrated in the rivalry between Phyllis Schlafly, an opponent of women's equality laws, and Gloria Steinem, who worked tirelessly for the emergence of gender equality. Phyllis Schlafly argued that women would suffer if further equality measures were taken because such changes would enter women into the draft, revoke protection from the law in sexual assault and custody cases, and—most importantly—destroy the traditional American family. Schlafly promoted the Stop ERA campaign, which worked against the efforts of feminists and proponents of women's rights and eventually caused a resurgence of concern with the sanctity of the traditional American family amongst the public.

Please, leave your Customer Review on Amazon

PERIOD 9

1980-Present

Transitioning to a new century filled with challenges and opportunities, the U.S. experienced renewed ideological and cultural debates and sought to redefine its foreign policy. It adapted to economic globalization and revolution of science and technology.

Major historical events of the period:

1979 – Iran hostage crisis

1986 – Iran–Contra Scandal

1987 – Reagan asks Gorbachev to tear down the Berlin Wall

1991 – Operation Desert Storm

2001 – September 11 terrorist attacks

2001 – War on Terror begins

PERIOD 9: 1980-Present

KEY CONCEPT 9.1: A new conservatism grew to prominence in U.S. culture and politics, defending traditional social values and rejecting liberal views about the role of government.

In reaction to the political failures and uncertainty of a disenchanted public, conservatives had a revival during the 1980s which continued into the 1990s and the new century. The perception of the government shifted to a conservative viewpoint as people began to openly question and criticize their leaders. People lacked faith in the government and therefore wanted the government to be in control of fewer vital industries and programs. This drew people toward right-wing conservatives like Ronald Reagan who stood as staunch supporters of smaller government and deregulation of industries. While conservatism achieved gains and growth as a movement, conservatives were not fully successful, as numerous liberal systems and programs were difficult for them to change or defeat.

President Ronald Reagan

Reduced public faith in the government's ability to solve social and economic problems, the growth of religious fundamentalism and the dissemination of neoconservative thought all combined to invigorate conservatism.

As the 1970s came to a close, the U.S. government was struggling to maintain the faith of the people. The seventies were characterized by scandals and failures in the eyes of many Americans. Nixon's Watergate scandal led to a drop in public opinion, as the American people questioned the morality and legality of their president's actions. Nixon's eventual resignation left the people feeling betrayed and abandoned by their leader. It also led to a lack of faith in the office of the president itself, a position which had so often offered hope and inspiration. Public trust in the president of the United States took years to recover from the blow dealt by the Nixon scandal.

The OPEC oil embargo caused a widespread economic recession and a wave of unemployment and inflation. Most people put the blame squarely at the feet of the American government. After the Iran hostage crisis' paralyzing effects on the Carter presidency, which once again weakened the faith of the American people in their government and president, it was obvious that the United States was ready for a change in leadership. Ronald Reagan, more able to harness the waves of religious fundamentalism and the neoconservative movements than his liberal opponents, ushered in a new wave of conservative values and policies.

Public confidence and trust in government declined in the 1970s in the wake of economic challenges, political scandals, foreign policy "failures," and a sense of social and moral decay.

Political movements and changes are based on a hope for the future and a reaction to the past. Thus, many of the social and political changes that took place in the 1980s found their start in the tumultuous 1970s. While the fifties and sixties had been characterized by growth and national pride, the seventies were characterized by several perceived government failures. The economy, which had thrived in the postwar years, was starting to settle. Several political scandals called the leadership of the country into question and led to a sense of moral decay. Foreign policy was a constant source of embarrassment and chagrin for the federal government, as American political power seemed weak at home and abroad.

Economically, the issues in the 1970s were multidimensional. The United States was producing as much oil as it could domestically, but demand was continuing to increase. To offset this demand, the United States purchased oil from abroad through OPEC, the Organization of the Petroleum Exporting Countries. This was a mutually beneficial agreement. The United States had one of the strongest economies in the world, and the American dollar was the currency of choice.

However, this also meant that the OPEC nations had fundamental control of a significant portion of the American economy because they controlled the means of energy production. As the United States bought more and more oil from OPEC, domestic production decreased accordingly. It was cheaper for businesses to purchase oil abroad than to produce it at home.

In 1973, several factors combined to severely impact the U.S. economy. First, the United States decided that the American dollar no longer had to have the backing of gold. This meant that the value of a dollar would be fluid and not depend on the amount of gold bullion in the Federal Reserve. While beneficial to Americans because it allowed the value of a dollar to fluctuate in response to the market, this affected the sale of oil as well. OPEC sold oil by barrels based on the American dollar. As the dollar fluctuated, the price of oil fluctuated accordingly. In reaction to this discrepancy, OPEC decided that they would instead base the price of a barrel of oil on the gold standard. This instantly made oil more expensive.

In October of 1973, Egypt and Syria launched an attack on Israel, in a conflict now known as the Yom Kippur War. Egypt and Syria wished to reclaim territory that they had lost to Israel during the Six-Day War of 1967. President Nixon recognized Israel as an asset to the United States after World War II and came to the country's aid with economic and military supplies. The OPEC nations were furious that the Americans would intercede on behalf of the Israelis and decided to issue an oil embargo. The terms of the embargo caused the price of oil to nearly double and sparked an international recession.

Gas rationing in 1974

The oil embargo caused a ripple effect through the economy. Increased oil prices meant a decrease in oil stores in the United States. This led to gasoline rationing as a way to avoid rapid consumption. The system of rationing was simple and based on license plates: an individual with a license plate that ended in an even number could only buy gas on even dates and an individual with a license plate that ended in an odd number could only buy gas on odd dates. In theory, this would help avoid a run on the gas stations. In reality, lines were long and often the station ran out of gas before it ran out of customers.

Petroleum is also used for the production of materials like plastic, which created its own impact. Beyond the cost of gasoline, the demand for household products was starting to outpace the supply. This meant that price inflation rapidly became a problem.

As inflation started to rise, people needed an increase in wages to counteract the increased cost of living. However, as the cost to produce and transport products was skyrocketing, businesses were unable to provide the desired wage increases to their employees. Instead, Americans took other measures to stave off the increase in the cost of living. People became very conscious of their cars. Smaller models which consumed less gasoline became popular. People were also very considerate of how they drove. The national speed limit during the period was fifty-five miles per hour, the optimal speed for fuel conservation. Household energy consumption was also closely monitored, as people tried to conserve energy.

As the oil embargo rocked the American economy, several other factors added to the economic downturn. Loss of faith in the economy meant that the stock market began to drop. It lost 40 percent over eighteen months and took nearly a decade to regain the people's faith. With inflation on the rise, unemployment also rose. The percentage of unemployed Americans reached double digits over the course of the decade. Interest rates hit 20 percent, which meant that some items, like houses and cars, became unaffordable for Americans.

With the economy struggling throughout the whole nation, anger and resentment came to a head in the West over land. The federal government owned about 60 percent of the land west of the Rocky Mountains. This land was open for public usage to an extent, but the industries that utilized this land balked at the amount of government regulation and the expensive fees and fines. Ranchers, for instance, spent an inordinate amount of money on grazing permits and didn't understand why they were being charged for what was essentially a public service.

This led to many westerners feeling that they were being exploited, as they cared for the land that the government actually owned. They also complained that the government was unresponsive to the needs of the local population. Things like irrigation rights were established in Washington without any input from the local population. As tempers rose, the Sagebrush Rebellion was started to fight federal control of the land.

The Sagebrush Rebellion gained momentum as the federal government passed the Federal Land Policy and Management Act (FLPMA) in 1979 which stated that federal land would never be sold to private and public investors. The FLPMA also set aside land for federal parks. This meant that even though the land had previously been open to the public, it was no longer usable. Things like irrigation, which had formerly been allowed, were no longer options. This infuriated westerners who felt that their land was essentially being stolen. President Reagan eased some of the anger when he appointed one of the Sagebrush leaders to his Department of the Interior, but the resentment did not fully fade until the 21st century.

Another event that had a major impact on the way that American's viewed their government during the 1970s was the Iran hostage crisis. The causes for the crisis go back to the 1950s when Iran's leader Mohammad Mossadegh decided that he wanted to nationalize Iran's petroleum reserves. The United States, however, had a controlling interest in Iran's oil reserves and wanted to maintain their hold. Therefore, they planned a coup to replace Mossadegh with the more pro-Western Mohammed Reza Shah Pahlavi.

Iran hostage crisis

In August 1953, the coup, code-named Operation TP-Ajax, was successfully implemented. While the Western world embraced Iran's new leader, the Iranian people were resentful. They felt that the Americans shouldn't have a role in their sovereign nation and, as the Shah revealed himself to be a brutal dictator, anti-American sentiment grew. By 1970, the image of the Shah had reached an all-time low, and some Iranian people were ready for a change in leadership. They turned to Ayatollah Ruhollah Khomeini, a radical Islamic cleric. The Shah fled to Egypt as the new regime took over in 1979.

Later that year, in October 1979, President Carter allowed the former Shah to enter the United States to seek medical treatment. The Shah was suffering from lymphoma and appealed to the president's moral conscience. The people of Iran were furious. A group of college students stormed the U.S. Embassy in Tehran and took sixty-six individuals hostage. The United States responded immediately with diplomatic overtures and economic sanctions. All Iranian holdings in the United States were seized. Still, they had little success.

Thirteen hostages were released soon after they were taken but this was mainly because they were not Americans, or were Americans that had felt oppression themselves, like African Americans. Later, another would be released after developing medical problems. This added to the constant fear of the hostages. They didn't know from one moment to the next whether they would live, die or be tortured. They were often paraded around by their captors and several times the watching American public feared for the lives of the hostages as they were presented to angry mobs.

President Carter wanted desperately to bring the hostages home. Morally, he felt that it was his duty as president to fight for his people and the ineffectiveness of his actions frustrated him personally. Politically, this was compounded by the continual media coverage of the crisis and Carter simultaneously running for reelection. In April 1980, Carter decided that the diplomatic route wasn't working. He gave the orders for Operation Eagle Claw which would allow an elite team to enter Iran and free the hostages.

Two U.S. Navy aircraft parked on USS Nimitz for Operation Eagle Claw

The plan might have worked, but a sandstorm caused one of the planes to crash, killing the servicemen onboard. Carter looked desperate and ineffective to the American people who had once again witnessed their leaders fail them. The people didn't trust a government that couldn't protect its citizens. When Election Day came in the fall of 1980, Ronald Reagan won by a landslide. Knowing that he had less than three months left as president, Carter redoubled efforts to bring the hostages home during his term. His efforts failed, however. The hostages were freed on Reagan's inauguration day, after being held for 444 days.

The rapid and substantial growth of evangelical and fundamentalist Christian churches and organizations, as well as increased political participation by some of those groups, encouraged significant opposition to liberal social and political trends.

The 1980s gave rise to several fundamentalist and evangelical groups that opposed the more liberal social ideas of the 1970s. They saw a decrease in public opinion and felt that the best way to fix the government was a back-to-basics fundamentalism that focused on religion and family values. These groups were surprisingly effective, if sometimes short-lived. They played a definite role in the political sphere and opposed many of the new legislative initiatives of the time. The Moral Majority and Focus on the Family were two particularly popular groups.

The Moral Majority is often considered a fundamentalist Christian organization, and at its core, it is. However, the founders of the movement, Richard Viguerie, Paul Weyrich, and Howard Phillips, quickly realized that they needed to branch out and welcome all disenfranchised conservatives who could support the same goals. In the end, they wanted a group that could unite these factions and enact change through political power; a real conservative voting block that could maintain the conservative morality of the nation.

Their political platform was very clear-cut but covered a wide range of issues. The Moral Majority was socially conservative; they opposed abortion and campaigned against the Equal Rights Amendment, which had passed in Congress in 1972 and was making its way to the states for ratification but fell short. They also opposed the idea of homosexuals' rights. Their ideas on sex, in general, tended toward the puritanical, and they opposed sex education and pornography. Instead, they wanted strong national defense, which led to opposition of the Strategic Arms Reduction Treaties with the Soviets. They supported the strong nuclear family and family values. They wanted prayer in schools and what they described as "Bible morality." They were anti-Communist and pro-Israel.

The Moral Majority was led by their President, Jerry Falwell, and primarily used direct mail as a technique to spread their ideas. They published a circular called *The Moral Majority Report* and shipped it monthly to—according to Falwell—over 600,000 supporters. Falwell also claimed that almost the same amount of targeted funding letters went out weekly. They claimed a supporting constituency of 50 million Americans and, especially in the 1980s election, focused on making sure that conservative leaders were elected.

The Moral Majority also had a targeted political strategy for elections. In 1982, they crafted the "Top-Secret Battle Plan for 1982." In the plan, they outlined a set of targeted objectives: the desire for a Human Life Amendment to fight abortion and support for the Family Protection Act, among others.

Dr. Jerry Falwell, President of the Moral Majority and the founder of Liberty University

In 1984, they pushed for the election of pro-Israel politicians and publicly supported Reagan's anti-Communist Central American policies. In 1988, the Civil Rights Restoration Act became their focus, though they were criticized for some of their comments.

While the organization had a lot of influence, they were not always the most political organization and they were criticized for many of their actions. Splinter organizations like the Focus on the Family group emerged from differing opinions in the organization and decreased the power of the Moral Majority by separating its base. The Moral Majority was eventually disbanded in 1989, as Falwell redirected his attention to his Liberty University in Lynchburg, Virginia and his work as an evangelical minister.

Focus on the Family was founded by psychologist James Dobson in 1977. Like the Moral Majority, Focus on the Family wanted to support fundamental Christian social conservatism. They created a family-centric political platform that blended fundamentalist ideals with family issues. They supported an education program that taught creationism and abstinence and supported public and school prayer. They also had a back-to-the-Bible approach to gender roles. They stood against anything that they felt would threaten the traditional family values they used as their bedrock, including rights for the LGBT community. They opposed abortion and pornography like their Moral Majority counterpart, but also addiction problems like gambling and substance abuse which they felt might tear a family apart.

While the Moral Majority focused on targeted mailings, the Focus on the Family movement tried to branch out into other media types. They had a daily radio show hosted by the group's president, Jim Daly, published resources and a magazine for readers, and provided video and audio recordings of their programs. The organization continued the spread of information in targeted programs, focusing on specific audiences that they wanted to hold and those that were receptive to their message. Two popular radio broadcasts were *Adventures in Odyssey*, for children, and *Family Minute*.

Like their targeted radio shows and programs, Focus on the Family separated its work into different ministries, each with a separate focus. Love Won Out was a Focus on the Family ministry until it was sold to Exodus International, who later stopped all activities.

Jim Daly of Focus on the Family

Love Won Out was a primarily anti-gay ministry that focused on rehabilitation. Wait No More focused on adoption. They worked to get children adopted from foster care, but only by what they considered appropriate households. No same-sex couples or couples living together outside of wedlock are assisted by the program.

Option Ultrasound is a program that provides grants for pregnancy crisis centers. The goal of the program is to allow women considering abortion to "see" their child before they decide. The hope is that women will change their mind when their baby is no longer abstract. To this end, the grants provided by the group are used to purchase ultrasound machines that can show a mother her child.

Conservatives achieved some of their political and policy goals, but their success was limited by the enduring popularity and institutional strength of some government programs and public support for cultural trends of recent decades.

Though the conservatives had been out of favor in Washington for several years, the failures of the liberal government in the 1970s meant that people were more open to the conservative messages of smaller government and social conservatism. When Reagan won the election against incumbent Carter in 1980, he was well liked for his optimism and his effectiveness as a spokesman for the government, which earned him the moniker "The Great Communicator." People rallied around Reagan as they rallied around their beliefs and set the stage for a period of conservative successes, a trend continued by his successor, George Bush.

Still, the success of the conservative movement was mitigated by several government programs implemented in reaction to social issues. Programs like Social Security and governmental healthcare were too deeply entrenched in the government to allow for true change. Similarly, any attempts to change aspects of these programs were often met with contention from the public.

Conservatives enjoyed significant victories related to taxation and deregulation of many industries, but many conservative efforts to advance moral ideals through politics met inertia and opposition.

The 1980s ushered in a period of fiscal conservatism. Conservatives believe that the government should remove itself as much as possible from economics, and that business runs best when it's not regulated. To this end, Ronald Reagan began a trend of tax cuts and deregulation that would continue into the next several decades. Reagan's economic policy, often called the trickle-down theory, was based on the concept of supply-side economics. This means that Reagan supported tax cuts for businesses.

The idea behind this economic policy is that if production is less expensive, it will encourage businesses to increase employment and business size, which will eventually benefit the consumer base by increasing the standard of living through less expensive and higher quality products. This is known as trickle-down economics because an increase in consumption by the wealthy and by businesses benefits the lowest income earners through increased employment and wage levels in the long run.

To this end, in 1981 Ronald Reagan signed the Economic Recovery Tax Act (ERTA) into law. The ERTA reduced individual tax rates by 25 percent across the board and was meant to be implemented over a period of three years. The ERTA also allowed for additional tax breaks for things like education and investment. This meant that someone investing in business would pay less in taxes as a reward for their investment in the economic market. Individuals who pursued higher education would also receive a tax write-off. In 1986, Reagan signed another tax act into law which cut taxes for high-income taxpayers from around 70 percent to 30 percent in another effort to boost his trickle-down policies.

While Reagan's economic policy was later criticized, it was a good fit for his presidency. His policies favored investment in businesses which lead to an advent for venture capitalism and entrepreneurship. He also had tax incentives for education and the new opportunities were reflected in the number of students enrolling in higher education. In turn, Reagan's first term as president saw a revolution in the information industry with the creation of some of the most influential tech companies, including Intel, Dell, Microsoft, and Cisco. With promised tax benefits, Americans were more willing to put some of their hard-earned money at risk, and the stock market also began to make a comeback.

In 1994, as Democrat Bill Clinton served as President, more than 300 Republican Congressional candidates signed a promissory document called the Contract with America in support of several key conservative values. Newt Gingrich, Speaker of the House of Representatives, led the contract presentation at a press conference in September 1994. The contract was based on three core principles of accountability, responsibility, and opportunity.

Accountability meant being accountable to the American people to counteract the disconnect between the people and their politicians. Responsibility spoke to the personal responsibility of the American people; the conservative Republicans felt that it was important for the government to let their citizens be responsible for themselves.

President Bill Clinton

This is augmented by the opportunity section. People need to have personal responsibility, but they also need to be able to achieve. The opportunity section was therefore focused on restoring the opportunities of Americans and immigrants to achieve the American dream.

Newt Gingrich, Speaker of the House of Representatives (1989-1995)

The contract had ten bills submitted to Congress that would be used to achieve eight basic goals. The first goal was to bring Congress back to the people by mandating that all laws that applied to others applied to Congress. The second goal was to make the best use of government resources by hiring an independent company to audit the federal government for waste or misuse. A reduction of the number of committees by one-third was planned to help decrease waste, a term limit for committee chairs was meant to increase productivity and encourage new ideas and a ban on proxy votes in committees would now be open to the public for observation. The seventh goal was to limit taxes by requiring a three-fifths majority for any new tax increase.

Finally, the contract called for a zero-baseline budget to keep the country accountable and monetarily sustained. In the end, the success of the contract was mixed. Several of the proposed bills were unable to come to fruition because of either a lack of support or vetoes issued by President Bill Clinton. Several did pass, however, and their success helped to bolster conservative values under a liberal leadership.

When George W. Bush became president in 2001, recession came in with him. Bush quickly reacted in an effort to help bolster the economy. Like Reaganomics, Bush's tax cuts were multi-pronged and included further incentives. Bush reduced income tax rates across the board to be implemented over a number of years. Despite popular rhetoric, these tax breaks did not focus on the wealthiest members of society. Instead, Bush focused on the middle class and had several tax breaks and incentives that were directed toward them in particular. For instance, Bush doubled the child tax break.

President George W. Bush

Bush's tax breaks did not change the country's momentum fast enough. In 2003, Congress stepped in and added several other tax code changes. They phased out the "Death Tax," or the estate tax on inheritance. They also encouraged people to invest their money by cutting the cost of investments. Their interference worked, and the economy started to stabilize and grow. Bush's tax cuts were unique, however, because they had a ten-year timeline before they became defunct unless reissued.

Some policies were renewed while others were allowed to expire, meaning that the current tax rate is higher than under President Bush.

Not all conservative initiatives were met with success, however. Many conservatives opposed abortion because they saw it as an immoral action. Religious groups equated abortion with murder and protested *Roe v. Wade* extensively. In 1992, conservatives were thwarted when *Casey v. Planned Parenthood*, which had its roots in the original *Roe v. Wade* decision, upheld and structured the abortion debate. Many states that disagreed with *Roe v. Wade* tried to limit abortions in their states by creating regulations or obstacles.

In 1982, Pennsylvania passed a law that included several obstacles to abortions. The Abortion Control Act required all women seeking an abortion to give informed consent and undergo a twenty-four-hour waiting period. Minors could not seek abortions without parental consent, and wives had to get consent from husbands. The act also mandated that abortion clinics report to the state.

Planned Parenthood quickly challenged the act, claiming that it violated *Roe v. Wade*. The Supreme Court took the case into review and in 1992 issued their decision. They ruled that many aspects of the Pennsylvania law were constitutional but that a woman's decision to receive an abortion is protected from the State. The Court ruled that abortions before the viability point could not be regulated except to protect the health of the mother and that states could not interfere with an abortion if the mother's health was at risk.

They deemed that any "substantial obstacles" that prevented a woman from seeking an abortion were in violation of the Constitution, but this did not include Pennsylvania's twenty-four-hour waiting period. The consent of the husband, however, was deemed unconstitutional, as it took away a woman's right to autonomy by forcing her to put the will of her husband above her own.

Although Republicans continued to denounce "big government," the size and scope of the federal government continued to grow after 1980, as many programs remained popular with voters and difficult to reform or eliminate.

While conservatives celebrated many economic victories during the eighties and nineties, there were some programs that they could not limit or eliminate, such as Medicare and Medicaid. The debate for national health insurance started during the Great Depression when the majority of people could not get the care that they needed. The initiative failed but continued to spark debate. In the 1960s, bills were passed to encourage states to provide health care for the elderly. Not all states did so, and those that did often provided inferior care.

Eventually, Medicare was signed into law in 1965. Its basic premise was to provide health care for all Americans over sixty-five years of age regardless of their financial situation. In 1972, this was expanded to include younger adults who had disabilities. Medicaid, also founded in 1965, is an assistance program. This program is open to people of all ages, provided they can demonstrate financial need. Both programs work to offset medical costs for those who cannot afford private medical insurance.

Several steps have been taken in an effort to limit Medicare and Medicaid spending, but the programs are so popular with voters that it's difficult to achieve real change while remaining responsible to a constituency. The 1988 Catastrophic Coverage Act, for instance, was celebrated as a great way to protect seniors from the stress of nursing home bills until it became obvious that Reagan's administration was expecting the elderly to pay for the new coverage without a tax on those not receiving coverage.

Seniors were furious, and the Act was eventually expelled. Many people worry about the spending on Medicare and Medicaid, but funding has been projected to exceed demands for the baby boomers, meaning the program is likely to survive. The newest addition to the healthcare debate is the highly contested Affordable Care Act or Obamacare. The ACA is an attempt to expand coverage to all Americans while limiting spending through restrictions on insurance companies.

Social Security is another social welfare program that conservatives have tried and failed to restructure. Social Security provides funds for individuals who are unable to work or are retired. The program is called a "pay-as-you-go" program, which means that every month money is collected from workers and their employers through Social Security deductions from paychecks. This money is then paid out to those who have retired or are disabled. It is estimated that one out of every four families is receiving Social Security payments of some kind.

*President George W. Bush discusses strengthening Social Security at the
Lake Nona YMCA Family Center in Orlando, FL (2005)*

The concern with the Social Security system is, of course, monetary solvency. As the life expectancy in the United States continues to rise, the federal government is paying out more and more Social Security dollars to more and more citizens. With the baby boomer generation soon reaching full retirement age, many economists are concerned that the program will run out of funds. A number of options have been considered, including raising the full retirement age; however, change is slow and laborious.

By current estimates, Social Security could run out of solvency within two decades. The concern is that if these programs are not solvent, they will require an increase in taxes and money borrowing that the country cannot afford. Conservatives tend toward fiscal conservatism and worry about what will happen in the event of defaulting on a debt of this size. These issues are compounded by the national debt, which hit $18.2 trillion in April 2015.

KEY CONCEPT 9.2: The end of the Cold War and new challenges to U.S. leadership in the world forced the nation to redefine its foreign policy and global role.

As the Cold War ended, the United States was forced to redefine its place in the global theater. This was affected by a number of factors. The collapse of the Soviet Union meant a restructuring of former Soviet republics and Soviet-bloc countries and a shift in international political power that had to be filled by other nations. It quickly became apparent, during the period immediately after the Cold War, that the United Nations also needed to be strengthened and reformed. While the United States pulled back and attempted to act mostly through the United Nations during the 1990s, they were called upon to function as "police" during several major conflicts. The 2000s saw America return to the forefront of international politics after the September 11, 2001 attacks. The resulting War on Terror redefined both domestic and foreign policy.

The Reagan administration pursued a reinvigorated anti-Communist and interventionist foreign policy that set the tone for later administrations.

When Reagan entered office, it was with a definite focus on anti-Communist policies, especially as they related to Latin America. El Salvador, Nicaragua, and Cuba were of particular interest, but the president was determined to stop any new Communist regime in the Western Hemisphere. He proved this when, after a successful Marxist coup in the Caribbean nation of Grenada, he authorized troops to invade and reinstall an anti-Communist government. The invasion included the death or capture of some 700 Soviet-supported Cuban soldiers and drew a hard line in the sand for any government factions considering a Communist regime in the Western Hemisphere.

This hard line on Communism gave rise to what's known as the Reagan Doctrine, which provided American support for any anti-Communist revolution. Reagan supported the anti-Soviet freedom fighters in Afghanistan with weapons and training, for example. In 1979, after Nicaragua fell to the Sandinista Marxist group, a decade of civil war followed which was the greatest test of the Reagan Doctrine.

Reagan approved covert training of Nicaraguan rebels, colloquially called Contras, and the CIA provided assistance until commanded by Congress to end all aid. Reagan quietly looked for ways to side-step Congress' decree and permitted the CIA to sell weapons to the Iranians provided that all proceeds went to the Contras. In 1986, the plot was revealed and the Iran–Contra scandal had serious political backlash for all involved, including the president. Four years later, however, the Marxist government of Daniel Ortega was routed in a national election.

Reagan's administration also wanted to strengthen ties with China as a way to contain the Soviets, but the president would not allow any policies which did not support Taiwan. The Taiwanese have been in conflict with China since the 1940s when they first sought independence. During the height of the Cold War, the United States made a declaration that any attacks on Taiwan would be met with American retaliation.

This meant that the United States could not strengthen relations with China unless an agreement of some kind was made. However, this also meant that military support for Taiwan was essentially a threat to the Chinese government. While the official relationship with China improved under the Reagan administration, the central conflict was not solved during his presidency.

Reagan did, however, structure a policy for foreign influence. His tendency toward hard lines in the sand and sticking to a set of ideals was supported, for the most part, by the American public. This inspired other leaders to try similar approaches after Reagan's term in office ended. In particular, both Bush Presidents fought foreign wars using the same sort of techniques that Reagan utilized.

President Ronald Reagan, who initially rejected détente with increased defense spending, military action, and bellicose rhetoric, later developed a friendly relationship with Soviet leader Mikhail Gorbachev, leading to significant arms reductions by both countries.

Ronald Reagan became president during the later years of the United States' Cold War with the USSR. He, like most Americans at the time, saw Communism as a threat to American interests. Therefore, in 1983, the Strategic Defense Initiative (SDI) was founded under Reagan's administration. Colloquially, this program was known as "Star Wars" because it was a missile defense system in space.

The point of the program was to find a way to protect the United States from nuclear attacks. The program relied on technology that wasn't available at the time but could be developed, particularly a super-computer system that could identify nuclear warheads as threats and use lasers to destroy them while they were still in the atmosphere.

The program garnered a lot of criticism. Many people thought that the SDI violated the Strategic Arms Limitation Talks (SALT); others felt that the SDI was an excellent idea but were concerned as to costs; some others felt that a successful implementation of it would give the United States too much of an advantage over the USSR and might cause them to strike preemptively. Due to constant setbacks and struggle to find funding, the SDI was eventually put aside.

In the end, it was probably for the best that the SDI was never completed, as an unlikely relationship began to develop between Mikhail Gorbachev, then the leader of the USSR, and the Reagan presidency. In 1981, President Reagan had attempted to implement better communication between the White House and the Kremlin. At the time, the USSR was controlled by Leonid Brezhnev who was unresponsive to Reagan's attempts. Brezhnev died in November 1982. His direct successor, Yuri Andropov, died less than two years later and was succeeded by Constantine Chernyenko, who died a little over a year later.

Gorbachev (left) and Reagan (right)

It was Chernyenko's successor Mikhail Gorbachev that finally responded receptively to Reagan's overtures. In an effort to improve relations, the two met in Geneva, Switzerland, in November 1985. They spoke about the differences and similarities between their two countries and tried to find common ground on which to build a relationship. The first meeting was a success, and a year later they met again at Reykjavik, Iceland. This summit didn't go as well as the first due to a disagreement about America's missile defense systems. Gorbachev wanted a promise that America would end its plans for a space-based missile defense system. Reagan refused to hinder American security in that way but offered to share the technology with the USSR so that both countries could be protected. When Gorbachev refused, the summit was called to an end.

Many people thought that the failure in Iceland would keep Reagan and Gorbachev from being able to achieve anything. Eight months later, however, Reagan demonstrated his faith in the relationship when he successfully called on Gorbachev to tear down the Berlin Wall that separated East and West Berlin in Germany. In December 1987, Gorbachev and his wife were welcomed to Washington for their third summit. The third summit in Washington was an unprecedented success, with both leaders signing the Intermediate-Range Nuclear Forces (INF) Treaty which eliminated ground launching ballistic and cruise missiles.

The next year, the Reagans returned the favor and traveled to Moscow for the next summit. There they signed the INF Treaty, which had been ratified by both governments.

The fifth and final summit meeting happened in December 1988 as President Reagan and George H. W. Bush, who was both the vice president and president-elect, traveled to New York where Gorbachev came to meet them. Reagan considered this a way for him to hand off the official relationship between the two countries to President-Elect Bush.

Reagans arriving in Moscow, May 29, 1988

Reagan's call for Gorbachev to tear down the Berlin Wall was an important moment in their relationship. In 1945, after the defeat of the German army and an end to the Western Front of World War II, the Allies met to determine what to do with the German territory and people. They decided to split the country into four occupation zones: for the United States, the USSR, Britain, and France. The German capital of Berlin was in the Soviet territory, but the Allies agreed to split it up as well, which annoyed the Communists. The USSR was rankled to have a Western capitalist city in the middle of their territory, so they attempted to slowly force the Allies out through starvation, cutting off all supplies to the western side of Berlin.

Instead of leaving, the United States, Britain, and Canada began airlifting food and supplies to their sections of Berlin. Realizing that starvation was not going to work, the Soviets turned to other pursuits but soon had to refocus on Berlin, as thousands of people began defecting from East to West Germany. At the height of the defections, in August 1961, nearly 2,400 Germans defected in a single day. Embarrassed by the flow of people from East to West, the Soviets decided to end the privilege of free movement across occupational zones.

Within two weeks, the Berlin Wall was constructed and in place. Once separated, the two halves of the city grew independently from one another. East Berlin suffered under inflation and lack of resources, while the capitalist Western half was rapidly rebuilt and flourished.

Woman waving over the Berlin Wall, 1961

On June 12, 1987, President Reagan stood in front of the Brandenburg Gate in Berlin and called for Gorbachev to tear down the wall because it was an outdated symbol. Two years later, on November 9, 1989, that dream became a reality as the gates were opened and citizens began removing the wall from their city. This, perhaps more than any other action, symbolized the ending of the Cold War and strengthened the relationship between the East and West.

While good relations between the East and West were primarily accredited to Reagan, his counterpart, Mikhail Gorbachev, also affected real change, leading to the end of the USSR and improved economic prosperity in the Soviet nations. When Mikhail Gorbachev assumed the leadership of the USSR, he knew that things needed to change. His country was stagnant and weakened by oppression.

President Reagan Giving a Speech at the Berlin Wall, Brandenburg Gate, June 1987

In an effort to combat this, he introduced two new sets of policies. The first was "glasnost," or political openness. Glasnost encouraged Gorbachev to connect with Reagan and it also had amazing effects on his own nation. It allowed people to relax in new liberties, like freedom of the press and real open and honest elections. The second policy was "perestroika," which means economic restructuring. Gorbachev realized that the Soviet policies of a Communist command-based economy were not working, and he shifted the control of the means of production from the state to private citizens and businesses. While these policies would eventually mean economic prosperity, that prosperity did not manifest before the old system collapsed, causing frustration and outrage throughout the USSR.

With the command economy in tatters and rationing a reality, it was no surprise when the Soviet Union began to crumble as individual states pulled away and fought for their independence. The Polish revolutions in 1989 were quickly followed by the Velvet Revolution in Czechoslovakia. Quickly, the other states began pulling away, and soon the USSR was officially disassembled.

While the end of the USSR looked like a failure to many of the people living in it, the rest of the world viewed it as progress. In 1988, *Time* magazine named Gorbachev their "Man of the Year" in support of his continued efforts to work with the United States for peace and a diplomatic end to the Cold War. In 1989, they upgraded him to the "Man of the Decade." While only a single magazine, it became obvious that they spoke for the world when Gorbachev was given the highly coveted Nobel Peace Prize in 1990 for his work to end the Cold War and the Nuclear Arms Race.

Bush's term as president saw continued good relations with Gorbachev, as both men continued the work that had been started in their own countries and abroad. It also saw the completion of the first Strategic Arms Reduction Treaty (START I). The treaty was a huge success and limited the United States and Russia (after the USSR was divided in the early 1990s) to 6,000 nuclear warheads each. Each country was also limited to 1,600 nuclear delivery vehicles. This limitation was an amazing success and dramatically reduced stockpiles. It also served as an example for the New START Treaty in 2010, which further reduced the limits.

The end of the Cold War led not only to new diplomatic relationships but also to new U.S. military and peacekeeping interventions as well as debates over the nature and extent of American power in the world.

As the United States and Russia ended the Cold War hostilities that had long polarized international relations, the question of American power and intervention arose. Most people favored a new international approach and placed their faith in the United Nations, whose military and peacekeeping forces are donated by member countries. In response, the United Nations changed the way it approached missions, with a focus on agreements that led to sustainable peace. Peacekeeping was no longer just a military role. Instead, the United Nations realized that peacekeeping had to include an effort to change all of a country's ills, including things like infrastructure and government.

Several peacekeeping efforts were successful, but it soon became clear that there were problems with the new systems. Yugoslavia, Rwanda, and Somalia were three places, in particular, where the peacekeeping efforts failed, and the United Nations was criticized for its ineffectual practices and structure. Many Americans questioned their place in an organization that would allow genocide to occur without attempting to stop it. The United Nations looked to reform and change to address their weaknesses and failings. They have since moved on once again to more complex missions and have maintained an effective role.

The United States could not remain behind the United Nations, however. In 1990, Iraq, under the leadership of Saddam Hussein, invaded their neighbor Kuwait. Hussein's validation for the invasion was that Kuwait was actually a part of Iraq and not a separate territory. He claimed that the Western powers had carved out Kuwait and had used the country, as well as other neighboring nations like Saudi Arabia, to keep oil prices artificially low.

Saddam Hussein

The other countries of the Middle East were concerned by Hussein's actions and condemned them. President of Egypt Hosni Mubarak attempted to host a negotiation between the two countries, but Hussein was not receptive, and on August 2, 1990, Iraqi forces invaded the country, causing King Fahd of Kuwait to flee into exile.

The other Middle Eastern Nations immediately called upon the West to intervene. The United Nations responded the next day, issuing instructions for the Iraqi forces to leave Kuwait and return to Iraq. They were summarily ignored by Hussein. After several days, King Fahd of Kuwait came to the United States directly and requested military and political aid.

Within several days, a coalition of American and NATO troops joined Middle Eastern troops in Saudi Arabia. The plan for Operation Desert Shield was to serve as a barrier between the Iraqi forces and Saudi Arabia, containing the problem until a solution could be met. Seeing that his position was weak, Hussein tried a number of measures to garner support for his invasion. He tried to claim that he was fighting a jihad, or Muslim holy war, against the coalition. He also attempted to garner the support of the world by turning the occupation into a political move to represent the struggle of the Palestinians. He offered to leave Kuwait if the Israelis would leave Palestine, the land that had become Israel after World War II. When it became obvious that these measures were not working to sway public opinion and that violence was imminent, Hussein made a deal with Iran to swell his military's ranks and prepared for war.

At the end of November, the United Nations gave Iraq a deadline. They were to withdraw all troops from Kuwait before January 15, 1991. Two days after the deadline passed, Operation Desert Storm began. The hope was to end the war quickly and decisively with the least amount of damage to Kuwait and its citizens. To this end, the United States and allied nations used the newest technologies available to them. They thought that an air offensive would create the least amount of damage in total. Therefore, utilizing planes and "smart" bombs, which had a built-in laser guidance system, the allies attacked Iraqi planes, runways, communications systems, and weapons plants.

Members of the coalition forces drive a tank during Operation Desert Storm

These air attacks were effective but did not lead to the end of the war as quickly as hoped. The air attacks were soon being carried out on ground troops as well as the high-profile targets. With the air operations working as effectively as they could, ground troops were soon necessary to finish the job, and Operation Desert Sabre managed to last less than a week before the Iraqi soldiers retreated. The United States pursued them deep into Iraqi territory.

A ceasefire was declared by the United States on February 28, 1991. In return for their withdrawal, the allies negotiated for Iraq's recognition of Kuwait's sovereignty. Iraq also agreed to get rid of all weapons of mass destruction (WMDs) like nuclear missiles. While the war was considered a definite success for the allies, it's important to know that the effects of the war were felt for several years. Non-compliance with the UN regulations and mandates meant that people continued to question the validity of the United Nations as an international peacekeeping body. Resentment also grew in the area and, eventually, several unresolved issues sparked another war with Iraq in 2003.

America has continued to question its own role in the international arena. Due to the unpopular wars in Iraq and Iran and several illegal forays into sovereign territory—like the 2011 killing of Osama bin Laden in Pakistan—the United States has been criticized internationally for acting as the world's police. An effective balance between action and inaction has yet to be determined.

Following the attacks of September 11, 2001, U.S. foreign policy and military involvement focused on a war on terrorism, which also generated debates about domestic security and civil rights.

America changed drastically at the turn of the century when terrorists carried out the first international attack on American soil since the bombing of Pearl Harbor. Much of America's political and economic future changed seemingly overnight. The terrorist attacks of September 11, 2001 drastically impacted the U.S. economy, as the World Trade Center literally disappeared and American airlines were crippled. Recession, already building from Clinton's time in office, was imminent.

Politically, the United States had soon pledged itself to two costly and unpopular wars which set them at odds with several other political leaders and earned them an international bias. At home, the political sphere became polarized and people began to question the federal government, as liberty and privacy were quickly put aside by the need for security. The place of the United States in world politics was once again in question. Additionally, the country and citizens had to revisit the founding documents, as the issues of security and privacy appeared to be at odds.

In the wake of attacks on the World Trade Center and the Pentagon, U.S. decision-makers launched foreign policy and military efforts against terrorism and lengthy, controversial conflicts in Afghanistan and Iraq.

The United States was fundamentally changed in September of 2001. The Middle Eastern terrorist organization known as al-Qaeda, headed by Osama bin Laden, had planted sleeper agents inside the United States. These agents prepared to perpetrate an attack on American citizens by learning how to fly commercial airliners. On the morning of September 11, 2001, these al-Qaeda terrorist operatives hijacked four American airline flights and crashed them into various political targets.

The first plane to crash was directed into the North Tower of the World Trade Center in New York City. Like each of the planes, it was filled with enough jet fuel for a cross-continental flight, and the damage was extreme. It was followed eighteen minutes later by the second plane, which crashed into the South Tower.

Another of the hijacked planes was directed to Washington, D.C., where it crashed into the E Ring of the Pentagon, the central hub of the United States military. As the Pentagon burned, the situation in New York became even more critical. The towers of the World Trade Center, unable to handle the burning jet fuel and structural damage, collapsed. Only six of the people who were left in the towers at the time of their collapse survived.

World Trade Center on September 11, 2001

A fourth plane was hijacked but was late in taking off. The passengers learned of the situation in New York and grew suspicious when they were not immediately returned to the airport. The current belief is that this plane was supposed to crash into the White House, Camp David, or a nuclear power plant. Wherever it was intended to crash, the plane did not reach its final destination. Instead, the passengers rose up against the four hijackers and the plane crashed in an empty field, killing all forty-five of the people on board.

More than 3,000 people lost their lives in New York. Over 10,000 others were treated for injuries, many quite severe. In Washington, 125 people died in the Pentagon, and 64 people died on the plane.

The nation was shaken by these events and citizens had a difficult time comprehending what they were seeing. President George W. Bush was in a Florida classroom making a public appearance at the time of the attacks. He quickly returned to Washington in an effort to aid the country in rallying behind the rescue efforts and to offer direction and leadership as the country mourned. In an address to the American people that night, he promised that there would be no distinction made between the terrorists that had perpetrated these attacks and those that protected them.

Al-Qaeda claimed responsibility and, within one month of the attacks, Operation Enduring Freedom, an international effort to end the Taliban regime in Afghanistan and bin Laden's associated terrorist network, had boots on the ground in Afghanistan. Within two months, the Taliban was officially removed from power, but they continued to utilize guerrilla tactics as they fought the U.S. troops from a base in Pakistan.

In 2003, the War on Terror extended. Seeing America's vulnerability, President Bush was moving decisively against anyone he felt posed a threat to the United States. Iraq, under the control of Saddam Hussein, was funding the terrorist organizations that Bush was attempting to destroy. This, coupled with erroneous reports that Iraq still had Weapons of Mass Destruction (WMDs) despite a UN Mandate, led to a joint American-British invasion. Like the war in Afghanistan, the war in Iraq easily achieved its first objective: the overthrow of the government. The occupation and guerrilla violence led by an insurgency followed this overthrow.

President Bush discusses the War on Terror

In 2007, violence in Iraq began to decrease. In response, the United States started to pull out troops until the withdrawal was completed in December of 2011. The United States still has troops in Iraq, but as advisors and teachers only. In May of 2011, Osama bin Laden was finally tracked down and killed by American Seal Team Six. One month later, President Obama called for a reduction of troops in Afghanistan, with a full withdrawal by the end of 2014. As with Iraq, some troops still remain to maintain peacekeeping efforts in the area.

The war on terrorism sought to improve security within the United States but also raised questions about the protection of civil liberties and human rights.

The wars in Afghanistan and Iraq—as far as human lives are concerned—were not the costliest of wars, yet both wars eventually became unpopular. It was very difficult for the United States to make any sort of headway in countries where the terrorist organizations were so deeply embedded as to actually become part of the government or the ruling faction of the government. When it became clear that the reports of WMDs in Iraq had been incorrect, public opinion for that war soured.

The war in Afghanistan was relatively well accepted. People felt that it was taking too long and that it wasn't as effective as it should be, but most people viewed the war in Afghanistan as important. The war in Iraq, however, made people nervous. People were unsure of why the war had started and many people were concerned that the war was actually a ploy to gain control of Iraq's oil resources. Some critics also raised the concern that Bush Jr. was using the War on Terror as an excuse to finish what his father started during Desert Storm.

Americans were also concerned as to how these terrorists had managed to infiltrate the country and plan these attacks without being identified by authorities. Americans were outraged by the fact that the attacks had been perpetrated under the nose of some of the best investigative organizations in the world, particularly the FBI and the CIA. In response, these organizations attempted to determine whether or not pre-knowledge of the attacks had been held by any American individual. They also wanted to know if another attack was imminent. The 9-11 Commission was created to answer these and other questions.

The end result of these fears was The Patriot Act, passed just forty-five days after the September 11, 2001 attacks. The Patriot Act harkens back to a long history of warnings by former American presidents after the American Revolution. They were worried that the American Revolution would encourage people to give away their liberties for the security of the new government. They warned that those who are willing to give up their liberties for security are destined to lose both. A similar argument happened in response to the Patriot Act immediately after 9/11.

Americans were terrified that another attack was imminent and that the investigative agencies that had failed to identify the first attack would fail again. This led to several measures being put into place that violated — according to many critics — civil liberties held by the American public. The Patriot Act expanded the authority of the federal government and gave the newly created National Security Agency the ability to monitor domestic phone and email communications. It also allowed for the collection of financial records and metadata from an individual's cell phone and Internet history. The Patriot Act is controversial and has been accused of unconstitutionality several times. Public approval plummeted as citizens perceived the acts and unpopular wars as the government's attempt to aggregate power.

> **KEY CONCEPT 9.3: Moving into the 21st century, the nation continued to experience challenges stemming from social, economic and demographic changes.**

The 21st century, marked by the ensuing conflict of the post 9/11 War on Terror, can be characterized as a period of social, economic and demographic changes. Economically, the country attempted to adapt to the new global market and the associated problems. Demographically, waves of immigrants from Latin America and Asia changed the American landscape, politically and socially. Both of these new challenges meant that the society could not stagnate and was forced to adapt as the people adapted.

The increasing integration of the United States into the world economy was accompanied by economic instability and major policy, social and environmental challenges.

The American economy, one of the most powerful in the world, had to change in reaction to outside forces and the globalization of the world economy. This led to fear and instability as investors and businesses took advantage of new policies and practices while the workforce often felt the negative impact of these newer and cheaper alternatives to American labor. The government attempted to aid both sides, while still considering the fate of America as a whole over any particular group.

As the business composition of the United States changed in reaction to the government and policy changes, the workforce was also forced to change. As the United States moved from domestic manufacturing to a more service-oriented economy, with production outsourced to foreign nations, it also had to consider how to maintain a thriving economy without the means of production in the United States.

Economic inequality increased after 1980 as U.S. manufacturing jobs were eliminated, union membership declined, and real wages stagnated for the middle class.

In the wake of World War II, the American economy saw a period of rapid growth. Most of this growth was due to new methods of production and businesses manufacturing goods and materials for sale worldwide. Not only were Americans enjoying new manufactured goods like Maytag appliances and Levi Strauss jeans, but the rest of the world was also looking to America to fill the gap left by the destruction of their own means of production. Germany and Japan, in particular, had been decimated by the war and needed to rebuild a nation and an economy from the ground up.

American products suddenly became the gold standard worldwide. New industry also meant new jobs and job growth, spurring the rise of a middle class that was composed of well-educated citizens who filled highly profitable production or management roles. By 1965, just over 50 percent of the economy was tied to manufacturing jobs. However, as the global economy rebounded from the war and foreign nations began to develop their own means of production, the demand for American goods started to decrease. In less than twenty-five years, manufacturing went from 53 percent of the economy to 39 percent. By 2004, manufacturing accounted for less than 10 percent.

The loss of manufacturing jobs had several immediate and long-term impacts. During the 1970s, it was estimated that one-fourth of the nation was working for manufacturers. By 2005, it was less than 10 percent. Perhaps the best example of this decline can be seen in the automotive industry. In 2005, General Motors had to cut over 30,000 jobs and closed nine American plants to make the business competitive internationally. The same year Ford also cut 30,000 jobs and closed ten plants nationwide. In one year, these automotive giants alone accounted for the loss of 60,000 jobs and nearly twenty factories. Citizens began to ask why these jobs were disappearing. It should be noted that these losses did not result in a permanently lower level of employment in the U.S.A., as they were offset by the creation of new jobs in other areas.

General Motors headquarters in Detroit

Two factors impacted the loss of manufacturing jobs inside the United States: globalization and outsourcing. Globalization speaks to an international economy where goods and services can be traded quickly and inexpensively over national borders. Outsourcing is when a domestic industry moves the means of production overseas, typically to take advantage of lower regulation and labor costs. The North American Free Trade Agreement (NAFTA) in 1994 allowed many countries to set up factories in Mexico. CAFTA, a similar agreement with Central American countries, continued the trend. India and China are also home to many American businesses because of their cheaper labor costs.

Outsourcing has meant a significant decrease in the number of people who join labor unions because as manufacturing jobs decrease, competition for those jobs increases. Businesses are less willing to meet the demands of the unions when other workers are willing to come in as strikebreakers and keep the jobs after the strike is broken. Union members began to fear for their place in the business if they spoke out too much, and union membership deflated rapidly. However, some unions stayed strong because jobs in their industries cannot be outsourced (e.g., teachers' unions) and because, in most instances, all new employees are required to join the union and pay membership dues.

Outsourcing allows for large profits for American businesses, but much of that money is spent in foreign countries to create the means of production. For instance, when factories were built in America, they were built by Americans and staffed by Americans. This meant that most of the investment money was eventually returned to the American economy. With the advent of outsourcing, American companies pay foreigners to construct and staff their factories.

This means that the only money returning to the economy is from advertising, corporate taxes and state sales taxes. As more money is leaving the country via imports than there is entering the country through the sale of exports, America is experiencing a trade deficit. Some commentators argue that products are cheaper, but Americans are poorer, as most service industry jobs pay lower wages than manufacturing jobs.

Policy debates intensified over free trade agreements, the size and scope of the government social safety net, and calls to reform the U.S. financial system.

As the economic and political atmosphere changed, the policies put in place for their regulation changed. Public debates characterized the end of the 20th century, as Americans attempted to determine the direction that American foreign and domestic policies should take. Globalization legislation, like NAFTA, characterized international relations while domestic policy debates focused on welfare policies.

NAFTA was designed as a contract between the United States, Mexico, and Canada. The idea was to phase out the tariffs and trade regulations between these three powers in an effort to achieve economic growth in all three nations. Since one-third or so of all economic imports and exports were headed from or to these two countries, the agreement had great promise for the American economy, though experts disagree on the outcome. On the one hand, all three countries did experience economic growth. On the other hand, that growth could have been coincidental and would have occurred without the new agreement. A similar argument can be made for many of the harms associated with NAFTA. While NAFTA made it easier for businesses to move to Mexico, it didn't impact movement to Asia as businesses were still moving there.

President Bill Clinton signing NAFTA

Domestically, the debate focused instead on social welfare programs like health care. The primary concern with programs like Medicare, Medicaid, and the new Obamacare is that these programs are hard to implement and sustain, and some have gone so far as to deem them unconstitutional. Many people fear that nationalized healthcare is a step towards socialism and that the problems seen in some countries with socialized medicine will happen in America as these programs continue to expand.

A common problem in socialist countries is the wait time to see a doctor, as the number of physicians decreases due to lack of financial incentive; however, many view this as an opportunity to perfect methods and encourage innovation in medicine. Others argue that any program which still allows citizens to opt out of the national plan in favor of a private plan cannot be deemed socialist. Constitutionality was a concern raised by the Obamacare taxes. The Affordable Care Act requires all citizens to have health insurance and taxes them with a fine if they do not comply. Proponents of the act claim that Congress is allowed to impose taxes and carry out programs for the wellness and betterment of the American people. Opponents of the act remind Congress that they are not allowed to force individuals to buy products that they don't want from private companies.

Similarly, the questions regarding Social Security reform do not question if changes need to be made, but what changes need to be made and when. Social Security is on the precipice of failure. Some believe that this is because of population increase, while others see mismanagement as the problem. With the baby boomer generation approaching Social Security retirement age, it is projected that the Social Security system will be unable to fund all claims by the year 2033, as the government will not collect enough taxes to fund the payouts and the trust funds held in reserve for crisis years will be depleted.

Thus, the government will have four options: increase income through taxes, reduce spending in other areas and divert the funds to Social Security, borrow the money from another source, or eliminate the Social Security program. The impending deadline for changes worries many economists, and only 50 percent of the American public have indicated that they have faith they will receive payouts when they reach retirement. Others say that small changes made over a number of years will fix the problem and create continued solvency.

Conflict in the Middle East and concerns about climate change led to debates over U.S. dependence on fossil fuels and the impact of economic consumption on the environment.

The world governments consume an amazing amount of oil and gasoline every year. Not only do these fossil fuels allow for transportation, but they provide electricity and the means to produce materials like rubber and plastic. Yet the amounts of oil deposits in the earth are finite and once they're used, they cannot be replaced. This, among other impacts, has caused many to question the United States' consumption of fossil fuels.

Availability is a primary concern. While energy demands increase, the amount of oil does not. What's more, the ability to refine and produce usable oil is also limited. Infrastructure limits the capacity and amount of a product that can be produced at any given time. Many nations have started to express concerns over their own stores of energy and are moving to stockpile in the event of natural disasters or political events like the 1970s embargo.

The United States has several refineries and plans for the Keystone Pipeline, an oil pipeline running from Alberta, Canada to refineries in Texas and Illinois. Many people support these measures because they would return the means of production to the Americans and would drastically decrease the dependence on Middle Eastern oil. This is a concern especially when one considers that the sale of oil to the United States and other Western powers may be funding anti-American terrorist organizations. Yet, opponents of this self-sufficiency plan claim that the environmental impact would be too severe.

Environmentalism is another question to consider when analyzing fossil fuel usage, particularly climate change. Every year the climate changes minutely but, over the last century, the climate's total change was 1.4 degrees Fahrenheit. Many environmental groups are concerned that global temperatures will continue to rise and that most of this change will come from greenhouse gases, like carbon dioxide, that are released into the air when fossil fuels are burned.

These gasses act like a greenhouse around the earth, thus giving them their name. They trap warmth by absorbing the sun's rays and allowing less radiation to leave the atmosphere. This makes the earth slowly warm. Because of these negative effects, many forms of alternative energy are attempting to achieve saturation the way that fossil fuels have. The issue with alternative energies is that they are dependent on uncontrollable factors. Wind energy only works in places where there is enough wind to be harnessed. Solar power only works during the day, and while it can be stored in battery packs, these batteries are often more harmful than the original fossil fuels would have been. Until a sustainable form of energy is created that allows the ease of use and low cost of gasoline and oil, it is unlikely that any real change will occur.

Wind farm in Power County, Idaho

While the United States was unable to answer the energy crisis alone, the United Nations worked to solve many of the world's energy concerns through collaboration. The United Nations created their United Nations Framework Convention on Climate Change (UNFCCC) in 1992 with the goal of affecting real change. The UNFCCC worked for several years developing what they felt were achievable goals and standards for countries and their environmental impacts.

The piece of legislation that they put forward was known as the Kyoto Protocol because it was ratified in Kyoto, Japan in December 1997. Fifty-five countries agreed to the Protocol, which was considered enough for ratification. Further meetings amongst the UN delegates better defined the goals and standards of the Kyoto Protocol. But in 2001 the United States refused to participate, claiming that they had no interest in the Protocol. Since then, many other countries have ratified it, and in 2007, 191 countries were signed to the Protocol.

The goal of the Kyoto Protocol was to stabilize the amount of greenhouse gas in the atmosphere in an effort to mitigate the gas and stop global warming. To do this, there are some legally binding practices. All member nations were asked to submit emissions status reports periodically and attempt real change within their nation by promoting climate conscience technology and educating the public about emissions and prevention. The end goal was to reduce emissions, but only industrialized nations were actually asked to meet any sort of commitment.

Developed nations like the United States and most European nations were asked to reduce their emissions levels to pre-1990 levels. These nations were also asked to share any technology that they might develop to aid in these efforts with developing nations. Developing nations are nations that are still industrializing. Industrializing is an important process in the economic growth of a country, and it was considered impractical for industrializing nations to conform to the same policies as industrialized nations. Therefore, their agreement to emission reduction levels was voluntary. To help industrialized countries meet their goals, the Kyoto Protocol implemented three innovative programs: the clean development mechanism, joint implementation, and emissions trading.

While many nations believe the United Nations is progressing in the right direction with climate change, some nations have expressed concerns. In 2011, Canada left the group, claiming that while they valued the efforts and goals of the Protocols, there was no point in remaining a member considering that the world's largest emissions producers had not signed the agreement. As of 2013, China led the world in greenhouse gas emissions, producing almost 30 percent of all emissions worldwide. The United States generates a level of emissions equal to half of China's emissions. This meant that even if every nation were to reduce emissions, there would be almost 45 percent of emissions that could not be changed. The Kyoto Protocols have been extended into 2020, but the United States has not made a move to rejoin.

The spread of computer technology and the Internet into daily life increased access to information and led to new social behaviors and networks.

The Internet has been around for over twenty-five years, over the span of which much has changed economically and socially. The Internet has revolutionized communication, the job market, and social behaviors. Communication has been vastly changed by the Internet and its associated technologies. Before the Internet, the only options available were letter writing, phone calls, and actual face-to-face interactions. With the advent of computer technology and the birth of the Internet, this has drastically changed.

Instead of letters, people can send instantaneous emails and text messages. Cell phones have moved beyond mere phone calls with FaceTime. Computers and tablets allow users to Skype with anyone from around the world. Even media has changed tactics; instead of continuous news coverage and newspapers alone, there are clips and articles online. The speed and frequency of our communications have also increased, as most forms of online communication happen in real time and are near instantaneous.

The Internet has also revolutionized who can be contacted. It's estimated that about 2.5 billion people are online on any given day. This means that contact can be made outside of the immediate vicinity. Online dating and networking sites allow personal and professional relationships to develop between people who would never have met otherwise. Image sharing sites like Reddit receive traffic from around the world. Twitter played an integral role in the Arab Spring rebellions in the Middle East by allowing protesters to coordinate online. This sharing of instantaneous news, knowledge, and culture has revolutionized the way that people see and interact with the world around them. It also has changed the way cultures are perceived and has led to connections and understanding between people of widely different backgrounds.

2011 uprising in Egypt

Business has been similarly affected by the technology revolution. Machines are making many humans obsolete in factories and production. The competition for jobs has also increased as sites allow web conferencing and individuals can E-commute daily without being physically present. All files are digitized, allowing for easy access, maintenance and storage. This also, however, puts them at risk from hackers who can access databases remotely. Even colleges offer online courses and classes. Some businesses are suffering though. For instance, mom-and-pop bookstores are finding it harder and harder to compete with stores like Barnes & Noble and Amazon, that offer electronic books, as well as printed copies available for online purchasing from home.

The Internet has also given rise to a multitude of cultural and social changes, including the creation of new words. An entire vocabulary has developed over the Internet. Individuals can email or tweet or Facebook their friends. The pound key (#) has now become the hashtag, and the art of the "selfie" is practiced by people worldwide. Entirely new language variations have emerged, such as leetspeak. Developed by computer hackers, leetspeak is a cipher version of English, where letters are substituted by numbers and symbols. Thus, "leet" might be spelled "1337" or "l33t".

There's also chatspeak, which is made from common texting acronyms. Chatspeak is designed for speed and shortening communication. LOL, for instance, means "laughing out loud" and has infiltrated even offline communication. Nude images and online rants live on the Internet forever and have become warnings to those who act inappropriately online. They've even given rise to entirely new industries that can be hired to clean up an individual's online image, which is important as employers have begun to investigate potential hires online.

The U.S. population continued to undergo significant demographic shifts that had profound cultural and political consequences.

As the government and the economy changed, so did the composition of the American people. In the last several decades, the U.S. birthrate has started to decline. With an average of 1.9 children per family, Americans are producing fewer children every year, leading to a slow decline in population. This means that if no immigration was allowed into the country, the population would start to slowly decrease.

A birthrate of two children per family would create a sustained population as each family produced only enough children to replace them. With a birth rate under two, immigration accounts for all population increases in the United States. Most of these immigrants are people of color who come from vastly different backgrounds, particularly Asians and Latinos in recent years. This has encouraged Americans to consider their own cultures and beliefs as the country moves forward.

After 1980, the political, economic and cultural influences of the American South and West continued to increase as population shifted to those areas, fueled in part by a surge in migration from regions that had not been heavily represented in earlier migrations, especially Latin America and Asia.

As immigrants came to the U.S. from Latin America and Asia, they tended to settle in areas that were less heavily populated or where a number of their countrymen already resided together. This led to a new political climate in the southern and western parts of the country. Each immigrant group had a different culture and influenced the development of those areas differently.

In 1960, Latinos accounted for less than 4 percent of the nation's population. In the last fifty-five years, that number has jumped to 16 percent, representing approximately 50 million people. A number of those Latinos are Mexican. The United States took much of its western territory from Mexico during the mid-1800s. Many people decided to stay with their homes and became Americans instead of relocating within the new Mexican boundaries. Many Mexicans crossed the border in the late 1800s in response to the California gold rush.

By the early 1880s, the U.S. government was restricting the number of Asians allowed to immigrate to the country for work. Instead, they encouraged Mexicans to come and fill the jobs Asians were doing, like building the transcontinental railroad. The American government also reached out to Mexican laborers during the Second World War, when it became obvious that the labor force was not large enough to meet demands. America promised the workers a fair wage, human rights protections, food, and housing.

In turn, the Mexican government signed the Emergency Farm Labor Agreement. This program lasted for two decades and had several unforeseen effects on immigration, as Mexican nationals could get accurate information from these migrant workers about labor conditions and decided, in ever increasing numbers, to move north. It also started the illegal immigration movement, as many individuals didn't want to wait for the legal channels and moved north illegally.

Puerto Ricans, as citizens of a protectorate of the American government, enjoyed the same rights and privileges as American citizens when on the mainland. This led to several waves of immigration from the island to the mainland as the people sought work and an escape from the island's endemic poverty. The U.S. government, in turn, tried to bring new industry and economy to Puerto Rico to reverse the flow of immigrants. This was relatively ineffective but did help those who remained on the island.

Fidel Castro (right) with fellow revolutionary Camilo Cienfuegos (left) in Havana

While Cubans had always lived in the United States, their population underwent a mass exodus from 1950 to 1960 as the Cuban Revolution occurred with the overthrow of dictator Fulgencio Batista. The population grew by almost 100,000 in a single decade. Fidel Castro soon put a ban on Cubans attempting to leave the island, though he lifted the ban once to allow Cubans to reunite with their loved ones. 300,000 Cuban refugees came to America, and amnesty laws allowed the United States to welcome another 125,000 during the 1980s, as the federal government considered them refugees from Communism.

A number of Central American immigrants traveled to America during the 1980s. While most of these immigrants came illegally, they came to escape violence, revolutions, and dictators in their home countries.

In total, Central Americans reached a population of 1.3 million people by 1990. The different groups traveled and settled in different places, establishing immigrant neighborhoods that became part of the local government. Guatemalans, for instance, tended to cluster in Texas and California while Nicaraguans settled primarily in Miami.

Although the programs meant to help workers legally enter and exit the country came to an end, Latinos continued immigrating to the United States. By 1965, the Immigration and Naturalization Service (INS) was reporting an apprehension rate of approximately 100,000. This was exacerbated by the 1965 Immigration and Nationality Act which created a first come, first served basis for visas and put a quota cap on immigration from the Western Hemisphere. While most people assume that the immigrants were mostly working-age males, a significant number of females entered the country illegally in the 1980s and 1990s. Not all of these immigrants were unskilled laborers, either. Many educated individuals fled their home countries for the opportunities only available in America.

The immigration of Asians to the United States was very different, primarily due to their location in relation to the United States and the anti-immigration laws of the 1800s. In the early 1800s, many Chinese immigrated to the United States to take part in the California gold rush and the building of the transcontinental railroad. Discrimination soon led to a ban on Chinese immigration, called the Chinese Exclusion Act. This did not stop other Asians from entering the country, but America soon reached out to other countries to put an end to the immigration of unskilled laborers.

From 1917 to 1945, Asians were not allowed to enter the country at all due to the Asiatic Barred Zone. The only exceptions were the Japanese and Filipinos, though this changed with the Japanese attack on Pearl Harbor. Due to discrimination and lack of connection to their home, immigrants already living in the United States tended to band together for mutual support, creating cultural enclaves like Chinatown.

The last of these discriminatory acts would be repealed in 1965, two years after the first Asian American man was elected as Senator for Hawaii. The end of these restrictive measures led to a surge of immigrants, especially after the various wars turned many Asians into refugees and several acts allowed the refugees special permission to enter the United States regardless of the quotas. In 1965, America passed the Immigration and Nationality Act, which allowed Asian immigrants to become citizens.

Department of Homeland Security Secretary Janet Napolitano
swears in ten people as U.S. citizens under the Immigration and Nationality Act

By 2000, 4.2 percent of the U.S. population identified as Asian. In seven years that number rose to almost 5 percent. Yet Asian Americans do not experience the same cultural backlash as Latinos. This is primarily due to the significantly lower number of Asians who enter the country illegally, which gives them the ability to be legally gainfully employed.

The new migrants affected U.S. culture in many ways and supplied the economy with an important labor force, but they also became the focus of intense political, economic and cultural debates.

While both Asians and Latinos served as very necessary additions to the labor forces, they were also a central point for several cultural and political debates. These debates tend to focus on the perceived issue of illegal immigration and therefore tend more towards Latinos than Asians. While many people fear that the number of immigrants is growing too large, it's important to note that the economic slump of the early 2000s actually saw thousands of people voluntarily leaving the country as work become scarcer. After the signing of the NAFTA and CAFTA agreements, the economic disparity between the countries lessened, and coming to America was no longer the only way to improve the quality of life.

This hasn't stopped some groups from speaking out against Latinos, however. Native First movements spread panic about the aging of the white population and try to convince people to take action against the Latinos. This is compounded by the lack of progress by the federal government to answer the illegal immigration question.

Some states have responded by taking matters into their own hands and enacting state laws that limit opportunities for those who cannot prove citizenship. The South and the West, particularly Arizona, passed over 300 regulations in 2010 alone, banning illegal immigrants from renting homes, procuring state drivers licenses, even attending school. As these measures are reviewed in court, the question still remains as to what to do with the people living in America illegally.

While many people see immigration reform as a Latino issue, there are actually a large number of illegal Asian immigrants as well that have been at the fringes of the immigration debate. In California alone, it is estimated that there are over 400,000 illegal Asian immigrants. Nationwide the estimate is close to 1.3 million, making Asians the second highest illegal group in the United States. Typically, they have remained quiet, but as the possibility of real immigration reform is discussed, more and more Asians are speaking out and confessing their illegal status. They point out that they, like Hispanics, have been productive members of society and deserve to have a role in the place where they live.

Demographic changes intensified debates about gender roles, family structures, and racial and national identity.

As debates rage on about immigration and potential reform, it's important to also remember the social aspects of the shift in demographics. While the issue goes beyond immigration, one of the most important social bills affecting demographics does deal with immigration directly. The Immigration Reform and Control Act of 1986 was a landmark bill that analyzed the impacts of immigration into the United States with a particular focus on illegal immigration and how to control and contain it.

Immigration to the United States after World War II increased significantly, as many people saw the United States as a place where they could achieve financial opportunities not available in their home countries. This was particularly true for those who lived in Latin American countries, where poverty was endemic, and in Asian countries that were impacted by the Korean War and the Vietnam Wars. As immigration increased, American citizens indicated their concerns about the impact this new labor supply would have on employment. The fear was that illegal immigrants would take jobs previously held by American citizens because they would be willing to work for lower wages.

The Immigration Control and Reform Act was a way to assuage these fears. It required all employers with three or more employees to verify the identity of all employees, as well as their immigration status. Any employer who was found employing illegal immigrants would be fined. The Act also granted amnesty for a number of illegal immigrants living inside of the country, essentially about 3 million individuals.

While the act has been considered mostly successful and is still in place today, there were loopholes. For example, instead of a firm or business hiring employees themselves, they would hire a contractor who would then loan them subcontractors for specific jobs for a specific length of time. The subcontractors were then the responsibilities of the contractor and not the business. Therefore, the business could not be fined if these subcontractors were not legal citizens or legal foreigners using work visas.

This loophole also meant that some of the subcontractor pay went instead to the business's contractor. Businesses that didn't want to use subcontractors were still wary of hiring foreign citizens who might be in the country illegally. While immigration has continued to be an important topic and many presidents have pledged to continue immigration reform under their presidencies, the Immigration Reform and Control Act of 1986 is one of the few acts that has actually been put into place to answer the question of immigration laws inside the United States.

Another social law that indicated the huge shift in public opinion and demographics, as the United States reevaluated its social culture, was Don't Ask, Don't Tell (DADT), which dealt with the public perception of sexuality and began one of the newest civil rights campaigns. Don't Ask, Don't Tell is the colloquial name given to efforts by President Clinton to end discrimination against homosexuals in the U.S. military.

Clinton's original intention was to create a bill that would immediately overturn the ban on homosexuals in the U.S. military branches. However, this was met with immediate backlash from political contemporaries, including those in charge of military regulation committees. The argument was that by allowing gays to openly serve in the military, the functionality of the armed forces would be weakened. In the end, Clinton managed to reach a compromise he named Don't Ask, Don't Tell.

The compromise allowed gays and lesbians to serve in the U.S. military provided they did not disclose their sexual orientation and did not engage in any sexual practices. In turn, the bill would also protect homosexual soldiers against superior officers inquiring as to their sexual orientation and making decisions based on their answers. This compromise did not make either side particularly happy.

Those who felt that having gays openly serve in the military would affect military effectiveness were worried that the same effects would occur with gays serving in the military and keeping it secret. Similarly, homosexuals were upset that Clinton's complete repeal of their military ban had been reduced to a secrecy agreement. Still, from 1993 to 2011, Don't Ask, Don't Tell illustrated the military's policies toward homosexuals. This compromise did not stop homosexuals from being discharged from the military, and over the course of the ban, many service people were discharged for refusing to hide their homosexuality.

When Barrack Obama became president in 2009, one of his policy goals was the repeal of Don't Ask, Don't Tell. While he hoped to get DADT repealed immediately, it was felt that the impacts of the repeal needed to be examined beforehand. Therefore, the Pentagon began a study of how DADT's repeal would affect military effectiveness. They polled soldiers and commanding officers who overwhelmingly indicated that they were minimally or completely unconcerned about the prospect of open homosexuality.

Chief of Naval Operations Adm. Gary Roughead (left) testifies about the comprehensive review working group report regarding "Don't Ask, Don't Tell"

In the end, the ban on disclosure of one's sexual orientation was overturned when the study concluded that military operations would be minimally affected by any changes to the Don't Ask, Don't Tell policy. While this change was considered a major victory for the LGBT community, the change in sexuality demographics is still a continuing issue. DADT symbolized a first step forward in one of the newest civil rights movements.

Please, leave your Customer Review on Amazon

We want to hear from you

Your feedback is important to us because we strive to provide the highest quality prep materials. Email us if you have any questions, comments or suggestions, so we can incorporate your feedback into future editions.

Customer Satisfaction Guarantee

If you have any concerns about this book, including printing issues, contact us and we will resolve any issues to your satisfaction.

info@sterling-prep.com

We reply to all emails – please check your spam folder

Thank you for choosing our products to achieve your educational goals!

IMAGE CREDITS

Period 1

Pueblo girl winnowing beans, Lummis, Charles F. "The Land of Poco Tiempo." *Scribners.* Dec. 1891: 760-771.

Pueblo cart, Beadle, J.H. *Western Wilds and the Men Who Redeem Them.* Washington, D.C.: Clark E. Ridpath, 1917.

Algonquin Indian, Hutchinson, H. N. ed. *The Living Races of Mankind.* London: Hutchinson & Co., ca 1910.

Iriqouis dwellings, Lossing, Benson J. *Our Country.* New York: Johnson and Bailey, 1895.

Spanish explorers: Cortés, Coligni, de Soto, and Verazzani, Lossing, Benson J. *Our Country.* New York: Johnson and Bailey, 1895.

Meeting of Cortés and Montezuma, Buel, J. W. *Around the World with Great Voyages.* Philadelphia: The Columbia Syndicate, 1892.

Heroic defense of Cuzco, Adams, Davenport W. H. *The Land of the Incas and the City of the Sun.* Boston: Dana Estes and Company, ca 1885.

Colonial slave market in the 17th century, Lossing, Benson J. *Harper's Encyclopedia of United States History.* New York: Harper and Brothers Publishers, 1912.

Typical Cayuse and his mount, Humfreville, J. Lee. Twenty Years Among Our Savage Indians. Hartford: The Hartford Publishing Company, 1897.

Christopher Columbus, Baldwin, James. *Baldwin Reader: Fourth and Fifth Years Combined.* New York: American Book Company, 1897.

Introduction of slavery, Ellis, Edward S. *The Youth's History of the United States.* New York: The Cassell Publishing Company, 1887.

Thanksgiving before the image of the Virgin, Lossing, Benson J. *Our Country.* New York: Johnson and Bailey, 1895.

Landing of Columbus, Spencer, J. A. *History of the United States.* New York: Johnson, Fry, and Company, 1858.

Spaniards gambling, Lossing, Benson J. *Our Country.* New York: Johnson and Bailey, 1895.

Caravel with oars, De Oliveira, Brás. *Caravel with Oars.* 1894. *The History and Development of Caravels, Graduate Thesis.* By G. R. Schwarz. Texas A&M U, 2008. N. page. Print. Wikimedia Commons

Portuguese galleons and carracks, João De Castro, D. *Portuguese Galleons and Naus (Carracks) Routemap of the Red Sea Roteiro Do Mar Roxo 1540 Galleon Nau (Carrack).* 1540. Universidade De Coimbra, Portugal. *Wikimedia Commons.* Media Wiki, 3 Nov. 2013.

Spanish Armada, Lossing, Benson J. *Our Country.* New York: Johnson and Bailey, 1895.

Henry Hudson, Drake, Francis. *Indian History for Young Folks.* New York: Harper and Brothers, 1912.

Spanish explorers raising memorial cross, Lossing, Benson J. *Our Country.* New York: Johnson and Bailey, 1895.

Dutch selling slaves to the Virginia planters, Mace, William H. *A School History of the United States.* Chicago: Rand, McNally and Company, 1904.

Spaniards destroying Mexican idols, Lossing, Benson J. *Our Country.* New York: Johnson and Bailey, 1895.

Sugar plantation, Bryant, William Cullen and Sydney Howard Gay. *A Popular History of the United States.* New York: Charles Scribners' Sons, 1881.

John Brown at Harper's Ferry raid, Lossing, Benson J. *Our Country.* New York: Johnson and Bailey, 1895.

Period 2

Cultivation of tobacco at Jamestown, Scott, David B. *A School History of the United States.* New York: Harper & Brothers, 1883.

Settlers in North Carolina, Lossing, Benson J. *Harper's Encyclopedia of United States History.* New York: Harper and Brothers Publishers, 1912.

Queen Isabella of Castille (left) and King Ferdinand V of Aragon (right), Ellis, Edward S. and Charles F. Horne. *The Story of the Greatest Nations.* New York: Francis Niglutsch, 1906.

Indians at a Hudson Bay Company trading post, Indians trade furs at a Hudson's Bay Company trading post in the 1800's. Digital image. *Hulton Archive.* Getty Images. Wikimedia Commons

The Dutch trading with the Indians, Ellis, Edward S. and Charles F. Horne. *The Story of the Greatest Nations.* New York: Francis Niglutsch, 1906.

Domestic slave trade, Bryant, William Cullen and Sydney Howard Gay. *A Popular History of the United States.* New York: Charles Scribners' Sons, 1881.

Depiction of a tobacco wharf in colonial America, Depiction of a Tobacco Wharf in Colonial America. Digital image. *The Mariner's Museum and Park.* The Mariner's Museum. Wikimedia Commons

Slave auction, Ellis, Edward S. *The Youth's History of the United States.* New York: The Cassell Publishing Company, 1887.

Exploring northern Georgia, Stephens, Alex H. *A Comprehensive and Popular History of the United States.* Chattanooga: Hickman and Fowler, 1882.

Roger Williams building his house, Bryant, William Cullen, and Sydney Howard Gay. *A Popular History of the United States.* New York: Charles Scribners' Sons, 1881.

Quaker woman preaching in New Amsterdam, Bryant, William Cullen, and Sydney Howard Gay. *A Popular History of the United States.* New York: Charles Scribners' Sons, 1881.

Savannah, from a print of 1741, Bryant, William Cullen, and Sydney Howard Gay. *A Popular History of the United States.* New York: Charles Scribners' Sons, 1881.

Arrival of the Indian allies at the French camp, Stephens, Alex H. *A Comprehensive and Popular History of the United States.* Chattanooga: Hickman and Fowler, 1882.

Scene on a plantation, Lossing, Benson J. *Harper's Encyclopedia of United States History.* New York: Harper and Brothers Publishers, 1912.

Carolina rice field, Bryant, William Cullen, and Sydney Howard Gay. *A Popular History of the United States.* New York: Charles Scribners' Sons, 1881.

King Philip, or Metacomet—Wampanoag chief, Wood, Norman B. *The Lives of Famous Indian Chiefs.* Aurora: American Indian Historical Publishing Company, 1906.

Trading with Indians, Drake, Francis. *Indian History for Young Folks.* New York: Harper and Brothers, 1912.

Sugar cane, Richardson, Abby Sage. *The History of Our Country.* Boston: Houghton, Mifflin and Company, 1883.

William Penn, Stephens, Alex H. A Comprehensive and Popular History of the United States. Chattanooga: Hickman and Fowler, 1882.

French Métis, Sellier, Charles-Auguste. *Metis Francais. La Nouvelle-France.* By Eugene Guenin. Paris: Hachette, 1900. 415. Print. Wikimedia Commons

Puritan, Lossing, Benson J. *Our Country.* New York: Johnson and Bailey, 1895.

Portrait of John Locke, Kneller, Godfrey, Sir. *Portrait of John Locke.* 1697. Oil on Canvas. State Hermitage Museum, St. Petersburg, Russia. Wikimedia Commons.

Interior of Christ Church, Boston, Pratt, Mara L. *American's Story for America's Children: The Early Colonies.* Boston: D.C. Heath & Company, 1901.